RICK SANDERS
IN THE MOMENT

Copyright © 2022 by Bahne Bahnson

All rights reserved. No part of this publication may be reproduced, scanned, uploaded, stored in a retrieval system, or transmitted in any form or by any means, electronic, mechanical, photocopying, recording, or otherwise, without the prior written permission of the publisher, except for brief quotations covered under fair use.

Permission to reprint photographs is courtesy of David Stockner, and Amateur Wrestling News.

Author: Bahne Bahnson
Developmental Editors: Emily Jones, Michael Larson
Copy Editor, Typesetter: Josephine Funk
Cover Designer: Kelsie Pehl
Proofreader: Mike Chapman

SandersInTheMoment@gmail.com

Library of Congress Cataloging-in-Publication Data

Names: Bahnson, Bahne, author.
Title: Rick Sanders In the Moment: Biography of an Olympian
Description: IngramSpark publishing [2022] | Includes end note references.
Identifiers
LCCN 2022913552 (Hardcover)
ISBN: 979-8-9865386-0-0
Subjects: Sports | Biography | Amateur Wrestling | Marijuana | ADHD | History
LC record available at https://lccn.loc.gov/2022913552

Printed in the United States of America.

10 9 8 7 6 5 4 3 2 1

RICK SANDERS
IN THE MOMENT

BIOGRAPHY OF AN OLYMPIAN
BY
BAHNE BAHNSON

Edited by Josephine Funk

For David Stockner
Brother, mentor, patriarch, and
Keeper of the Scrapbook!

Preface

My high school years in South Dakota spanned 1969-1972. Wrestling was a big part of my life during that time, and Dan Gable was "The Guy". The media followed his remarkable collegiate win/loss record, his 1970 upset by Larry Owings, and his rebound at the 1972 Munich Olympics. There was nobody bigger in amateur wrestling than Dan Gable, then—or now. But viewing the ABC media clips coming from the Olympics that summer of 1972, another wrestler caught my eye, and the attention of many. His name was Rick Sanders.

Sanders had personality. He was unabashed on the mat. His long hair and beard stood out like the legendary Tasmanian Devil. He was so unlike anyone else on the U.S. freestyle team, or really anyone competing in the demanding sport of wrestling, especially in the conservative Midwest. Even more alluring, Sanders was from the "Wild Pacific Northwest"—a place of mountains, trees, oceans—a far cry from my life on the northern plains. I was a Gable worshipper, but I converted to Sanders and hopped on a bus to Oregon for college. By the time I had settled in to my freshman college dorm, Sanders was gone.

Fifty years later, I found myself retired and looking for a project. Sanders popped into my head. I wondered whether anything had been written about Rick. The verbiage is slim, but the record is astounding. I decided to write Sanders' biography in an attempt to help preserve his legacy in a sport he absolutely loved and flourished in; U.S. amateur wrestling.

The 1972 Munich Olympics were televised by ABC. Television coverage of wrestling was much improved over the 1968 Mexico City Olympics where Sanders won a silver medal. Rick's accomplishment received little media comment and zero T.V. coverage in '68. Sanders took full advantage of photo-ops at Munich. His 1960s counterculture hippie persona was in full bloom by then. High school wrestlers witnessed brazen personal freedom and unorthodox wrestling style. Sanders was the electric guitar in a 1950s ten-piece band. He was a catalyst for change.

Culture changes the man—the man rarely changes the culture. However, occasionally a meteor may strike, altering the course of history. There are the Einsteins and Edisons, George Herman Ruths, and Richard Joseph Sanders. Sanders was described as a meteor in his 1987 National Wrestling Hall of Fame induction. It said, "He was a stroke of brilliance." Sanders moved the culture, announcing by his approach that wrestling—an arduous, exacting sport—may be enjoyed in pursuit of excellence. This is Rick's story.

Introduction

He moved to the edge of the wrestling mat with a confident yet nonchalant demeanor of one accustomed to victory. He appeared to have a slight smirk on his face; in his hazel eyes, a mischievous twinkle. It was, after all, the 1972 Olympic Games, and athletes were expected to be ready to perform at the highest echelons of sport. This was freestyle wrestling, the international style of a sport that Rick Sanders had spent his lifetime honing, practicing, and perfecting.

Rick had come to dominate at the 57 kilogram, 125.5-pound class, which was often called a bantamweight—a term derived from the similarly named Bantam Rooster, a small but cock-sure fowl known for strutting around barnyards and picking fights to impress the females. An appropriate analogy for Sanders.

Across the mat, his opponent, Japanese Hideaki Yanagida, waited. Yanagida was an Asian Games champion and a two-time world champion. In his career, he was as yet undefeated.

Sanders: In the Moment

Though the two were competing at the same weight class, that was where the similarities ended. Yanagida, under pressure to perform, shifted warily from foot to foot, in contrast to Sanders' easy strides. Yanagida stood an inch shorter than Rick and gave off an austere disciplined air, his close-cropped hair and clean-shaven face in line with traditional Japanese custom for wrestling at the time. Sanders, on the other hand, was shockingly unconventional even for his time, sporting a hippie's long hair, full beard, love beads, and pot pipe as he stepped up to the edge of the mat.

Even within the U.S., Rick's "free love" hippie status was controversial to the sport. Counterculture was evolving rapidly on the coasts, but in the conservative breadbasket states where wrestling powerhouses were focused—Iowa, Oklahoma, Michigan—people were unaccustomed to hippies, drugs, rock music, and political unrest. Rick Sanders, from Oregon, often clashed with his more conservative superiors, who feared his wild West Coast ways would poorly represent the United States on the international stage.

Times were changing, though. The '60s and '70s saw an unprecedented level of political unrest, both within the U.S. and on the international level. The growth of television was a catalyst, allowing folks at home a glimpse of things they'd never seen before. Today, ABC Television's cameras loomed large at mat-side, ready to catch the action. The Games were the pinnacle of amateur sports competition, and the title of 'Olympian' was a lifelong accolade anywhere in the world. Sanders was a survivor. His unorthodox style found him undefeated and poised for this fourth-round match. He was aware of ABC's commitment to cover this year's Olympic matches, and with all eyes on him, he was ready to take the stage.

Sanders: In the Moment

Swapping Tiger sneakers for wrestling shoes retrieved from his ever-present canvas bag, Sanders deftly cinched the laces tight.[1] He shed his beads and pot pipe. Around him, fans claimed seats at mat-side, clamoring to watch. He heard their chants, intoxicating in his ears—Sanders! Sanders! Sanders!—and gave his characteristic smirk.

Preparations complete, Sanders shook hands with his coach and cornerman, gave a truculent chin lift to conservative U.S. Wrestling Federation chieftains in attendance, then strolled his Hobbit-like physique out to meet the Japanese stud Hideaki Yanagida in what would be the deciding match of his career.

Ricky Sanders in Bly, Oregon.

Chapter One

Richard Joseph Sanders was born January 20, 1945 in Lakeview, Oregon, to Anita and Melvin Sanders. The family of six resided in Bly, a small town in south central Oregon located forty-five miles to the northwest. Rick was born at the June Robertson Maternity Home located in Lakeview after the Sanders family had arrived fourteen hours earlier. Rick was the last baby born to Anita, who was thirty-seven at the time. Rick was born into the capable, caring hands of the blended Sanders family.

Anita had two children from a previous marriage to Cecil Stockner, an auto mechanic from Libby, Montana. Stockner was as excellent an auto-mechanic as he was an imbiber and a womanizer. Anita could not reconcile Stockner's assets with his liabilities and she relocated with her children, Kay and David, to Klamath Falls in southern Oregon. Melvin Sanders followed Anita from Montana and convinced her she was in need of his solid credentials. Melvin, at five foot one inches tall, was two inches taller than Anita. He evolved into a gambler and an alcoholic—iniquities unmanaged by whatever solid character he possessed.[1] Patricia, Rick's older sister by three years, was born in due course. David and Kay

Sanders: In the Moment

Stockner, a decade older than Patricia and Rick, resided half-time as members of the Sander's family.

Melvin worked at the sawmill in Bly. His job was to shovel waste sawdust into a cone-shaped incinerator, a common practice at the time. The family lived crowded in a shack with stud walls covered by cardboard and then wallpapered by Anita. Building materials were scarce, with World War II just coming to an end.

In time, the family of six moved into the back of a storefront building. Anita's father was a professional photographer, and Anita followed him into the trade. Anita used the storefront to pursue her photography business.[2]

Rick's half-sister, Kay Hirons, remembers a normal upbringing, not one out of the ordinary, of duress, or of poverty. Anita adamantly instructed her children that they were never to allow anyone to call them "white trash." They could become whatever they wanted to be.[3]

The family did not have a car when Rick was born. The doctor lived in Lakeview, nearly fifty minutes away. Melvin traded WWII gas rationing tickets and a cord of wood for use of a neighbor's car. The family planned to take the other children to a sister who lived in Klamath Falls, still further away in a nearly opposite direction. Anita called her sister at Klamath Falls when Rick was born. Patricia, now three years old, learned of her brother's birth in her very first phone call. Not only did the Sanders family not have a car, they didn't have a phone either.[4]

Life in Bly kept Anita busy. Her daughter, Kay, remembers Anita fondly as kind, very loving, with many close friends, but perhaps a little weak at enforcing the rules.[5] Along with raising four children, Anita ran her photography business and worked at the local tavern playing piano by ear and accomplishing other sundry chores. Melvin's job in the timber

Rick's three-year-old sister Patricia and half-sister Kay Hirons.

industry was transitional and employment was often tenuous. Oregon's unemployment rate in 1949 was quite high at 8.3 percent.

Bly is renowned for a tragedy known as The Japanese Balloon Bomb that occurred on May 5, 1945.[6] Rick was five months old. A Sunday school group, held just north of town, discovered what they thought was a weather balloon on the ground near their picnic area. However, as they prodded the payload, its 15-kilogram high-explosive anti-personnel bomb exploded. All members of the Sunday school class were killed. Rick's sister Kay was a member of the Sunday school group, but luckily, exhausted from a dance the night before, she decided to sleep in that morning.

Federal authorities investigating the incident determined the balloon to be one of over 6000 released by Japan in retaliation for the American bombing of major Japanese cities as WWII neared its end. The bombs were designed to start forest fires and cause consequent forms of calamity in the Pacific Northwest. Authorities warned locals not to mention the incident or talk to the press so that Japan would not learn of the diabolical scheme's effect. "Loose lips sink ships" was common parlance.

The Balloon Bomb tragedy nonwithstanding, after a four-year run in Bly, the family moved further north to Oakridge, Oregon. Kay, turning seventeen in Bly, eloped with a boyfriend to Reno. She married, became Kay Hirons, and moved to California. Melvin found work in Oakridge with the Pope and Talbot lumber company.[7] Melvin allegedly frequented the local taverns, but David Stockner remembers him as being an adequate provider. Melvin worked on the lumber mill's sorting pond, a challenging job requiring nimble footwork to avoid wet feet; perhaps an inherency passed on to the advantage of Rick. In addition, Melvin was remembered by Stockner as being "flighty", a quality reminiscent of Rick as well.

Oakridge is forty miles east of Eugene and 150 miles southeast of Portland. Today, the town's main industry is recreation, billed by many as the Mountain Bike Capital of the World.[8] The Middle Fork Willamette River runs through town. Beautiful forests of new growth Douglas fir surround Oakridge. In the 1950s, the old growth forests had trees 250 feet tall, with trunks measuring five to six feet in diameter. Those trees are gone today, as is the sorting pond and Pope and Talbot lumber company. But while they lasted, those old growth forests and the small-town life in Oakridge cultivated Rick's lifetime love of nature and the outdoors. Rick would spend much of his childhood in Oakridge with his three-year-older sister, Patricia. David finished high school at Oakridge in three years. He was able to skip an entire year when his school records did not follow from Bly.

David Stockner was a solid adult role model for Rick. The Korean War was half over when David graduated from Oakridge High School in 1952. David joined the army as a paratrooper. His primary goal, however, was to earn the GI Bill as a ticket to a college education. He realized that goal. Rick respected his half-brother's sense of adventure, travel, and accomplishment. Rick's impetus for self-improvement came from Stockner. Conversely, Stockner cataloged myriad newspaper clippings in a scrapbook marking Rick's wrestling odyssey. Researchers have found the information a Sanders treasure trove owing to Stockner's meticulously developed archive. David built a distinguished career as a teacher and principal in the Portland area. He became patriarch of the Sanders family, with Rick receiving respite, counsel, and financial support in the later years of his life from David.

Rick had an affectionate relationship with his sister Patricia. She remembers her first day of school in Oakridge and waiting to be picked up by the bus. Four-year-old Rick picked a bouquet of flowers from a bed in the yard and fondly presented them to Patricia on her momentous day.[9] Observing the kindness, Anita whispered advice in Patricia's ear suggesting she take the flowers on her inaugural journey to Oakridge elementary school. An intimate kindness created an eighty-year-old memory. Love blossomed for the Sanders in Oakridge for a time.

The Sanders' home was meager—a wood burning stove, an outdoor privy, and small living quarters. Seventy percent of Oregon homes at the time were heated by wood; thirty percent did not have flush toilets. A backwater swamp created by a Willamette tributary served as their backyard. It provided recreation for Rick and Patricia through the summer. Although television expanded rapidly during this time period of the 1950s,

Sanders: In the Moment

Rick's Family. Seated on the sofa, left to right: Dave Stockner, half-brother; Anita, mother; Melvin Sanders, father; Melvin's mother. Seated on the floor, left to right: Patricia, sister and Rick Sanders.

—

"transforming the nation as no invention had done since the automobile," [10] the Sanders home remained unaffected. They did not own a magic box; still no telephone either. The outdoors became their entertainment.

Rick loved family excursions in the local area hunting for mushrooms. On many occasions, they found shaggy mane mushrooms along Oregon's gravel roads, picking trunk-loads. Dipped in egg and milk, then coated with breadcrumbs and fried, the mushrooms became a delicacy. Many Sunday afternoons of harvesting nature's bounty ended with the family enjoying the fruits of their labor.

For Rick, the freedom of the outdoors may have been more of a blessing than expected. Patricia and teammates of Rick suggest that in today's parlance, he may have been diagnosed somewhere on the

Attention Deficit and Hyperactivity Disorder (ADHD) spectrum. Symptoms of ADHD that Rick seemed to manifest included those related to hyperactivity: often unable to engage in leisure activities quietly; often "on the go", acting as if "driven by a motor"; talking excessively; difficulty waiting his or her turn; often interrupts or intrudes on others.[11]

To be sure, Rick was a feisty little kid. He once, while living in Oakridge, started a fire on top of a rabbit cage, then threw a bullet into the fire to test what would happen. In effect, he had created a three-ring circus to satiate his hyperactivity—a fire, an explosive, and a terrorized rabbit to placate extraordinary childhood exuberance. When the bullet exploded, it grazed his forehead. He escaped the episode unscathed—the rabbit's fate was unrecorded.[12] This incident was just one of many anecdotes of a life full of freedom and risk-taking.

Despite his shorter attention span, Rick loved listening to stories. Anita was an avid reader and read to her children frequently. After high school, she had gone to normal school, a program in the 19th and early 20th century that taught high school graduates to become primary school teachers. Anita earned a teaching credential, and taught school for a time in Montana. Despite her efforts, by the time Rick was in fifth grade, Anita realized Rick was memorizing the stories she read to him. He couldn't read. Anita immediately consulted Rick's teacher and together confirmed the inability. The teacher experimented with Rick until she found a subject that interested him enough to work at reading himself. "The Oregon Trail" by A.B. Guthrie captured his imagination and created his love for reading.[13] Another favorite author was J.R.R. Tolkien and his fantasies, *The Hobbit* (1937) and *Lord of the Rings* (1954).[14] Sanders was about ten years old when he began listening to the tales. He began reading them during the 1960s, at the height of their popularity, as a way to pass the time while sweating it out in hot boxes on a regular basis.[15] Sanders took a liking to the Tolkien Halfling Hobbit, Frodo Baggins, who traveled extensively on mythical quests, but also struggled with temptations of power, pride, and humility. Sanders, whose stature never exceeded 5'4", likened himself to the miniature Baggins. Rick puzzled over Frodo's adventures to Middle Earth, while he himself journeyed to world-wide wrestling venues. And, like Baggins returning to his home and the safety of the Shire, Rick returned home to Portland and familiar wrestling rooms, surrounded by the green and verdant mountains, valleys, forests, and rivers of Oregon. The simplicity of the Hobbit lifestyle—good food and good friends, and needing little else to sustain a full life—resonated with Sanders, whose worldview was constructed from similar values.[16] Of course, Tolkien's mythical masterpiece held deeper meaning, and as Rick matured, so too did his appreciation and identification with additional Tolkien themes. Sanders wasn't alone in his love for books. Frodo Baggins' popularity in the 1960s had a run similar to the contemporary character Harry Potter, in the titular series by J.K. Rowling, written four decades later.

The Sanders family began to change during the 1950s. As mentioned, David was in the military. Half-sister Kay Hirons was established in California.[17] Occasionally, Anita would package Patricia off to Kay while stabilizing the family's current state of duress due to marital problems. Patricia rode the bus back and forth between Oregon and California. Anita pinned a name tag and address to Patricia's coat to ensure she ended up at the right location.[18]

Anita and Melvin's marriage was beginning to fall apart. The divorce rate during the 1950s was less common at 2.1/1000. Nothing like the country's high of 5.3/1000 in 1979, and clearly a negative stigma for children and families at that time.[19] The dissolution of the marriage was quiet but unequivocal. It was rumored to have involved infidelity, something for which Anita had experience and no tolerance. Anita initiated a split with her second and final husband, migrating to Portland with Rick, now twelve, and arranging for Patricia, fifteen, to go to California where she continued high school under Kay's care.[20] Melvin Sanders subsequently disappeared for half a dozen years. He reappeared when Rick turned eighteen, an age at which Melvin was no longer liable for child support payments. Melvin Sanders was rarely part of Rick's life, nor do any other family members recollect anything of his existence after the marital break-up.

Portland is located at the confluence of the Willamette and Columbia rivers. Snow-capped Mount Hood at 11,250 feet is fifty miles to the east and sits majestic within view of Portlanders. Named after Portland, Maine, the city began in the 1830s, a terminus of the Oregon Trail. The city was approximately 370,000 when Anita and Rick arrived in 1957. It has doubled since, and is now the 26th largest city in the United States. When the two arrived, downtown Portland had not changed from the 1930s. It was dingy. But beginning in the 1960s, Portland began to assume its reputation for progressive political values and evolved as a bastion of the counterculture. The downtown Chrystal Ballroom was the counterculture core in Portland. It had an eighteen-month run mixing "weird music, light shows, drugs, and kids wearing funny clothing."[21] Notwithstanding, Portland is historically billed as the "City of Roses"—one of the greenest cities in America.

When the Sanders family moved to town, Interstate 5 and 84 were just being constructed. Anita found a place to live on Third Street in downtown Portland. It was an area known as skid row at the time. She was on welfare until she found work as a framer in a photography shop. When she received her first employment check from the new employer, she took the remaining welfare money back to the welfare office and insisted they take it back. She was now gainfully employed.[22]

Anita ultimately got a full-time job with the City of Portland in its microfilming department. In addition, she worked part time as a grocery cashier. She never owned a car or learned how to drive.[23] When Patricia rejoined the family to finish her junior and senior year of high school, Anita had established a schedule wherein she was often compelled to run to work. She was chronically late. Patricia adapted to her mother's schedule, mapping rendezvous points where she could intercept Anita, run with her, and discuss relevant family issues. Rick shared the proclivity for being late. It was not out of character for him to show up at wrestling practice in nothing but a jock strap carrying workout clothes under-arm or in his omnipresent duffle bag.[24] ADHD is characterized by inattention to time parameters. Needing to be somewhere at a specific time is only meaningful when the deadline hits. Planning in advance of an appointed time is of little concern.[25] However, when it is that time, as when the whistle blows at the start of a wrestling match, complete concentration to the task at hand is characteristic. Rick's on-mat focus was extraordinary, his ADHD advantage.

Despite her lack of punctuality, Anita was nothing if not attentive to her son's schooling. She received occasional letters from the school district regarding Rick's progress. In the beginning, these letters were addressed to "Melvin Sanders." Anita was having none of that. Using her lunch hour one noon, she ran to the school district office located in downtown Portland and straightened the matter. She made it quite clear that Melvin Sanders was no longer a part of the Sanders family living on Third Street and that she indeed was the responsible parent for Richard J. Sanders. Further, she should be the addressee on all future correspondence.[26] And she was. Anita's fortitude under duress was a solid example for Rick. If it was a contest between individualism and the establishment, Rick, like his mother, could be unwavering and ready to take it on.

Rick was finishing seventh grade when the move to Portland occurred. By the time he was in eighth grade, his low grades were becoming an issue. He still struggled at reading, but when test questions were read to him, he scored in top percentiles.[27] But an ability to read is foundational to intellectual growth and confidence. Confidence emboldens, and for an adolescent in Rick's situation—undersized physically, socio-economically distressed, lacking paternal support, and academically challenged—he likely began feeling himself disappearing from view. Kay Hirons, Rick's half-sister, recalled he was a quiet boy during his middle school years. But despite his introversion, as he grew older, Rick's need for attention began to take root.

Rick began high school in 1959. He attended Lincoln High School, the oldest public high school in the Pacific Northwest. He had a flat top haircut that he maintained through his senior year (the Beatles, importing the long hair fashion, wouldn't arrive in Portland for another five years), and a physique more recognizable as a junior high kid. He made an attempt at school participation by going out for cross country—looking for that high school niche where he could fit in, possibly excel, and be noticed. The Lincoln harrier squad was vigilant in effort but wanting in reward. It lacked appeal.

Physical education classes were compulsory for freshman and sophomores. Larry Keck was the P.E. teacher and wrestling coach. Keck noticed Sanders had an aptitude for wrestling as he observed the lightweights during a gym class unit on wrestling. He encouraged Rick to try out. Lincoln High School had a generally poor wrestling program due to transient coaching and the team never having a winning season during

Rick's high school career. Nonetheless, Rick became a city champion as a freshman—quite a feat considering he had no prior wrestling experience, and the fact that the Portland Interscholastic League (PIL) consisted of twelve public high schools. Dennis Fuller, wrestling historian, noted in Bob Allen's *55 Years of Excellence: Oregon High School Wrestling*, "He was so unorthodox that people just couldn't deal with his style. He was dominant right from his freshman year." When Rick found in himself a talent for wrestling, his course was struck. Wrestling better suited his physical and mental predilection.

Many youths of the day expanded their aspirations and began developing a worldview by watching TV. Television continued to influence the public as the 1950s merged into the 1960s. American capitalism and politics exploited the medium for all it was worth, conveying entertainment, sports, news, consumer goods, and political doctrine, all through the venue of television. American culture changed. "Americans conflicted over two contradictory sets of values. One set was necessary for traditional economic production: discipline, delayed gratification, good character, and the acceptance of hard work. Competing values included: expanded personal consumption, immediate gratification, egalitarianism, and hedonistic pursuit of self-expression."[28] Americans struggled developing new rules to live by. Newfound freedoms and affluence challenged many to reevaluate their moral compass.

Dwight Eisenhower was Rick's president during his freshman year at Lincoln High School in downtown Portland. By the end of his sophomore year, John Kennedy would assume that role. Crooner Frank Sinatra's hit single *'High Hopes'* endorsed Kennedy's youthful campaign promising a "New Frontier" for America.

Rick was largely on his own at this time and for the remaining thirteen years of his life. Wrestling provided him the aforementioned traditional values: discipline, delayed gratification, good character, and acceptance of hard work. Yet he relished freedom of conscience, later indulging in the hedonistic pursuit of self-expression. Many of Rick's close friends would notice his esoteric manifestations as his career evolved—and would wonder. He would smoke cigarettes, imbibe, and search out the ladies, none of which were uncommon dalliances, but Sanders' unabashed approach was uncharacteristic for a rising star in the ascetic wrestling culture.[29] But, growing up largely unsupervised in the cauldron of the '60s Portland counterculture, what's to wonder? *'The Times They Are a-Changin',* according to Bob Dylan's 1964 folk-rock ballad. By that time, Rick would be humming along.

<u>Chapter Two</u>

Dale Thomas, Olympian and esteemed former long-time wrestling coach at Oregon State, commented that Sanders had "thighs like a baseball catcher." Though perhaps not perfectly suited for high school cross country, Sanders' brief foray into the sport did give him an edge. Running is integral to wrestling—both for conditioning and weight loss. At all levels of the sport, from high school to international wrestling, high mileage running is a necessity to help lightweight wrestlers cut pounds.

Don Behm, a 1968 Olympic silver medalist, shared a lot of similarities with Sanders, from a childhood spent on the West Coast—Behm lived in Vancouver, Washington just across the Columbia River from Portland, practically Rick's neighbor—to competing at the same weight class for the right to represent the U.S. in international tournaments. Though they never met in a high school wrestling match, thanks to Behm's family relocating to Lansing, Michigan early on, their high school training experiences still paralleled each other.[1] Behm describes his weight cutting regimen in Dale Anderson's insightful book, *A Spartan Journey*:

> It was simple: run my ass off and don't stop till I made weight—just run, run, and more running. It also had the effect of putting me in great shape. Out of season I would be at 145 pounds.

Sanders: In the Moment

I could diet to about 135 pounds, and the rest was just one pound per mile. So, to make 125.5 would be 9 or 10 miles. The key to it was to plan for the running at the end, which I did by running every morning and after every practice—at least 5 or 6 miles every day. That also meant not eating for the last 2 days.[2]

When training, Rick was often seen running along the shoulder of the road ten or fifteen miles outside of Portland. David Stockner, Rick's half-brother, also remembers Rick running an *Oregonian* paper route through high school. Rick ran the route, putting papers in a box at each house. When President Kennedy was assassinated in November 1963, Rick looked at the extra edition as an opportunity for another workout.[3]

Ron Calhoun, an Oregon state high school champ, as well as a future Portland State University (PSU) and Multnomah Athletic Club (MAC) teammate of Sanders, remembers road trips dropping Rick off along the route to competition venues. Rick would run two to three miles, then teammates rolled him up in blankets to keep the sweat going and put him back in the car.[4] Similarly, PSU coach Howard Westcott always reserved station wagons from the PSU motor-pool for road trips so Rick had space in the back to work out and keep a sweat going. Last minute training was vital; Sanders rarely made weight on time.

Wrestling in high school during the 1960s was one of the few winter sport options. The other was basketball. For those who weren't tall enough or athletic enough to play on the hardcourt, wrestling was the best alternative at most schools. Famed American novelist, John Irving, always a champion of amateur wrestling and a long-time high school coach, wrote several award-winning novels including *The World According to Garp, The Cider House Rules, A Prayer for Owen Meany, The Hotel New Hampshire,* and interestingly especially for wrestlers, *The Imaginary Girlfriend*—a memoir of writers and wrestlers who played a role in his development as a novelist and as a wrestler. Irving competed as a wrestler for twenty years beginning in the late 1950s and coached wrestling until he was forty-seven. *The Imaginary Girlfriend* is, in part, an epistle to the "half-way decent" wrestler. Irving suggests, "for wrestling, good balance is as important as quickness; it is also as uncoachable. And by balance, I mean both kinds; the ability to keep your balance—to a small degree this can be taught, by maintaining good position—and how quickly you can recover your balance when you lose it. The latter ability is unteachable."[5] Sanders had Olympic levels of unteachable balance, a skill which allowed him to wrestle with ease at the unique confluence of unorthodoxy and innovation. Hall of fame Olympian Wayne Baughman would observe, "I first encountered Rick at the 1964 Olympic Trials. Rick had tremendous hip flexibility and thigh power and the most uncanny sense of balance I ever saw."[6]

Jerry Groover was a sophomore at Cleveland High School in Portland when he met Rick for the 1959-1960 PIL 98-pound city championship. High school and college wrestling seasons generally run from November to March. Rick's first season ran from November 1959 to March 1960. Rick was just completing his first ever season in the sport. Groover dieted and cut weight to make the 98-pound weight limit where he felt he would have his best chance to compete. Sanders weighed in at eighty- seven pounds. Groover started with a four-point lead. Sanders never stopped moving and won 7-4. "His counters were so good," remembered Groover.[7] To Jerry, Rick seemed a bit introverted and humble. The following year, on seeing Groover, Rick remarked, "I'm glad you're up a weight class." Groover was charmed, and also glad—not needing to face Sanders.

Rick was involved in other organizations at Lincoln as well. He was a member of the Lords, an all-male service club that did benevolent outreach for the Red Cross and various rehabilitation centers. The club

Sanders: In the Moment

Sanders, second row, 1st from left. Rick was a member of the Lords—an all-male service club that did benevolent outreach for the red Cross and various rehabilitation centers.
Picture courtesy of the Cardinal Lincoln Yearbook, 1962.

---

conducted fundraisers and hosted school dances and social events. He participated in Chess Club. Members met weekly and played matches in a league with other Portland schools. Finally, as an athlete, Rick was a member of the "Order of L." Athletes held fundraisers and established a treasury of funds used to purchase athletic equipment. Despite his involvement in all of these various clubs, in the yearbook group photos, Rick appears rather disinterested. The spark that fired his enthusiasm, energy, and identity was time on the mat.[8]

Sanders only loss in high school competition was to Gary Head of Klamath Falls. Rick was a freshman when he met Head, a junior. Delance Duncan was wrestling coach at Klamath Falls who recognized Head as an undersized football player, but nevertheless an excellent athlete. He

Sanders: In the Moment

convinced Head to try wrestling. So, while Sanders was a freshman phenom, Head was a first-year wrestler as well, but physically more mature. Head beat Sanders in their only high school meeting. Sanders won his first state championship the following year at 98 pounds. Gary Head became a state runner-up that same year as a senior wrestling at 106 pounds. Many find it difficult to hold "runner-up" status, but being the only wrestler to beat Rick Sanders in high school is an appropriate letterhead for a lifetime of correspondence.[9]

Rick won his second PIL city championship in the 1960-1961 season. The top two wrestlers in each weight class of the PIL city championships were eligible for the 1961 state meet. Rick was the city defending champion at 98 pounds. He pinned opponents in each of the first three rounds of the Portland high school tournament and was awarded a decision in the championship match. At the state meet, held March 3rd

Rick's HS team. The Lincoln Cardinals rarely had a winning record with transient coaching and lackluster numbers of participants.
Sanders, bottom row, 3rd from left.

and 4th at Oregon State University in Corvallis, Sanders became the first state champion in Lincoln High School's history. He pinned his opponent in the first round and then gained three decisions. He won the championship in a close 1-0 final over Jerry Abaas of Redmond.[10]

Rick began his junior year at Lincoln in the fall of 1961. Much was happening at the beginning of the decade. The birth control pill was approved for use in 1960. By 1962, it had become an instant success with 1.2 million women using it. The door was opened to a more promiscuous regard toward premarital sex.[11] Sanders would learn to appreciate a more liberal approach toward sexual freedom. The number one song on the radio was "Travlin' Man" by Ricky Nelson, the lyrics ironically reflective of Sanders' off-mat international experiences. And at the 1960 Olympic Games in Rome, three U.S. wrestlers won gold medals. Perhaps an impressionable Sanders lifted an eyebrow at the possibilities.

Sixty-two wrestlers were in the Lincoln High School wrestling room for the 1961-1962 campaign. The varsity won three duals of ten contested duals. Sanders won his third PIL city championship—the best in his weight class among Portland high schools. Rick Sanders and Al Stebinger were the only Lincoln Cardinal mat men finding their way into the state tournament.[12] Oregon State University, home of the Beaver wrestling team, is located in Corvallis and is the only D-I program remaining in the state today. Rick moved up to the 106-pound weight class for the season. Rick pinned his first opponent at state. He won by decision in rounds two and three, 10-2 and 3-2 respectively. He prevailed over Steve Ando from Grant High School, also a Portland high school, by pin in the third period for his second state championship. Al Stebinger, the other Lincoln wrestler, lost in the first round 6-2 in a hard-fought battle. The Portland *Oregonian* reported, "Rick was pleased with the outcome of the meet, but said, "I'm sorry I didn't pin them all." Grants Pass, Oregon won the team title. Three Portland high schools were in the top nine. Stebinger's first round loss left Sanders as the only Lincoln wrestler able to earn team points. Lincoln finished out of the top ten.[13]

The high school wrestling season came to a close by the end of March. Rick's energies could be devoted to academic pursuits in the final quarter of the school year. He showed some measure of commitment. Rick displayed talent in the arts during high school as well. He seemed to enjoy periods of introspection and dabbled in poetry to reflect his inner thoughts. Most of his work, he admitted, made sense only to himself. However, in 1962, his poetry resonated with judges at the annual PIL poetry contest. In the eighth edition of *Reflections,* the students of the twelve Portland public high schools wrote their thoughts, experimenting with ideas, words, and literary forms. Rick's 1962 work was one of the esteemed selections:

SUPERSTITION

It came with the dark,
    and stayed with ignorance.
It grew fast,
It grew strong.

It came into the mind.
    and there it destroyed.
There was no wisdom.
There was no reason.

It would not leave,
    and it fought to keep its place.
It was vicious.
It was cruel.

Sanders: In the Moment

> The light did not come,
> and it was secure.
> Its roots went deep.
> It was malignant.
>
> Richard J. Sanders, Junior
> Lincoln High School

"My poetry is like a diary," said Sanders. "I write for myself. The images are too personal to have much meaning for anyone else. But 20 years from now, these lines will remind me how I felt when I wrote them down."[14] Though Rick talked of only needing a nonpublic forum for his fine arts interests, he seemed in other public comments to covet the appreciation of others, and sought to display his own diversified identity. He wanted to be known as more than just a wrestler.

The wrestling identity seemed too prominent to augment by dabbling in fine arts, however. The media kept its focus narrow. "Pound for pound Sanders is as fine an athlete as the PIL ever produced in a specialized field," praised Leo Davis, long time sports writer for *The Oregonian*, the state's major newspaper. In his 1962-1963 senior season, Rick won his fourth PIL championship and his third state crown. He made the move up to the 115-pound weight class in his final year, where he met Ron Iwasaki.

Ron Iwasaki was a future two-time Division I All-American for Oregon State. Iwasaki is an affable, warm-hearted man. He had high regard for Rick, who he met in competition several times. Iwasaki said of Sanders: "I probably wrestled Rick 12-15 times in my high school, college, and post college career, but I don't remember one of them ending favorably for me. There was little intimidation," said Iwasaki. "Except that you did not know how the match was going to play out... but suspecting it wouldn't be pretty or enjoyable."[15] Iwasaki remembers Sanders as a terrific counter wrestler; "for timid opponents, at times he'd 'dare' you to try to grab a leg to get something going." Ron rarely got a takedown on Rick. "My best—and probably most memorable—was getting the initial takedown in the Oregon High School State Wrestling Championship Finals in 1963. He escaped then I got a second fireman's to end the first period up 3-1 (a second and any subsequent takedowns were only one point back then). Unfortunately for me, the final score was Rick 13 to my 5. None of my matches were close," Ron admits. "There were some surprising moments I suppose, maybe getting a couple cradles on Rick one time." Iwasaki recalled, "Rick got tougher as the match went on, sometimes while on top he'd relax to see what you might try to do… but if he was on a mission… it seemed unrelenting."

Sanders' resting heart rate measured in the low forties, an aerobic level on par with 1972 Olympian, Steve Prefontaine.[16] Sanders assessed his own capacities: "Technique-wise I'm not extremely good, but I have a lot of endurance and rely on conditioning. I don't get tired and my heartbeat, when I'm in top shape, is only 45 per minute." With that kind of endurance, Sanders might have competed well in the Robin Reed era of the 1920s. Reed, a lightweight also of Portland and a Multnomah Athletic Club (MAC) member, was a 1924 gold medal Olympian. The catch-as-catch-can wrestling style at that time, based on submission holds, might have a match last over an hour. All in all, if misery loves company, Iwasaki should've been quite comfortable. And as a measure of their respective ability levels, Oregon in 1962-1963 allowed two wrestlers in each weight class from each school to try for the same individual state championship. Iwasaki was unequivocally second best. There was little chance at dodging quality opponents.

Sanders: In the Moment

Rick Sanders displays with pride most valuable wrestling trophies.

Rick Sanders Captures Third State Wrestling Championship

"Pound for pound Sanders is as fine an athlete as the P. I. L. ever produced in a specialized field." This well-earned compliment was paid to Senior, Rick Sanders, by Mr. Leo Davis, sports writer for the Oregonian.

Wrestling his way to fame, Rick has established a record that has made the student body of Lincoln very proud of him. As a freshman he won the city's 98 pound title. This performance was repeated his sophomore year and he earned his first state championship. As a junior he gained the city and state championship in the 106 pound weight class. Rick's wrestling career ended in high school with the capturing of the city championship in the 115 pound division. This year he was presented with the outstanding wrestler in the P. I. L. trophy and gained the state championship. With this final victory, he became the second person in Oregon to ever hold three state titles.

For the past three seasons he has led in team points and pins. For all his hard work and devotion to wrestling, Rick has been honored by the Lincoln P. T. A. with the most valuable wrestler award for three consecutive years.

The best Portland Interscholastic Conference athlete ever produced. Photo and original caption courtesy of Cardinal Lincoln High School yearbook, 1963.

Sanders: In the Moment

Rick had a rather up and down year as a senior at Lincoln High School in 1963. His wrestling was par excellence. With his final victory, he became the second person in Oregon to ever hold three state titles.[17] Not only had he won his third state championship, this one at 115 pounds, but he was also presented with the Portland Interscholastic League outstanding wrestler trophy after winning his fourth city championship. He led Lincoln High School's team in points and pins for the past three seasons. The Lincoln P.T.A. honored him with the Most Valuable Wrestler award for the third consecutive year. But academically, he struggled. ADHD-affected students, though not unintelligent, often do not follow through on instructions and fail to finish schoolwork. They avoid, dislike, or are reluctant to engage in tasks that require sustained mental effort like homework. Whatever the circumstances, Rick lacked credits to graduate and left school in the last quarter under a disciplinary policy. A fifth of whiskey was allegedly found in his locker.[18]

Rick ended high school with a win-loss record of 80-1. His only loss was to the aforementioned Gary Head of Klamath Falls. Sanders' high school career is highlighted in Bob Allen's wonderful book, *55 Years of Excellence* (2017). The book documents Oregon prep wrestling dating back from the 2000s. In it, Allen queries 45 Oregon wrestling aficionados to rate Oregon's Best:

> "Part of the interview process was to ask the question: Who do you feel were the best five to eight wrestlers from each weight class from 1960 through today?" A scoring system of 10-8-6-4-2-1 was developed to reflect their opinions. The team that was formed involved moving the highest point producers into a weight the wrestler competed in *sometime* in high school. Without this method, Rick Sanders would have been the choice in three weight classes."(98#, 106#, & 115#)

Sanders: In the Moment

Allen's book profiles eleven of the toughest brackets over the last 55 years as well. A tough bracket is inherent in most tournaments: one that has parity among wrestlers, one or more superstars, and often an upset of a heavy favorite. The 1961 98-pound bracket for A-1 high schools was voted 9th out of 60 by a panel of coaches, officials, and fans. Sanders prevailed in that bracket as a sophomore in his first high school state championship 1-0 over Jerry Abaas of Redmond.[19]

Sanders completed his high school career admirably. Lincoln High School coaches recognized his talent early and they encouraged their protégé in a sport that demanded affirmation and confidence. It was fortuitous that the Sanders' move from Oakridge to Portland resulted in a downtown residence near not only Lincoln High School but also the Multnomah Athletic Club. Rick benefitted from the caliber of workout partners

Pictured, left: Rick sent this highschool senior picture to Melvin who, when Rick was twelve, abandoned him. Rick signed it: "To My Father With Love, Rick."

in both wrestling rooms. Even some of Sanders' adolescent deficits seemed to benefit his prep wrestling success. His attention deficit and academic challenges left Rick unhindered to focus on wrestling. But what to do now that high school wrestling was over and college requirements were sorely lacking? Could wrestling be pursued beyond high school? Did Sanders have the desire and talent to take wrestling to the next level?

To the casual observer, occasional fan, or even many dedicated wrestlers, the decision to endure the enormous physical and psychological commitment to completely expose one's vulnerabilities, one-on-one, on a wrestling mat before bleachers full of critics and fans, begs for some rationale. The desire to become a wrestler seems to be a quest for self-discovery. Its inherency exists at varying degrees and lengths of time for all humanity; a pecking order at a primal level. For grapplers, at an early age, attitude begins to manifest and a perceived notion of dominance over peers eddies forth in search of confirmation. Each time out on the mat, whether in practice or competition, more self-discovery occurs. It's painful and seemingly purposeless, but the drive is there and the chance for discovery overwhelms and indeed subsumes all negatives: hours of drilling technique, running miles and miles, dieting, cutting weight in steam rooms and rubber suits, strength training, spitting in a cup, peeing and pooping to make weight, mat burns, jammed digits, and so on. All of this strife ends on a prayer, a mantra of "I can get that guy!" For many, high school level wrestling is sufficient, the search fulfilled. Yet, at collegiate and international levels, it's more than winning or achievement. It's testing new hypotheses or the stretching of old ones, experimenting with confidence levels, and blending the results of those tests into the individual psyche.

Author J.R.L. Anderson recognizes the quest for self-discovery in his 1970 book *The Ulysses Factor*. There is some factor in man, some form of special adaptation, which prompts a few individuals to seek exploits which, however purposeless they may seem, are of value to the survival of the race. In *The Ulysses Factor*, the individual needs to engage physically in pursuit of a goal. Anderson described this as a personal experience, explaining, "Your own foot must tread the mountain top, your own eyes see the waves, your own hand be on the tiller."[20]

Sanders' drive to wrestle at the elite level was an effort at self-discovery. He was a champion at the high school level. With the dwindling scope for physical exploration of the world, men invented new goals. Rick's turf was the wrestling mat. His courage propelled him on his own through downtown Portland's Park Blocks neighborhood to world-wide venues. Sanders was uncommon among his peers however. He seemed to look forward joyfully to the intricacies unique to each match. There was a possibility in each match for fan approval, a smidgen of media notice, the balm of peer acceptance, the fascination of a new move created, even escape to or from the divine.

In Genesis 32:24, Jacob wrestles all night with an angel disguised as a man. At dawn the man wrenched Jacob's hip out of joint, yet Jacob would not let the man go until he blessed him. And the man did. There was no ostensible purpose for the match; no stadium full of fans; the man was incognito. But the match was concluded, the blessing bestowed by the enlightenment of God. Perhaps that was what Sanders unwittingly was searching for at the highest echelons—one enlightening match.

—

Rick would remain an itinerant of downtown Portland the remainder of his life. He resided at several locations, barely moving outside a square mile area. He lived with his mother through moves precipitated by urban renewal projects resulting from President Johnson's 1960s Great Society initiative. Inner city low income and dilapidated housing was raised and replaced using federal money funneled to city government. Sanders lived intermittently with teammates while he attended Portland State during his college years and after. Rick never owned a car, and so most of his employment through the years was at downtown restaurants and bars. Sanders learned how to wrestle freestyle (the international form of wrestling) at the downtown Multnomah Athletic Club (MAC) located a short jog from Lincoln High School. Rick practiced and competed in Amateur Athletic Union (AAU) wrestling tournaments supported by the Multnomah Athletic Club. The MAC remains an elite and vibrant club today with over 17,000 members. Wrestling is no longer in vogue, but the sport's heritage is rich with past members and Wall of Fame icons such as Robin Reed, John Miller, Henk Schenk, and Rick Sanders.

The AAU was the national governing body for U.S. competition in all amateur sports at the international level during the 1950s and 1960s.[21] At the time, U.S. wrestlers lacked opportunities to compete domestically in freestyle and Greco-Roman, the international forms of the sport. Their high school and college wrestling was folkstyle, a style significantly different from freestyle and Greco. Folkstyle places more of an emphasis on the ability to control an opponent on the mat, whereas the focus in freestyle and Greco is more on exposing a competitor's back to scoring positions and ultimately pinning an opponent. A proficiency in freestyle and Greco is excellent training for folkstyle, and Sanders benefited from his early exposure to all styles. The AAU sponsored tournaments at clubs around the country like the MAC, The San Francisco Athletic Club, Mayor Daley Youth Foundation Wrestling Club of Chicago, and the New York Athletic Club. However, the lack of wrestling programs and financial support provided by the AAU was a continuing frustration to

U.S. coaches and athletes. Don Schollander, a '64 and '68 Olympic gold medal swimmer from Lake Oswego, a Portland suburb, decried the ineptness of the AAU in his book *Deep Water*.[22] Likewise, Steve Prefontaine, the famed Oregon distance runner, and Sanders, both being honored at a MAC recognition dinner one night, spent much of that evening commiserating about their inherent frustrations with the AAU.

After the 1960 Olympics and the beginning of the Cold War era, the U,S. Government encouraged higher levels of athletic achievement that augured well for the AAU. The Soviet Union, under Premier Nikita Khrushchev, recognized the propaganda value of gold medals. The Rome Olympics produced three gold medal winners in wrestling for the U.S. It was the best wrestling team result in twenty-eight years. Terry McCann of Chicago won gold at 125.5 pounds. McCann was a University of Iowa product and two-time NCAA champion. Shelby Wilson also won gold. Wilson wrestled at 147.5 pounds. Wilson was a tough farm kid that battled for Oklahoma State while in college. Finishing runner up in two NCAA championships, his "never quit" attitude led him to Rome in 1960 and to the top of the award stand. The third gold medal winner was Doug Blubaugh. He was also an Oklahoma farm kid known for toughness born of an arduous farm-life and intense workouts. He wrestled at the 1960 Olympics in the 160.5-pound weight class, weighing only 152 pounds.[23]

Blubaugh would go on to become a college and international wrestling coach. He was esteemed as great a coach as he was a wrestler. Dale Anderson, who was a two-time NCAA champion at Michigan State, where Blubaugh was assistant coach on their 1967 national championship team, reflected, "Doug was the catalyst for those great Michigan State teams. I have always believed it was Doug who made us so darn tough. He was just so darn tough himself, both physically and mentally. He showed us what it meant to be a champion. It wasn't about his ego; it was about him teaching. He truly knew how to coach, as well as wrestle."[24]

The 1960 Olympic wrestling venue was perhaps the most unique of the modern era. It was held on mats beneath the ancient vaults of the Basilica of Maxentius, named after the emperor who envisioned and nearly completed the colossal building. The Basilica was meant to hold public gatherings and to display the power of Rome. However, before it could be completed, Maxentius was killed in a power struggle with Constantine I, who fortunately decided to complete the edifice. Built in the fourth century, much of the building has been destroyed by earthquakes. Yet its history and what remains of its mammoth structure created a stellar site for the wrestling competition. Even the ancients struggled to complete Olympic venues on time.

The Rome Olympics was the first to be broadcast on television. The persuasive value of the media was recognized early on, creating more national emphasis on physical fitness and scientific advancement spurred by the space race with the Soviet Union. Wrestling, as one of the traditional Olympic sports, deserved the grandeur of the ancient Basilica of Maxentius as its venue. The modern medium of television was a wonderful accent to American Olympic mat success.

The stellar performance at the 1960 Rome Olympics meant the pressure was on for future Olympic success. The Olympic success of McCann, Wilson, and Blubaugh would have been the first noticed by high school sophomore wrestling phenom Rick Sanders. They set the stage and helped inform his goals and ambitions. Sanders would compete for an Olympic team spot himself in 1964.

Rick's workouts with MAC partners were Herculean. When in high school, he would wrestle through practice at Lincoln then run over to the MAC a few blocks away and practice through the evening. The MAC wrestling room had the characteristic ambiance that pervades all "rooms" around the sport. It was cramped, overwarm, aesthetic-less, had the sole welcoming feel of Resilite mats, and exuded the unique smell of muffled sweat. Sanders belonged to the environment. It was home.

At one point, Rick's MAC membership was in jeopardy. He was allegedly apprehended running naked through a Portland Street. It would not be the last time that rumors of public indecency would be alleged against Sanders. Throughout Sanders' storied life, he was prone to inattention. On the conjecture that Rick fit somewhere on the ADHD spectrum, where sufferers often have difficulty organizing tasks and activities, he may have found himself late for practice, work, or a ride, and planned to dress en route. Lincoln High School's locker room was so close to the MAC wrestling room, Sanders may have gapped on decorum moving between practice sessions. The disciplinary committee of the gentlemen's club found in favor of the defendant, however, and Rick continued his club membership, a favorite though prodigal son.

The MAC was Sanders' portal to the world. Wrestling took him to Japan, Canada, Argentina, Sweden, Germany, Mexico, Finland, England, India, and Spain, as well as several states in-country. A photo of Rick is prominently displayed today in the club's public foyer, a lasting reminder of a hundred-pound waif who grew up in the neighborhood.[25]

The MAC not only provided a training venue for Sanders—it also became financial support for his wrestling quests. Rick would, on several occasions, cash in AAU and MAC sponsored travel vouchers to handle expenses and hitchhike to distant tournament venues. Athletes aspiring to compete as Olympians had to maintain amateur status. They could not endorse products or "cash in" on their notoriety as athletes commonly do today. High profile athletes were particularly at risk. Their relationships with employers, schools, private donors, et. al. were continually monitored by the AAU. The MAC's affiliation with the AAU protected Sanders from culpability for accepting financial support from a private organization.

Cyril Mitchell coached Rick under the auspices of the club, and Sanders won four national AAU championships competing on the MAC team. Mitchell was involved in wrestling at the MAC for sixty one years—fifty eight as coach and six years (from age 72) as a masters athlete. Masters-level competitors are established by age groups beginning as early as twenty-five and continuing through septuagenarian and octogenarian categories depending on the tournament. Cy won the 1922 Portland city-wide high school championship at 98 pounds, though he weighed barely 85 pounds. He went on to win several AAU open tournaments, becoming the second alternate on the 1928 U.S. Olympic team. His career at the MAC played in concert with his private insurance business. In addition, he served on wrestling's U.S. Olympic Committee and refereed in several Olympics. Pitted against his own age group in the masters wrestling program, he won six national championships.[26]

Sanders found in Cy Mitchell a solid mentor. Mitchell was a good leg technician from top position when both wrestlers were down on the mat. Sanders had unusually strong legs and was uncommonly flexible. Sanders' association with Mitchell and the solid competition provided by workout partners such as Johnny Miller, Ron Calhoun, Bob Bergen, and Marlin Grahn was serendipitous.

Sanders was quickly transitioning to the next level of competition. He was hanging on to wrestling at the MAC, which provided some sense of stability. His academic standing prevented matriculation to the college setting. He needed to finish some high school credits or earn a GED. Finding the inspiration to complete college entrance requirements could only evolve in service to Sanders' wrestling goals. Wrestling gave him purpose, routine, and stimulation, and it would ultimately get him into college.

The sixties culture was "tripping" along in 1963. Professor Timothy Leary was kicked off the Harvard faculty for experimenting with Lysergic acid diethylamide, commonly known as LSD. The drug was accidentally discovered by a Swiss chemist who, after the discovery, looking for potential medical uses and sources of remuneration, naturally sent it to the United States. Medical professionals found little medicinal efficacy. The drug ultimately was repurposed as a way to expand the collective mind of the youth counterculture. Acid trips were endorsed by Leary as a way to "Turn on, tune in, and drop out."[27] Many did, including Ken Kesey, a one-time University of Oregon wrestler and author of *One Flew Over the Cuckoo's Nest* and *Sometimes a Great Notion*. President Nixon, in his war on drugs during the early '70s, labeled Dr. Leary "Public Enemy Number One." Though Sanders would be accused of psychonautic acid trips, friends dispute the allegations. Sanders, on the other hand, may have enjoyed the accusation in the same way an adolescent enjoys the reputation of being caught smoking in the school bathroom.

At the end of summer 1963, across the nation, 250,000 people gathered at the Lincoln Memorial in Washington D.C. to advocate for civil rights. Martin Luther King, speaking for the disadvantaged, departed from his prepared speech and delivered impromptu remarks which became known as the "I have a Dream" speech, to wit: "I have a dream my four little children will one day live in a nation where they will not be judged by the color of their skin but by the content of their character..." The speech was covered by all three national T.V. broadcasting stations.[28] Millions were moved by the power of the suggestion that their own best nature might be revealed in a country committed to equal opportunity. King's message of hope tied to opportunity would not have been lost on

Sanders who, though originating from a poor socioeconomic background, was building an identity as an athlete of some renown.

The message Dr. King espoused, however, conflicted with the cavalier sixties counterculture message. Dr. Leary suggested, "live for today." Hope and character took time. A disciplined world view and deferred gratification was old school. Sanders lived the remainder of his life at the confluence of these conflicting worldviews. Wrestling took discipline and devotion. Personal freedom was an unbounded inalienable right. Handled with maturity, combining these worldviews had the potential to reach great heights. Sanders was still an adolescent finding his own way after high school.

Arising like a shaggy mane mushroom from the substrate of a youth spent on the streets of Portland's inner city, Rick was an emerging athlete—delicate, unformed, rare, and valuable. He sallied forth, looking for new wrestling conquests, undaunted by lack of a high school diploma or disciplinary infractions. He was ready to seek out his next challenge. The quest took him to Japan.

Chapter Three

The 1960 Olympics may have inopportunely affected Sanders' future Olympic aspirations. The Japanese wrestling team did so poorly in the 1960 Olympics, they shaved their heads in disgrace, and recommitted to the 1964 Olympic Games where they won five gold medals.[1] The renewed focus by Japan set the Japanese performance standard for future Olympic wrestlers Shigeo Nakata in 1968 and Hideaki Yanagida in 1972. Nakata and Yanagida became formidable opponents for Rick Sanders in future international competitions. Moreover, part of Japan's strategy was to create a conduit of Japanese wrestlers competing in American programs.

Oregon State's revered coach, Dale Thomas, was instrumental in developing a cultural exchange trip with Japan. A common theme within the sport suggests that to become a great wrestler, one must compete with the best. Coaches like Oregon's Thomas and Oklahoma State's Myron Roderick, following this maxim, encouraged and facilitated the cultural exchanges. A Japanese team toured Oregon during Rick's high school senior year, though his Lincoln High team did not compete in the exchange. Instead, the touring Japanese team competed against several Oregon prep teams, each assembled from local talent in their area. The outcome was predictable; the Japanese annihilated the Oregonians.[2] The return trip to Japan was scheduled for the summer of 1963. A different result was meticulously planned by Oregon prep coaches Delance Duncan and John Dustin. They assembled an Oregon All Star team to avenge the lop-sided losses.

Dale Thomas was a member of the 1947 NCAA Dream Team from Cornell College of Mount Vernon, Iowa. Cornell, at the time, was a private Methodist liberal arts college with 824 students. There was only one division of college wrestling at the time, with 102 member schools. The Cornell wrestling team, coached by Paul Scott, won the NCAA team championship in '47. Iowa Teachers College, now Northern Iowa, came in second; Oklahoma State, third. Dale Thomas was runner-up at heavyweight. Thomas completed his Ph.D. at the University of Iowa, was on two Olympic teams, and in 1957, took over the head coaching position at Oregon state where, according to Arno Niemand's *The Dream Team of 1947*, "He became the driving force behind wrestling in the state."[3] Thomas coached the Beavers for 34 years, amassing a never equaled dual-meet record of 616 wins. His teams won 22 conference titles and finished in the top ten at the NCAA tournament 14 times.

Coach Thomas was a force of character. He was supremely confident in the court of public opinion. His right ideas dominated his wrong ideas, and therefore, with few exceptions, challengers deferred to him. He was that rare coach whose personality is recognized among the greats, inclusive of anyone who lasted four years as a Beaver wrestler. A half nod from Thomas was gold to a student-athlete and the best to the least were in service to it. Steve Woods, a former Beaver, helped to define the undefinable Thomas in his book *Sorta Tough:*

> I remember little of my match that night but I do remember keeping one eye on "The Coach" as the match progressed. I do recall that I wrestled well, mostly out of fear, and distinctly recall the utter indifference shown by this intimidating presence that shared the mat with me and my

opponent. I was intimidated, my opponent was intimidated, the coaches were intimidated, and the crowd was intimidated.[4]

Dale Thomas made a habit of looking for kids from rural settings for his Oregon State teams. He characterized teams from certain communities as "the country club teams"—those that wouldn't persevere if times got difficult.[5] Sanders, being from Portland city center, therefore, did not fit the Thomas profile. Thomas once commented that, "Rick wrestled like a caged rat!" It was a positive reference, especially from a coach who did not coddle or recruit "city kids." Sanders gave little consideration to Oregon State for his wrestling future.

Yet Thomas is credited for the growth of youth wrestling in Oregon. Part of his legacy included the cultural exchange program with Japan, of which Sanders was a beneficiary. DeLance Duncan and John Dustin were the coaches at the reins for the 1963 return trip. Duncan, from Nespelem, Washington, wrestled for Washington State in the early 1950s. He became a high school coach in Oregon beginning at Klamath Falls for a half dozen years but finished at David Douglas High School in Portland with a 27-year run. He has the distinction of coaching Gary Head, the only wrestler to beat Rick Sanders in high school. John Dustin was a two time All-American for Oregon State and coached at Marshfield High School from 1962-1970 before moving into school administration. These two coaches avenged one of the "darkest competitive periods in Oregon high school wrestling"—The drubbing given by the visiting Japanese team the previous winter. The Japanese national team had flattened all eighteen Oregon teams it met. In response, Duncan and Dustin carefully assembled arguably the best prep team in the state's history.

A qualifying tournament was held at Corvallis, Oregon, using international freestyle rules to determine team members. Four hundred and twenty high school athletes entered the freestyle trials tournament following the high school state championships. Sanders lost his first post high school match in a best of three series with Jeff Batchelor, a state champion and eventual BYU collegian, but Rick prevailed, winning two of three matches and earned a spot on the historic cultural exchange team.

Team members joining Sanders on that junket to Japan included Rich Henjyoji, Grant Humphry, Keith Flack, Don Dykstra, Rollin Schimmel, Fred Fozzard, Henk Schenk, Don Kauffman, and Harold Weight. Many of these team members would go on to impressive collegiate and international careers. Henjyoji became a national AAU champion in 1965; Schimmel won a 1967 NAIA national title and Outstanding Wrestler award; Fozzard won a 1967 NCAA championship, three national AAU titles and a World Championship in 1969; Schenk was a six-time freestyle and Greco AAU national champion and a 1968 and 1972 Olympian; and Weight was a NAIA national champion.[6]

Governor Mark Hatfield sent Sanders a letter of encouragement: "In each of your appearances you will be given an opportunity to exemplify both a high level of talent and a respect for sportsmanship which can accrue to this nation's good reputation as well as your own self-respect."[7] It is likely each team member received the hand-signed letter. But the letter made the scrapbook. Well-meaning, avuncular, if not fatherly advice to an Oregon favorite son who navigated life with neither an uncle nor a father.

The Oregonians lost their first meeting in Japan. Sanders was taken to his back early in the first four-minute period and bridged for most of the time to avoid being pinned. He wrestled well in the second period, but had too much to make up. Rick was defeated a second time in Japan before finishing 7 and 2 for the tour. The American team finished the tour with a 65-19-3 win/loss record. The team out-pinned the Japanese 30-0. Henk Schenk was outstanding, pinning 8 of 9 opponents.

Sanders: In the Moment

The tour schedule was rigorous—five all night train rides, two involving transfers to and from ferry boats. Every city produced fatiguing schedules of sightseeing and official functions. The American team covered 2000 miles in three weeks. Yet the hospitality was intimate, with the athletes staying in the homes of Japanese opponents. The team met virtually every reigning politician in the country along with a few of the royalty. The Japanese were dominant in the lower four weights, but the heavier weight classes belonged to the Oregonians. Sanders wrestled at 120 pounds and was, according to Coach Duncan, the most popular American with the Japanese for his aggressive, high scoring matches.

The Oregon/Japanese cultural exchange trip. Sanders front-left.

—

Sanders: In the Moment

At the tour's end, several of the Oregonian wrestlers were homesick and looking to future college and post high school plans. Not Rick. He wanted to stay in Japan. To that end, Rick's mother Anita provided him with a letter of permission to stay, and it was clear his intent was to stay. Japanese officials were leery. They wanted to avoid any potential international incident. Delance Duncan spent no little amount of diplomacy convincing Rick of his need to return to the United States. Rick was interested in his chances of continuing international competition by way of the 1964 Olympic trials. He also needed to complete a few high school credits, and he risked losing his job in the circulation department at the *Oregonian* delivering the daily newspaper. Sanders heeded Coach Duncan's counseling and returned to Oregon with the team.

Delance Duncan has been involved with Oregon wrestling for five decades. In his estimation, Rick Sanders was the greatest Oregon wrestler, with the possible exception of Robin Reed.[8] That observation includes the likes of Jess Lewis, Henk Schenk, Fred Fozzard, Len Kauffman, Greg Strobel, Larry Owings, and Les Gutches. Duncan believes, "While other guys were working to get their bachelor degrees in wrestling, Rick had a masters, a doctorate, and was always working on his wrestling post doctorate. You could show him something new and he'd come back next week with three more ways to accomplish the same result and five ways in which to defend the move." All in all, Duncan looks back at the 1963 Japanese Cultural Exchange trip as the most important experience in his 50-plus-year association with Oregon wrestling.

Back in the states, Sanders worked out at the MAC during the 1963-1964 wrestling season while attempting to become academically eligible for college. Cy Mitchell was able to arrange dual meet matches between the MAC and area colleges. Sanders won matches against Central Washington State, Oregon State, Eastern Oregon College, and

Sanders: In the Moment

Washington State. The MAC team wrestled Dale Thomas' Oregon State Beavers twice in 1964. Rick wrestled Gary Head, the only wrestler to beat him in high school, at both dual meets. Sanders decisioned Head, now an Oregon State Beaver, in a match at Corvallis on January 11th, ten-zero. A month later in February, the two met again in Portland. Rick won that match, wrestled under international rules, by pin. Gary Head was a worthy opponent. He went on to win the Pacific Coast Intercollegiate conference tournament by pin in the championship match that year.

Sanders, wrestling for the MAC a week later in February, pinned his Washington State Cougar opponent in 1:46. The MAC won the Portland match over Oregon State 17-9, and beat Washington State 32-0. Nineteen-year-old Sanders was back in Corvallis two months later in April for the 1964 western regional Olympic tryouts.

While Sanders worked on entering college and adjusting from his cultural experience in Japan, he found American culture in a state of flux. President Kennedy, assassinated in November of 1963, was replaced by Lyndon Baines Johnson, the 36th President of the United States. Johnson's frenetic work ethic resulted in 184,000 U.S. troops in Vietnam by 1965, introduction of his grandiose "Great Society" policy including an unconditional war on poverty, and the Civil Rights Act of 1964. Urban renewal was part of Johnson's war on poverty. Portland officials demolished the homes and businesses of thousands of low income and minority residents and forced them to relocate under Great Society programs.[9] The city, like many urban centers, scraped away decaying areas and recast them in the modern mold despite protests from long-time residents who were proud of their homes and wanted to remain in them. The Sanders family relocated, yet remained in the downtown area where Rick's mother was able to continue to walk to work.

Sanders: In the Moment

Rock and roll, drugs, and protest evolved into the counterculture. But according to Chris Strain in *The Long Sixties*, "Before there were hippies, there were simply young people, normal in appearance but discontent and yearning for change, trying new things, and pushing the limits of convention."[10] Strain's analysis fits Sanders' counterculture assimilation quite well. It was not Sanders' objective to be a catalyst for change. Rather, he delighted in the novelty of new trends and a range of new personal freedoms to exercise. He enjoyed the music and the earthiness of the dress and hairstyles. The sexual openness of the era was not lost on Sanders, but he was not characteristically anti-establishment. That attitude would manifest later in his career.

Rick was unlike his contemporary, Cassius Clay, who self-proclaimed his solitary "greatness" from the start of his career. Clay was the light-heavyweight gold medal winner at the 1960 Olympics where he impressed as many people from his loquacious pontificating as from his athleticism. Later, Clay became the 1964 heavyweight boxing champion of the world, knocking out Sonny Liston. Clay would, soon after his victory, join the Nation of Islam, change his name to Muhammad Ali, and protest military service in Vietnam. Sanders was never that overt about drawing attention to himself using political ideology. Rick was more subtle in his attempt to gain attention. When he felt his wrestling prowess did not garner sufficient crowd appeal, he later resorted to long hair, a beard, and love beads. Rick could be ostentatious, however. 1964 AAU teammate Bruce Glenn recalls Sanders' entrance to the wrestling arena for a match wearing white sweatpants, his head covered with a white hoodie, and dragging his characteristic duffle bag behind him on a rope! Rick was bold, but his actions were clearly benign.

For Sanders, the era came and went fast and flashy. The change and freedom he was looking for is perhaps best exemplified by the introduction of what Henry Ford II billed as "The Working Man's Thunderbird"—the 1964 Ford Mustang. The style and name exuded freedom, wildness, and untamed libido, an identity Rick assumed with relish and no harm intended. An athlete at Sanders' elite level today can afford muscle cars and trucks. Sanders wouldn't have had money to fill the vehicle with gas.

Rick was fortunate, then, to be invited to join fellow Oregonian wrestlers Bruce Glenn and Joe McFarland on a cross continent trip to wrestle in the 1964 National AAU tournament. The grapplers traveled in a first-generation motorized camper.[11] The AAU tournament was held at Singer Bowl, located on the grounds of the New York World's Fair at Flushing Meadow from June 22nd through the 25th. Singer Bowl was one of the first athletic arenas that looked like most sports arenas on college campuses today. It held 18,000 fans with locker room facilities for 200 athletes. The facility was built by the Singer Sewing Machine Company. During the AAU tournament, the open-air competition area became so hot, mats had to be moved under the canopied areas, displacing World Fair exhibits displaying sewing machines, typewriters, vacuum sweepers, and new computing devices. The venue doubled one month later, lasting August 24th-29th, as the site for the "Final Squad Selection Tournament" for the 1964 Olympic wrestling team.

The 1964 Olympic wrestling trials had been held at twenty regional sites around the country. Sanders competed successfully in the Oregon regional at Corvallis on April 10th and 11th. Rick wrestled at 125.5 pounds, the international bantamweight class at New York in both the AAU and Olympic tournaments. His first opponent in the AAU competition was two-time NCAA champion from Cornell, Dave Auble. Auble was a tough veteran. He graduated from college in 1960, so he was seven years older than nineteen-year-old Sanders. Bruce Glenn recalls the

Sanders: In the Moment

Auble/Sanders match as a heated battle both physically and because temperatures were so hot. The competition took place outdoors and the temperatures were in the 90s. The mats were almost too hot to wrestle on. Sanders' unorthodox style and youth so frustrated Auble that when the match was over with Auble victorious, Sanders received a middle finger salute from his opponent.[12] Sanders would meet Auble again six years later at the 1972 National AAU tournament—Rick's last—and avenge the loss competing at 136.5 pounds. Gray Simons, perhaps even more accomplished than Auble, was next up for Rick at the 1964 AAU New York tournament.

Simons makes virtually every list of "best ever wrestlers." He emanated from one of the country's great high school programs—Granby High School coached by the esteemed Billy Martin.[13] Martin won 22 team titles in 23 years coaching. The Granby Roll, a move executed most often from bottom position, was developed in Martin's program and its ubiquitous use is indicative of Martin's success as a coach. From that solid base, Simons entered the college ranks wrestling for Lock Haven, an NAIA college in Pennsylvania. He became legendary, winning four NAIA championships and three NCAA titles in the 1958-1962 period. Accenting his seven college championships were six outstanding wrestler awards—four at the NAIA championships and two at the NCAA level. That record will likely never be matched. NAIA champions are no longer eligible to wrestle at the Division I level as they once were. Simons wrestled at 115 pounds throughout college and during two Olympics. In his final Olympic run in 1964, Simons met Sanders first at the AAU tournament in June after Rick's loss to Auble. Simons beat Rick and eliminated Sanders' chances of placing in the 1964 AAU tournament.

Though failing to place, Sanders had looked impressive against both Auble and Simons. Therefore, he was invited to an International Rules and

Sanders: In the Moment

Holds clinic to be held at Russ Houk's wrestling camp in Pennsylvania. The camp covered all expenses, but invitees had to get there.[14] The timing was great for Sanders since it provided him a place to train with the best and stay free of charge until the Olympic Squad Selection Tournament began August 24th back at Singer Arena in New York. This was the first of several times Rick would attend Houk's camp over his career. Typically, it was no problem for Sanders to sojourn in the Pennsylvania area. However, trouble would catch up to Rick along a Pennsylvania turnpike in the future that would significantly impact his career.

Both Sanders and Simons dropped down to compete at 114.5 pounds at the New York Olympic Final Squad Selection Tournament. Auble remained at 125.5 pounds. Rick had a respectable tournament but did not finish in the top two. Simons and Okla Johnson of Michigan earned the right to move on to the Final Olympic Team Selection held at the U.S. Naval Academy in Annapolis, Maryland. The final Olympic training camp began September 4th and lasted three weeks. The U.S. Wrestling Olympic Committee, at its discretion, added nine wrestlers to the Naval Academy challenge matches. Sanders was invited, and even as an alternate could continue to vie for the 114.5-pound Olympic featherweight spot.

Through a series of single elimination bouts, the number one man was determined. If an alternate, like Sanders, reached the semi-finals, he was required to win two of three matches in challenging the number two man for the right to meet number one. The Olympic spot on the team was determined in two of three final matches. Sanders worked his way through the gauntlet. Rick decisioned Okla Johnson 4-3 to get to Simons. Sanders had improved his skill level by competing with the best all summer long. However, Simons defeated Rick 6-1 and 2-0 in the finals.

The outcome of the final Olympic trials held at the U.S. Naval Academy in '64 sent Simmons to Tokyo, Japan and Rick back to Portland,

Sanders: In the Moment

Sanders (second row, 2nd from left) spent the summer of '64 in New York, Pennsylvania, and Maryland wrestling in the AAU Nationals tournament, the Olympic Trials, and at Russ Houk's legendary wrestling camp in Pennsylvania.

—

a first alternate on the 1964 Olympic team. Dave Auble won the Olympic spot at the 125.5-pound bantamweight class. Sanders had been in the New York, Pennsylvania, and Maryland area wrestling from June 22nd through most of September 1964. He was nineteen years old and on his own. His commitment to the sport was unwavering. He was something like a vaudeville performer, never quite knowing where he would lay his head or eat his next meal. It didn't seem to matter—he was "all in." Hall of fame Olympian Wayne Baughman observed, "I first encountered Rick at the 1964 Olympic Trials. He didn't make the team but he looked more impressive against Gray Simons than anyone had in a long time," said Baughman. "Sanders could wrestle as hard and fast as anybody who ever lived. It wasn't unusual for him to be behind 10 or 12 points and come storming back to annihilate his opponent."[15]

In a rare effort, Rick also competed for a spot on the '64 Greco-Roman Olympic team. He lost twice to Dick Wilson at 114.5 pounds. Wilson was a member of two previous Olympic Greco-Roman teams—1956 and 1960. The Greco-Roman wrestling style is different from freestyle in that Greco wrestlers may not use holds below the waist to score points. Therefore, the Greco wrestler attempts to score using headlocks, body locks, and arm drags to take their opponent down from a standing position. Gut wrenches are used to turn an opponent when on the mat. Wrestlers cannot attempt to move forward to escape when on the mat in the down position since the top wrestler would of necessity need to attack the legs to prevent the escape. The Greco wrestler also uses a move known as a suplex in which the attacking wrestler lifts their opponent in a high arch, exposing their opponents back to the mat in the process. Sanders was not at his best if not able to scramble on the mat, attack and use his legs. His tryout was unsuccessful. Sanders wrestled Greco-Roman internationally only one more time, when he failed to place as a member of the 1965 World Team competing in Finland.

It would be difficult to underestimate the importance of Sanders' 1964 summer/fall trip to the AAU national tournament and Olympic Trials at New York's Singer Arena. While Sanders was ultimately unsuccessful at any of the three tournaments, the experience and confidence he gained sharpened his wrestling skill set. The swath that Sanders would go on to cut through the collegiate ranks was clearly influenced by his formative matches with the likes of Auble and Simons. Also competing at Singer Arena were Bobby Douglas, Don Behm, and Tadaaki and Masaaki Hatta. Each wrestler influenced Sanders' future success.

Sanders: In the Moment

The United States freestyle wrestling team won one medal at the 1964 Olympics, a bronze by Dan Brand at 191.5 pounds.[16] The poor showing is attributed in part to the few falls achieved by the United States team—only four. A win by fall avoids any black marks and improves the wrestler's opportunity to move on and compete in succeeding rounds of competition. By contrast, the U.S.'s 1960 freestyle Olympians recorded fourteen falls, resulting in three medals, all gold.

Failing to pin opponents clearly influenced the American freestyle result, but subpar equipment also played a role. It's likely Gray Simons' success at the international level was compromised by the quality of European wrestling mats. The old horsehair and straw-filled canvas wrestling mats were eventually replaced by the PVC Rubber Nitrile foam and polyethylene foam mats in use today. The improved surfaces of the modern material would have better suited the faster style of finesse wrestlers like Simons. Not only did the old-style mats bunch up, preventing a consistent reliable attack, but they often caused injury, mat burns, and infection. Warren F. Tischler, a high school, college, and AAU wrestler, returned from WWII and developed the insular foam mat that is the standard in use in the world today. His firm, Resilite Sport Products, Inc., demonstrates the quality of its product by dropping a raw egg from the height of a two-story building to prove their mats' shock absorbency.[17] An unbroken egg, tantamount to an unscarred and unbroken wrestler. Sanders benefited from the new-age mats. His high school and college wrestling was done on Resilite-type wrestling surfaces. He was accustomed to the faster surfaces which would be in use at the 1968 Mexico City Olympics.

New products improved athletic performance in other sports as well. Pole vaulters and high jumpers landed in sand and sawdust pits for years. Descending from heights of six feet in the high jump to sixteen feet in the pole vault during the 1940s and 1950s, and commonly into loose to hard pack sand and sawdust, was inhibiting, often painful. Inventor Don Gordon developed and marketed a foam product revolutionizing track and field with what he labeled the Port-a-Pit. High jump records began to ascend. Dick Fosbury, the 1968 Olympic gold medalist from Oregon State University and founder of the Fosbury Flop high jump technique used almost exclusively today, commented after his Olympic triumph that he couldn't have won his gold medal without the Port-a-Pit's assurance of a safe landing.[18] Fosbury's style of flipping over the high jump bar backward and landing on one's shoulder and neck virtually replaced other techniques such as the scissors, western roll, and straddle, all used until the late 1960s. Technological advances were rapidly changing the limits of sports.

Despite Sanders' disappointing 1964 Olympic Trials finish, it wasn't for lack of focus. PSU teammate, Ron Calhoun, recalled Sanders' intensity on the mat. "Rick was totally concentrating the whole nine minutes he wrestled. He was always working for the pin. Even in practice, Rick was relentless."[19]

Mihaly Csikszentmihalyi is a Hungarian-born American psychologist who developed Flow Theory, colloquially known as "being in the zone."[20] Flow theory helps to explain Sanders' total concentration on the mat. An individual achieves flow when he or she is absorbed in an activity requiring absolute focus and application of his or her personal skill set. What the individual feels, wishes for, and thinks about is in harmony for the duration of the activity. Looking at the flow experience retroactively creates a sense of gratitude and happiness, joy, or euphoria. Csikszentmihalyi asserted that when people reflect on how the flow experience feels, they mention unique components of enjoyment so rewarding people feel that expending a great deal of energy is worthwhile simply to achieve it. The intensity of the enjoyment can seem so profound, minutes can stretch out to seem like hours while in the flow.

Wrestling is clearly an activity demanding extended focus and skill in order to accomplish the challenge. Csikszentmihalyi's "flow" is exemplified in the "on mat" experience. The enjoyment Rick experienced on the mat allowed him to exercise a sense of control over his actions. His sense of self emerged stronger after his flow experience. Rick rarely was defeated. He did not dwell on losses or offer much comment. It's likely he enjoyed the inherent joy in the matches he lost up until the final whistle blew.

There was never much grass that grew under Sanders' feet. With his high school career over, and the '64 Olympics underway without his participation, Rick needed a new venue. He'd obtained the credits necessary to enter college. But which college made sense for the next stage of his wrestling career?

He received a letter of interest from legendary coach Cliff Keen at the University of Michigan. Keen was a three-sport athlete at Oklahoma State University in the 1920s. He was undefeated in wrestling and won the Olympic trials in 1924, but was unable to compete in the Games because of a broken rib. His 45-year tenure coaching the Michigan wrestling team is the longest coaching career in wrestling history. His teams won 276 dual meets against 88 losses and 11 ties. Eleven national collegiate champions were crowned under his tutelage.[21] Coach Keen noticed Sanders at the Olympic Trials when Rick defeated Lansing, Michigan native Okla Johnson. Keen was interested in Sanders. A September 14, 1964 letter from coach Keen offered in part:

> Dear Richard:
>
> I am enclosing herewith, an application blank which you should send in as soon as possible... It was indeed a pleasure to meet you and to visit with you.

Sanders: In the Moment

  I am certain an opportunity to come to the University of Michigan would be one of the greatest things in your life. It will require the utmost effort on your part but I am quite sure that you have the determination to "make something of yourself" and to "go places."

  Please keep in touch with me and you can be sure that I will help you in every way possible.
  Sincerely,
  Cliff Keen   Wrestling Coach

Sanders never liked being called Richard, and perhaps that dissuaded him from attending Michigan. Keen would have been the most qualified coach Rick would ever have over his entire career. Sanders' free spirit might have fit with the times at Michigan, where Tom Hayden and the Students for a Democratic Society were active in the Civil Rights movement.[22]

  Instead, despite the potential possibilities, Rick stayed in the Pacific Northwest. Dale Thomas at Oregon State, ever in the parsimonious position of limited scholarship money, also was unable to attract the blue chipper. That honor would go to a different Oregonian coach. Right across the street from Lincoln High and the MAC, Howard Wescott of Portland State walked a couple blocks up the hill to the Sanders residence on Montgomery street and, flashing a broad smile, knocked on the door.

Chapter Four

Though Sanders' first attempt at the Olympic Games was unsuccessful, he was no doubt seasoned and perhaps inspired after the trials. Howard Westcott, Portland State University's wrestling coach, made his pitch recruiting Sanders right out of the Park blocks surrounding Portland State where Rick grew up. Clearly Westcott was aware of Sanders' wrestling ability. The PSU coach was also aware of Sanders' academic challenges. Westcott was an astute observer of the socioeconomic challenged athlete. He had been one himself.

Dr. Howard Westcott was a professor of physical education at Portland State University and perhaps the most eclectic college wrestling coach ever in the sport of collegiate wrestling. He graduated from Reed College in Portland with a degree in mathematics—a straight A student. Reed College is an elite liberal arts school with many notable students, such as Steve Jobs, founder of Apple and Pixar studios, who attended Reed as a freshman before dropping out of college. Reed is consistently one of the most liberal colleges in the United States, according to The Princeton Review. Westcott went on to graduate school, earning his MA and Ph.D. in mathematics from Columbia College. World War II was going on while Westcott was at Columbia. Howard tested at the highest level in the country in his P.E. military exam. Consequently, he was tasked by the military to develop a six-week basic training program for new recruits.[1] With his military obligation completed, Westcott became a wrestling assistant to Gus Peterson at Columbia College and taught health and physical education at Rice and Wyoming before returning to Reed as athletic director. Westcott joined the faculty at Portland State in 1952. He was head wrestling coach from 1952-1971 as well as assistant football coach. His grapplers never had a losing season.[2]

Westcott's approach to the sport had a uniquely cerebral aspect. He noted: "Our objective in the wrestling program is the growth of the individual, not only as a wrestler, but intellectually through the college program so he can achieve the highest possible professional level in his chosen career." Further, "Wrestling teaches the individual initiative, both on the mat and in his studies and a willingness to sacrifice. It is a highly developed team sport that teaches sacrifice for the good of the team and develops a tremendous amount of self-confidence and certainly self-preservation."[3] Most of Westcott's rather lofty platitudes could be concurred in by the athletes he coached. Clearly a collegiate wrestler will need to sacrifice to be a participant, and an individual sport like wrestling requires adequate levels of self-confidence. But perhaps no part of Westcott's philosophy was so valuable to Sanders as the assistance in keeping him academically eligible. Sanders was intelligent, but lacked discipline academically.

Sanders excelled under Westcott's tutelage, though Howard demonstrated very little wrestling technique. Even his practices were spare. Howard sat in a chair at mat-side beginning around 2:30 and monitored wrestlers coming and going as suited their schedules until about 5:00 or 6:00.[4] No calisthenics or team conditioning. Yet, the methodology was golden. PSU won an NCAA Division II National championship the second year in the division, with top four finishes in the first four years and one fifth place finish at the 1967 NCAA Division I championships at Iowa State.

Japanese high school phenom Masaru Yatabe, a Sanders' PSU teammate and two-time D-II national champion, was the de facto technician in charge of the room during the Sanders' years. According to Yatabe, "Rick was terrible at takedowns." Westcott's demonstration on how to set up a double or single leg takedown was comical. "One assumes a stance in front of your opponent, distract them by a single or double hand clap, then shoot for the legs."[5] The finer points of that approach were lost on Rick. He overcame his takedown deficiency in typical Sanders unorthodox approach. He offered his leg to an opponent, then proceeded with a maze of leg grapevines and hyperextended arm bars. A fan once asked, "Why do you let them in on your legs?" to which Sanders replied, "They don't have my legs, I've got their arms!"

Westcott's forte was his ability to recruit and maintain his legions in the program for four years straight when, typically, collegiate athletes come and go. Howard rarely recruited outside the Portland metro area. Ron Calhoun, a Sanders' teammate, remembered Howard using current wrestlers to recruit friends since they knew each other as part of the Portland prep wrestling culture.[6] Westcott put on clinics at city high schools, scouting for the right kind of kid—generally blue collar, hardworking, self-starters from broken homes, eager to show their worth. Westcott was kin to the downtrodden. He himself grew up in the Lents neighborhood of Portland, a poor and depressed area. Howard's father was a drunk and general son-of-a-bitch. According to Wescott's son Mark, Howard joined a neighborhood Boy Scout troop of similarly cast-off boys for respite. The association lasted a lifetime.

Sanders: In the Moment

Howard had an eye for talent and a strong sense of conscience that appealed to his grapplers. Mike McKeel was a two-sport athlete who matriculated at Portland State after a two-week freshman debut with the Willamette University football team at Salem, Oregon. Mike transferred after witnessing poor behavior from his previous coach at Willamette. The coach, incensed by another player's limited skills and practice performance, swore at the offender, ripped the helmet from his head, and punched the kid in the face. McKeel left the program in search of a more philosophical approach to a game he loved. Howard scored him a scholarship at PSU with the stipulation he join the wrestling team as well after the football season. McKeel became a NCAA Division II runner-up champion at 191 pounds on PSU's 1967 championship team. Mike became a successful dentist after college. McKeel counts Westcott as one of the three most interesting people in his life. He still remembers his favorite Westcott philosophical maxim: "If you need someone to do something for you, ask before 10:00 a.m. In the morning, they'll have optimal energy and you'll have an edge."

McKeel has enduring respect for Westcott, despite chuckling over some of his eccentricities. Howard was called Hayseed Westcott for habitually wearing the same clothes for days at a time. Many of the PSU Vikings accrued nicknames assigned by their teammates as well; Mike was Paky, named after the Portland Zoo's new elephant because of his physique; Sanders became "Alfie", due to his resemblance to Alfred E. Newman's Mad Magazine character. The team's use of pseudonyms was reflective of Westcott. His esoteric, innocuous nature was endearing to his athletes.[7]

Westcott's son Mark, a world class pianist, regularly attended home PSU wrestling matches. Mark observed Sanders as a 'diamond in the rough'; "...You couldn't teach his instincts; he did what was completely unexpected. He was homely, ears stuck out, was not at all a physical presence, but when he got in a crouch—he became a ballet dancer that could go beyond thrilling. He was artistry on the mat."[8]

According to Bob Bergen, a Westcott blue-chip recruit who went on to a remarkable Oregon prep coaching career with a dual meet record of 254-25-1, Howard was clandestinely known as the "Fixer" particularly with regard to football players having difficulties academically.[9] Westcott was well connected with faculty and administration. Sanders lacked credits to graduate from PSU in 1968. Even so, after his 1967 D-I national championship and Outstanding Wrestler Award, he gave Wescott credit for being his coach. Rick commented, "When my career is over, I hope that I can get into coaching—maybe take over for coach Westcott." That said, close friends recognized that it would be difficult for Rick to harness his frenetic lifestyle and manage the more mundane aspects of college coaching.[10]

Marlin Grahn, after two years in the Army, wrestled for Westcott, later becoming an assistant and ultimately head coach. Grahn remembers Howard as quite a character. "After we'd clinch a dual meet win, he'd go into the crowd and light up a cigar. As wrestlers we'd go 'Is this for real?'"[11] Masaru Yatabe recalls Westcott indulging in the occasional cigar as well. While on one memorable trip to Pullman, Washington to conduct a wrestling clinic at Washington State University, Westcott was enjoying a cigar and singing while driving across the expansive eastern Washington wheat fields. Mas, in the passenger seat, looked over to discover the chest pocket of Howard's blazer was on fire. They pulled to the side of the road and put Westcott out. Apparently, ash had fallen into the pocket somewhere mid-chorus.[12] Smoking among athletes was uncommon but not unheard of. Bobby Douglas remembers 1963 NAIA wrestler Bucky Maughan going up into the stands and smoking a cigarette after pulling off an upset championship win at the Division I NCAAs.[13] Maughan became the long-time North Dakota State Bison coach and distinguished National Wrestling Hall of Fame member. He was a lifetime smoker, occasionally lighting up right in the wrestling room. Clearly, over the ensuing decades, the harmful effects of smoking have been well researched, and most sportsmen eschew the habit, especially in the attempt to achieve elite athletic performance. During the 60s, smoking was socially accepted, included as part of the military rations given to soldiers, used as a means of weight loss, condoned by celebrities and businessmen, and sometimes recommended by doctors to treat anxiety. Perhaps Wescott's smoking provided sanction for Sanders' eventual smoking affinity. Rick conjured up all sorts of esoteric weight control methods through his career. Smoking in his era was as easily thought to be beneficial as it was harmful.

Sanders' relationship with Howard Westcott was solid—somewhat as a father figure. Sanders would indeed be back in the room after his college career, helping to coach and training for international events. Bob Bergen recalls looking to mat-side while engaged with a tough dual meet opponent one evening to see Westcott and Sanders in heated conversation, then coming off the mat to find the pair laughing with one another. Westcott had that undefined yet quintessential coaching persona that inspires acolytes to perform, often beyond their talent level. Howard could draw from multiple ranks. Masaru Yatabe was a Japanese transplant; Chuck Seal, joining the team a year later, was an Eastern Oregon bone-breaking cowboy; Rick Sanders was an inner-city child of the sixties counterculture. They all became national champions, leading the Portland State wrestling team to victory.[14]

Rick Sanders, Mike McKeel, and Masaru Yatabe started as freshman at Portland State in 1964. Yatabe could not speak English very well, having just arrived from Japan. Regardless, the three would become fast friends.

Yatabe was a soft spoken, unassuming man whose character belied an elite competitiveness and leadership ability. In Japan, he wrestled on a Tatebayashi team, sharing the mat with the great Oklahoma State three-time national champion and two-time Olympic gold medalist Yojiro Uetake, three years his senior. Yatabe wrestled Uetake daily for the one year they were in high school together. The team practiced 365 days a year—plus an additional three mornings a week on Monday, Wednesday, and Friday before classes started. In Masaru's senior year, he ended up second place in the nation after tying with his opponent at the end of regulation and the overtime period. They were immediately made to get on a scale. Masaru was a pound heavier, thus receiving the runner up trophy.

Yatabe became team captain of his Tatebayashi high school team during his senior year. His Japanese coach Mr. Kobuta wanted Yatabe to be a trailblazer on the American college mats. Yojiro Uetake, Yatabe's high school teammate—three-time NCAA champion, who went undefeated in college (57-0) for Oklahoma State—came to Stillwater through the relationship Oklahoma State coach Myron Roderick had with Japan's Olympic coach, Ichiro Hatta. Yatabe would follow in similar footsteps.

Arriving in the states to begin his college experience, Yatabe met Grant High School coach Bob Shewbert at the Portland airport. The Shewberts served as a host family to Yatabe for the next five years. Yatabe was supposed to join the University of Washington team, but at the time, it didn't have much of a program. In addition, the language barrier, rigors of college, and homesickness became issues during Yatabe's freshman year. But his countrymen had given him such a celebratory Japanese sendoff, he couldn't bear to let them down by quitting. Yatabe matriculated at Portland State, where Howard "The Fixer" selected course work and arranged for certain tests. The trailblazer strategy worked; five Japanese countrymen followed Yatabe into the ranks of American college wrestling.[15]

Clarence "Chuck" Seal from Eastern Oregon was the third blue chip wrestler in the 1965-1968 PSU lineup. Seal won three Oregon state high school championships. He was unique as one of the only teammates who was not a Portland metro recruit. Eastern Oregon is considered cowboy country, so Seal was often referred to as "Cowboy." He grew up in the tiny town of Terrebonne, Oregon and went to Redmond High School. He didn't start wrestling until his sophomore year in high school after having a career ending argument with the basketball coach as a freshman. He was married and had been out of high school a few years before Ron Calhoun drove over to Redmond and convinced him to wrestle for Westcott and PSU. Seal won two NCAA D-II Championships for PSU, one at 152 pounds, the other at 145. He was third in NCAA D-I in 1967. Calhoun commented, "Chuck was built like God ran out of parts." Seal had the upper body of a 190 pounder and the legs of a 130 pounder.[16] Long time PSU Coach Marlin Grahn referred to Chuck as "a man-child who could just torture people." Delance Duncan, longtime Oregon high school coach, observed, "Seal had formidable long arms and hand strength."

Though Seal was physically able to punish opponents, he didn't match Sanders for Rick's relentless pursuit. The combination of Yatabe's technical skills; Seal's physical talents; Sanders' relentlessness, and joined by McKeel, Garrison, Green, and Campbell, Portland State would build a stellar national wrestling reputation.

The Portland State wrestling team was made up of eclectic personalities, not the least of which was Sanders. Duncan, coach of the

Sanders: In the Moment

Oregon/Japanese prep foreign exchange team, related the following that typifies Rick; Coach Duncan needed to retrieve a document left with Rick and arranged to meet him at an apartment near Portland State shared with teammates Masaru Yatabe and Chuck Seal. After determining the document was not among the apartment's clutter, which included Eastern Oregon Chuck Seal's saddle in the middle of the apartment, Rick suggested they take his motorcycle over to his mother's apartment and continue the search. Duncan, acting *in loco parentis* asked, "Do you have

Rick was voted Outstanding Wrestler of the 1965 NAIA national tournament as a freshman. Sanders is the only wrestler to have been voted OW at the NAIA, NCAA D-II and D-I levels. He did it twice in D-II.

—

a license?" Sanders pulled out his wallet and responded, "Sure coach, here it is." They journeyed forth, Duncan on the back of the cycle. Less than a quarter mile down the road, they were pulled over for a missing plates violation. In classic Sanders' chatter, Rick convinced the officer to forego a citation. He was just home from an international meet in Sweden and overlooked the need for updated plates.[17] Rick had the operator's license but never considered the need for updated plates; another example of Rick's symptomatic ADHD. Duncan, having spent his youth on the Colville Indian Reservation, was accustomed to freedom of movement rarely interrupted. A fatherly nod from a knowing coach and all was well.

Portland State University's 1964-1965 NAIA season was filled with big college duals. They included: Idaho State, Utah, San Jose State, Fresno State, Oregon and Oregon State, Washington and Washington State, Brigham Young, Cal Poly, as well as Oregon Collegiate Conference and Northwest Conference teams. They finished the season 7-2-1. Sanders scored ten pins in eleven matches. Rick went on to the NAIA tournament held in Terre Haute, Indiana where Bloomsburg State of Pennsylvania won the team championship; Lock Haven was the runner-up, ten points back. Portland State was sixth, one point ahead of Adams State. Here, at 115 pounds, Sanders earned his first national championship. He beat Dave Hazewinkel of St. Cloud State. Hazewinkel was no chump. He would go on to become the first American to win two medals in world Greco-Roman wrestling—bronze in 1969 and silver in 1970. Rick was also voted Outstanding Wrestler of the 1965 NAIA tournament and was awarded the tournament's Gorriaran Award, given to the wrestler who records the most pins in the least amount of time.[18]

Sanders was ranked number one at 115 pounds for the 1965 NCAA Division I tournament. NAIA champions could wrestle in the NCAAs at that time. However, Rick was a freshman in 1965, and freshmen were not allowed to wrestle in Division I tournaments. Therefore, Sanders was unable to participate. That rule did not change until 1969. Tadaaki Haata, another Japanese/Myron Roderick recruit to Oklahoma State, won the 115-pound class over Glenn McMinn of Arizona State 9-6 in '65. The following year, Sanders would defeat Haata by fall in the semifinals; McMinn, seeded second, was defeated and out of the tournament by the second round. Would Sanders have defeated Haata if allowed to participate in the 1965 tournament? If so, Rick would have become a three-time NCAA Division I champion and would have competed in the D-I championship match four times.[19]

While Sanders won the Gorriaran Award at the NAIA national tournament, fellow Oregonian Len Kauffman won the Gorriaran at the NCAA Division I level. They were contemporaries in the ranks of Oregon State high school champions who had stellar collegiate careers: Sanders at PSU, Kauffman at Oregon State. Both had wide open, aggressive styles, always looking for the pin. National records indicate Kauffman had an 84 percent pinning ratio in college at the Division I level. Sanders and Kauffman wrestled on AAU national and world championship teams together. Oregon State coaching legend Dale Thomas called Kauffman "the greatest wrestler I ever coached."

Len Kauffman held Rick in high regard. Kauffman noted, "It was his intensity, his flexibility and his unorthodox and creative wrestling ability that set him apart. He was so different." According to Kauffman, Sanders was a world class wrestler because "he loved wrestling, studied it, worked at it, and surrounded himself with other good wrestlers. He wasn't conservative. He scored a lot of points. Rick was a free spirit who advanced without much coaching—learning the nuances of the sport on his own."[20] In the three NCAA Division I tournaments Sanders wrestled (1966, 1967, & 1968), he pinned seven of 12 opponents. In the other five

Sanders: In the Moment

matches, Rick scored a total of 68 points. Sanders averaged over 16 points a match on the five other opponents. Sanders always put on a show, whether at an elite tournament or a dual meet competition.[21]

Like Sanders at home PSU matches, Kauffman drew crowds to his Oregon State matches. The college radio station carried the Beaver duals. Kauffman wrestled at 177 or 191 pounds depending on where Coach Thomas felt the team needed him most. As his match approached, additional fans who had been following the match via radio would arrive, anticipating the excitement Kauffman's style of wrestling generated. Sanders' wrestling affected the crowds similarly. Mike McKeel, Sanders' PSU teammate at 191 pounds, remembers dual meets with the Beavers on the OSU campus at Corvallis: "Fans would start lining up at 4:00 p.m. for a 7:00 p.m. match."[22] Sanders' friend and workout partner Bob Bergen reflected, "High school kids would drive in to Portland for PSU home matches to watch a Sanders' performance."

In his final tournament at the 1972 Munich Olympics, former wrestling partner Marlin Grahn, always an enamored fan, remembers that each time Rick was called to wrestle, the fans in the Ringerhalle venue scrambled excitedly to claim new seats near his mat. Grahn reflected, "Dan Gable was the story of the '72 Olympics. But when Sanders was on the mat, all eyes locked on him. He was so far ahead of his time."[23] He was creative, aggressive, and relentless. Sanders brought an excitement to wrestling that put the word *grand* into grandstands. Workman-like in his early career, more showman for fans in his later career, Sanders began to want more from wrestling fans than just admiration for his wrestling skills. He wanted to squeeze their esteem into recognition of a larger character. Sanders became more altruistic, giving back by participating in youth clinics and occasionally making a comment at sports banquets.

Sanders: In the Moment

Sanders and MAC teammates occasionally traveled to California to run wrestling clinics at Cal Poly in San Luis Obispo. Rick's sister Kay would host the clinicians at her house. The Oregon crew slept on the deck facing the ocean—choice accommodations for wrestlers, often the most unheralded of athletes. Rick once admitted to Kay that "There is nothing duller than wrestling. People do not come to watch." Kay recognized Rick's passionate need for attention, perhaps the source of his unconventional drive to draw attention to the sport and himself in later years.[24]

The Amateur Athletic Union (AAU) sponsored a national tournament annually from 1888 to 1982. The first tournaments offered limited weight classes, but as wrestling popularity increased, more weight classes evolved. Some wrestlers won multiple classes at the same tournament, capturing a lower weight class and then competing at heavier weights held later in the tournament. Sanders began wrestling in national AAU tournaments, competing as a member of the Multnomah Athletic Club in 1964.

The AAU tournaments attracted top flight competition such as Wayne Baughman, Bobby Douglas, Don Behm, Wayne Wells, Gene Davis, and John and Ben Peterson. All these wrestlers would eventually become teammates of Sanders in international competition. AAU national tournaments diminished in the 1970s after the U.S. Wrestling Federation—later USA Wrestling—evolved as the national governing body for wrestling in the United States. Top flight competition begets top flight wrestlers, and many AAU champions were integral to Sanders' successful career.[25]

Sanders' wrestling continued beyond the 1965 college national tournament. In May, the Multnomah Athletic Club team won the national AAU freestyle tournament in San Francisco. Sanders at 125 pounds, Jerry

Sanders: In the Moment

Conine at 213.5, and Gary Stensland at heavyweight all earned points for the MAC. Sanders won the championship over Ikeda, a Japanese athlete. The level of competition attracted wrestlers from diverse and distant locations. The MAC championship was much heralded by the city of Portland, the MAC wrestlers having outpointed the New York Athletic Club by two points and the San Francisco Olympic Club by five.

Sanders often struggled with Japanese wrestlers. His early experience on the Japanese tour after high school was mixed. He lost the first couple matches on the Japanese tour. Those losses after an 80-1 high school record may have spooked Rick. PSU teammate Masaru Yatabe observed that Rick should have had more success wrestling his characteristic unorthodox style against the highly technical and quick Japanese wrestlers.

The 1965 national AAU championship was MAC coach Cyril Mitchell's second national championship after a twelve-year hiatus. Sanders and Conine won championships; Stensland was second. As a result of their respective individual championships, Rick and Conine were named to the United States team to wrestle in the Freestyle World Championships held in Manchester, England on the first of June. In Cy Mitchell's 36 years as coach, there were lucky times when one contestant was sent to regional tournaments by the MAC. A team championship was a clear indication of the surge in wrestling's popularity in the Pacific Northwest.[26] The AAU and the MAC gave financial support for the athletes' travel expenses, which included an extension to Helsinki Finland for the Greco-Roman championships.

Also as a result of the success at the 1965 AAU tournament, Sanders began his friendship with Bobby Douglas and Wayne Baughman as a member of the 1965 World Championship team competing in England and Finland. Bobby Douglas, a future Olympic and World Team teammate, was just beginning his international career. Douglas wrestled collegiately for Myron Roderick at Oklahoma State. Douglas and Sanders became lifelong friends. They were like brothers, even though Bobby was a Black American raised in Ohio. Both grew up in poverty with little parental support. They discovered a talent and affinity for wrestling that provided a conduit to rise above meager means. Bobby was three years older than Rick and sometimes found himself in the older brother role—encouraging and cajoling. They competed on the same team at the 1968 Olympics and on three World Championship teams. Bobby wrestled at 138.5 pounds; Rick at 114.5 pounds.[27]

Wayne Baughman remembers Sanders fondly as well. They had traits in common. Both were durable, rarely injured, and could be counted on as ready to take the mat. They were unquestionably tough. Both were raconteurs of some note. Baughman became a three-time All-American at the University of Oklahoma, winning the NCAA title in 1962. He won a total of 16 national titles, including five in freestyle, nine in Greco-Roman, and one in sombo (a form of wrestling similar to judo). He was a member of three Olympic teams and eight World Teams. Baughman went on to become an Air Force officer and coached the Air Force Academy Falcons for twenty-seven years. He was head coach of three World Championship teams as well as was head coach for the 1976 Olympic team. These were admirable ways to give back to wrestling beyond personal achievement.

Sanders lacked the substantive background that Baughman had groomed for himself, but Rick gave back to the community by working at wrestling clinics along the West Coast and in Pennsylvania. Sanders endeared himself to fans and journalists throughout his career. He worked in Portland area high schools encouraging and inspiring prep wrestlers.

Sanders: In the Moment

Steve Lawrence and his brother were high school wrestlers from The Dalles, Oregon, and longtime fans of Sanders. "When Rick won his first state championship, we were already fans," Lawrence reflected. "He had a habit of doing a standing back flip whenever he won a match. Our first reaction was, 'who the hell is that?' From then on, we followed him, watching him at state tournaments, Portland State, or at local wrestling tournaments. I remember sometime after I returned from Vietnam in 1969, the MAC team wrestled a Japanese national team in McMinnville, which I was lucky enough to attend," Lawrence said. "Rick kind of toyed with his opponent in the first round. Then suddenly, mid-way through the second, he quickly pinned his opponent in a leg split, applied so hard that the man could hardly exit the mat."

Baughman was deferential toward Sanders, referring to Rick as the ultimate competitor. He said of Sanders, "His mind was in the match all the time," and added, "Wrestling was Rick's total reason for life."[28]

The 1965 World Team was coached by Bill Smith of the San Francisco Olympic Club—one of the clubs edged out by the MAC at the 1965 AAU national championships. Sanders did not place in either of the Manchester England or Helsinki Finland tournaments. Larry Kristoff, at heavyweight, was the only American to medal, earning a bronze. Wayne Baughman was unscored on but ended up fifth; lack of pins and too many matches wrestled to a draw, under the international tournament black mark scoring system, made the difference for the Americans.

International wrestlers competed under the "black mark" scoring system adopted by the Federation Internationale des Luttes Associees (FILA), the international governing body for amateur wrestling, with headquarters in Lausanne, Switzerland. Under this scoring system, wrestlers are eliminated as they are assessed black marks. A win by pin equals zero black marks; a win by decision equals one black mark; a draw is given two black marks; a loss by decision is assessed three black marks; a loss by pin receives four black marks. Usually, when a wrestler has accrued six black marks, they are eliminated from further rounds of competition. It is a fairly easy system to manage, but subject to fraud when competitors conspire to throw matches to influence the accumulation of black marks.

It was Sanders' first international competition. In brief coverage by *Amateur Wrestling News*, "Sanders looked good in all three of his matches. He decisioned Mesenceli of Turkey; lost a close decision to Yoshida of Japan, an Olympic gold medal winner; and lost to Handari of Iran who drew with Gray Simons in the Olympics." Sanders' first World Team competition was impressive. Rick adapted quickly to the freestyle form of wrestling practiced for decades by foreign competitors. U.S. and foreign teams were beginning to notice the lightweight Oregonian.

Wayne Baughman began to catalog a few Sanders stories. Baughman recalled a delicate episode regarding an issue of weight loss between Sanders and the U.S. heavyweight Larry Kristoff at the 1965 England/Finland World Championship tour, causing some degree of consternation. Kristoff was a two-time NCAA Division II champion from Southern Illinois University Carbondale, winning titles in 1963 and 1964 at heavyweight. In the 1963 NCAA D-I heavyweight final, Kristoff narrowly lost the championship 2-1 on riding time. Kristoff made the 1964 Olympic team, finishing seventh. Kristoff's international tournament appearances often found him lining up with Sanders at team photo time.

After the freestyle competition in England and the day before the Greco weigh-in at Helsinki, Finland, Rick was several pounds overweight and was in the sauna trying to sweat them off. Larry, perhaps detecting Sanders' sometimes capricious attitude toward losing the pounds hours before a weigh-in, decided to lock Rick in the sauna. Kristoff, a

Sanders: In the Moment

JUST BEFORE their departure from New York en route to Manchester, England, the U. S. World's Championships team relaxed for this photo. Left to right (front): Jim Burke, Russ Camilleri, Richard Sanders and Bobby Douglas. BACK: Jerry Conine, Larry Kristoff, Lt. Wayne Baughman and Coach-Manager Bill Smith.

Sanders' first World Championships.
Photo and caption courtesy of Amateur Wrestling News, December 1965.

heavyweight unburdened by the need to cut weight, then went to a movie with a friend, intending to unlock the sauna after the show. He forgot Sanders in the sauna. When released several hours later, Sanders had to be put in a laundry basket and rolled across the street, where teammates lifted him onto the scale. He made weight. Following the weigh-ins, Rick drank six 6-ounce Cokes and immediately threw them up. He then drank four 6-ounce Cokes and threw them up. Finally, he drank two 6-ounce Cokes and was able to hold them down. On seeing Kristoff, Sanders chased Larry with a butter knife for a bit of pre-match warm up. Neither Kristoff nor Sanders placed at Helsinki. Rick never wrestled Greco-Roman style again. Alas, the Kristoff episode did not serve to improve Sanders' ability to make weight on time. Making weight for Sanders was never important until it was dire.[29]

Coach Smith was a gold medalist at the 1952 Olympic Games in Helsinki, Finland. Perhaps that is in part why he was selected to lead the 1965 World Team to compete in Finland. But Bill Smith was also a two-time NCAA champion for Iowa State Teachers College, now the University of Northern Iowa. His coaching career was stellar as well, having amassed a 57-5 high school record at Rock Island, Illinois; later, Smith coached Clayton Valley high school of Concord, California to a state high school championship. Serving as coach of the Olympic Club of San Francisco, his teams won three national team titles in freestyle and four in Greco-Roman wrestling.

Smith would coach Rick on future World Championship teams, offering encouragement, adulation, and commendation for Rick's wrestling and conduct. Smith offered a backhand compliment to Rick after the 1966 World Championships; "Your way of wrestling gives ulcers to people watching, but I enjoyed every second of it." Smith had much in common with Sanders at the collegiate level. Both were two-time NCAA champions with stellar collegiate records: Smith undefeated during college, Sanders with only two losses against 103 victories. Like Sanders, Smith believed that the caliber of competition in the practice room made those possessing inherent talent into champions. If the environment at practice was to either toughen up or get killed in that room, you had a chance to become a champion.[30]

Rick's summer wrestling tour was not complete after the Manchester/Helsinki World Championships. In August of 1965, Rick was invited by 1964 Olympic coach Dean Rockwell to a training camp at Adams State College in Alamosa, Colorado. The United States Olympic Committee on Development approved funds to conduct an "International Wrestling Holds and Rules Camp".[31] The camp was designed to afford outstanding wrestlers in the U.S. an opportunity to work together on the international styles of wrestling under top coaches. U.S. high school and college wrestling employed folkstyle wrestling whereas international competition at world championships and the Olympics was either contested in freestyle or Greco-Roman style. The objective for the camp was to better prepare U.S. wrestlers for competition at the 1968 Olympics, held in Mexico City, so that "more medals could be won." Alamosa, Colorado, at 7,000 feet in elevation, is similar to the elevation at Mexico City. The physical effect of competing at the higher elevation was of concern to athletes from many countries. Panels of U.S. doctors conducted a myriad of studies to determine the effects on athletes competing at altitude. Nothing conclusive was determined. Long distance runners seemed most susceptible. However, negative effects varied by athlete. Ultimately, officials decided to hold trials at elevation to determine which competitor best performed at 7,000 feet. The camp held two two-hour sessions per day for ten days. It was excellent training with only top wrestlers and Olympic hopefuls invited.

Sanders: In the Moment

To recap: Sanders, during the summer of '65, after his first year in college, found himself continually engaged on the mat. He wrestled in an AAU tournament in San Francisco in May which the MAC team won; made his first World Team competing in June—freestyle in England and Greco-Roman in Finland; then finished the summer in August at a ten-day Olympic training camp in Colorado. Sanders was finding himself in more and more team photos.

After the summer camp, Sanders continued his peripatetic existence, often at home where mother Anita relocated, sometimes living a few houses up Montgomery Street with a house full of wrestlers, propitiously as coeds availed themselves. He was largely unaffected and unbothered. Sanders' time seemed to be taken up largely by the wrestling room, either at Portland State, the MAC, or at some tournament venue distant from inner city Portland. Other times he found intermittent work usually in bars or restaurants—not the best environment for a lightweight wrestler trying to make weight.

Around him, the world continued on the move as well. The Free Speech Movement (FSM) began in 1964 at the flagship college of California, U.C. Berkeley. Students were frustrated with school administration for subjecting them to antiquated disciplinary rules, treating them more as children rather than young adults. Students held demonstrations, with many protests headed by high profile alleged radicals, attracting media attention. Several ended in arrests. A youth counter-culture morphed into a quasi-revolution laced with sex, drugs, and rock and roll.[32] Most young people were largely observers, but interested in change, trying new things and pushing convention. Six hundred miles north, nineteen-year-old Rick Sanders, college freshman, was open to the revolution. He started to smoke grass and spent many of his off hours head banging to burgeoning rock and roll on the radio. He kept his hair trimmed however, and did not yet have a beard.

The Midwest was slower to synthesize the changes occurring on the coasts. If a visitor from the Midwest, say for example Dan Gable from Waterloo, Iowa, got off the bus at the station in downtown Portland sometime in the mid 1960s, he would experience quite a different youth culture than his own. As Dan walked uphill the few blocks from the depot to his future teammate, Rick Sanders' sometimes employer, Montagues Pizza, near Portland State University, he likely would have met several free loving hippies—flower headband laced through shoulder length hair, a tie-dye tee shirt, love beads, sandals, and an easy smile. "Would Gable care for some beads?" one woman might ask. Gable might have felt out of vogue. But in the hippie spirit of brotherly love, the casual conversation might have continued along the route: "Do you have 'papers'?" A confusing request until clarified by Rick later—"papers", the wrappings necessary for rolling a marijuana joint. Gable would have spent most of the ensuing evening at the restaurant listening to electric guitars, cranked to impressive volume, as he breathed a continual waft of unfamiliar smoke laced with incense. Sometime after 10:00 p.m., Sanders, according to habit, may have led Gable to the Portland State or MAC wrestling room for an hour or two of practice, letting Gable finally relax in a familiar environment.

Sanders had a good stereo system according to Freeman Garrison, friend and four-year PSU teammate.[33] By the early '70s, Sanders often had with him a boombox. Sometimes called a "ghetto blaster", the boombox was a large radio with removable speakers and was often carried on the shoulder of pop rockers. Top songs in 1965 included 'Wooly Bully' by Sam the Sham & the Pharaohs and 'I Can't Get No Satisfaction' by the Rolling Stones. But despite the fact that The Beatles played in Portland in

Sanders: In the Moment

August 1965, Rick leaned a little more into folk rock. Bob Dylan wrote and performed the 1965 hit 'Like A Rolling Stone.' The song's less political theme was more in keeping with Sanders' nascent world view.

Gene Davis, a future 1972 Olympic teammate, recalled how Rick loved music, "especially loud music."[34] Wayne Wells was another Sanders' teammate at several AAU and international events. He was a keen observer of Ricky Sanders' wrestling career. Sanders, as an emerging headbanger from Oregon, had a skewed if not polar opposite approach to international wrestling competition than the mid-continent Oklahoman. "Rick always needed his music," Wells remembered. Rick would listen to the radio all night long. On one occasion, according to Wells, to avoid disturbing other team members, Sanders removed the acoustic ceiling tile, covered himself and the radio with the tile, and spent the night so disposed.[35] Wells turned it off after Rick fell asleep.

John Prine was one of Rick's favorite musicians. Prine's folkstyle lyrics offer insight into Sanders' personality and the value he placed on the "in the moment" experience and ordinary people.

Prine's first album was released in 1971, and therefore provided the only Prine songs Rick would have heard and identified with. 'Far From Me' is a ballad on the album describing the sorrow felt when a waitress shows no interest in the overtures of a protagonist busboy. 'Donald and Lydia' describes sexual exploits both real and imagined. The lyrics in 'Illegal Smile' are commonly understood to describe LSD or marijuana use. Other songs on the John Prine 1971 album flesh out the zeitgeist of the times—the human catastrophe of Vietnam and drugs in 'Sam Stone'; some of the first acknowledgement of environmental destruction - 'Paradise'; and neglect of the aged - 'Hello in There.' The fetish Sanders had for Prine's music reveals something of his own persona. Rick dabbled in creating his own poetry. Perhaps the rhythm helped him self-express or perceive his world in finer detail. Poetry may have been therapeutic in a way different from some of his more well described vices. The humor and friendliness of Prine's ballads have a rare ability to connect with the heart. Prine was a mailman prior to his success as a musician, occasionally penning a song while delivering the mail. Humble heritage combined with rare talent and a desire to live in the moment catapulted him to stardom. Sanders' wrestling trajectory reflected a similar pattern. Rick was not a vocalist or an instrumentalist. The music of the era captured his attention, as it did for many, through the uncomplicated message of peace, love, and hope—lyrics that helped form his identity in early adulthood.[36]

In other matters, the second of the four tragic '60s era assassinations occurred in 1965. Malcolm X was assassinated at the Audubon Ballroom in Harlem on February 21, 1965. He was presumably killed by members of the Nation of Islam, the organization he used as a forum to preach his world vision for social change—a vision that initially preached armed revolt against white society but had recently ameliorated after a pilgrimage to Mecca. Malcolm X's fiery and effective oratory was juxtaposed to Martin Luther King's message of nonviolent protest. Voices in tandem added confusion to the tumultuous '60s. Malcom X's world view was shared by Huey Newton and Bobby Seale, who advocated for Black Power and founded the Black Panther Party. Their message was carried to the 1968 Mexico City Olympics in the form of the iconic black gloved victory stand protest demonstrated by Tommie Smith and John Carlos.[37] Sanders would be witness to that message while competing at the Mexico City Olympics and rooming with black friend and wrestler Bobby Douglas.

President Johnson escalated the Vietnam conflict by feeding a fable to the American public about an unprovoked torpedo attack on U.S. Naval destroyers off the coast of Vietnam. The August 1964 torpedo attacks were never verified, but the resulting "Gulf of Tonkin" incident allowed LBJ to initiate the bombing of North Vietnam and subsequently expand the war through a compliant congress. Later in the decade, Rick would wear the occasional activist button. He and Greco teammate Buck Deadrich wore "Ban the Bomb" buttons while attending an Olympic function with President Nixon prior to the 1972 Olympics. Sanders was not politically astute but knew the significance of his action at the reception. He was asked by the United States Olympic Committee to take it off while at the White House function. Perhaps Rick's action was more an example of oppositional defiance towards authority, which was characteristic of the era.

Further domestically, The NCAA D-I Wrestling Championships were held at the University of Wyoming at Laramie in 1965. Iowa State won the team title by one point over Oklahoma State, 87-86. Fourth seeded Don Behm of Michigan State met first seed Yojiro Uetake of Oklahoma State in the 130- pound semi-final. The invincible Uetake moved on to the final with a two-point win. The two would compete in the 1968 Olympics at 57k, Behm for the United States, Uetake for Japan, though interestingly, they would not wrestle each other. Such were the idiosyncrasies of the international black mark scoring system. Behm and Sanders would begin a friendship at the 1968 Olympic training camp in Alamosa. By blending their skills in workouts at Alamosa, they would become the only medalists for the U.S. at Mexico City.[38]

Behm created quite a legacy collegiately and internationally. Today, he's known for his many accomplishments: he was a NCAA runner up in 1967 for the national champion Michigan State Spartans; he won Midlands twice at 134 pounds; he was an Olympic silver medalist at Mexico City; he was a silver medalist at the 1969 World Championships in Argentina; he was 136.5-pound gold medalist at the first USA

Sanders: In the Moment

Wrestling National Freestyle Senior Open in 1969 wrestling for the Mayor Daley Youth Foundation. Behm was the 125.5-pound gold medalist at the Pan American Games held in Cali, Columbia in 1971; perhaps most auspiciously, Behm was the first U.S. wrestler to win the prestigious Tbilisi tournament held in Georgia, a province of the former Soviet Union. Tbilisi is recognized as the toughest international tournament in the world.

Behm and Sanders wrestled against each other multiple times in trials tournaments through the years. The matches were classics and the pair always remained close friends. Perhaps more than any other friend of Sanders, Behm seemed to understand the source of Ricks' esoteric behavior—Behm the analytic pragmatist; Sanders the romantic.[39]

Chapter Five

Portland State University moved from the NAIA division of college sports to NCAA Division II for the 1965-1966 wrestling season. There were never more than fifteen wrestlers on the PSU team, but the nucleus of Sanders, Yatabe, McKeel, Garrison, and Rich Green allowed the wrestling program to move in relative comfort. Chuck Seal, the Eastern Oregon cowboy, would dally up at PSU the following year, joining the team at 152 pounds. Portland State managed a dual meet season record of 14-3-1 in their inaugural 1966 D II season. By mid-season, Sanders in the 115-pound weight class was listed as honorable mention at the Division I level by *Amateur Wrestling News*. Ernie Gillum of Iowa State, Glen McMinn of Arizona State, and Tadaaki Haata of Oklahoma State, the defending NCAA D-I champion at 115, were ranked first, second, and third respectively. The three had been top medal winners at the 1965 national tournament.[1]

Sanders had already competed in national AAU tournaments often with Division I wrestlers and trained with elite wrestlers working out at the MAC. Furthermore, Portland State garnered dual meet wins against Oregon State, University of Oregon, Washington State, Fresno State, and wrestling powerhouse Cal Poly during the 1965-1966 transition year.

Sanders: In the Moment

Sanders prevailed by fall in all matches except against his Fresno State opponent, who he decisioned 12-0. The higher-level competition only improved his skill set.

The 1966 college division or NCAA D-II tournament was held in Highland Arena on the campus of Mankato State College, Mankato, Minnesota. It was the largest tournament in the history of college wrestling at the time. Three hundred wrestlers among 200 teams competed. Sanders spent much of the 1965-1966 season wrestling up at 130 pounds. He had trimmed down to the 123-pound weight class for the tournament—still up from 115 where he won his NAIA championship and Most Outstanding Wrestler Award in March of 1965. Rick met Gerald Smith of South Dakota State University in the first round, pinning Smith in 4:59. His next opponent was William Neumeister of St. Olaf College. Rick won by fall in 1:54. The third round was against Charles Anderson of Northern Illinois. Rick won again by fall in 2:21. The fourth round upset the pattern. Despite Rick's sensational dual meet season, Warren Crow, wrestling for Division II Albany State at 123 pounds, met Sanders and became the first to defeat Rick during his collegiate career. It was a high scoring match, ending 19-12 for Crow. Sanders worked through the consolation finals to place third, though narrowly winning in overtime, but again by fall in 1:42 over Davis Johnson of Luther College. Rick moved down to 115 pounds for the 1966 D-I national tournament. Crow, remaining at 123, finished fourth at the 1966 D I nationals. It's doubtful Sanders moved down to avoid Crow at the D-Is; Crow might have moved down as well. Rick probably anticipated tougher overall competition at the next level and it would be his first D-I national tournament. Commonly, wrestlers feel their chances are better at the next lower weight.[2]

Warren Crow was a formidable opponent. He was a New York high school phenom, compiling a 25-0 record as a senior with 20 pins. He secured a scholarship to Cornell where, as a sophomore, he was ranked mid-way through the 1963-1964 season at number one by *Amateur Wrestling News*.[3] Then, at the national tournament, Crow lost in the first round to eventual champion Fred Powell of Lock Haven. Crow left Cornell after his sophomore season. Earlier in his career, he placed fourth at the 1964 U.S. Olympic trials at 125.5. Sanders wrestled at 114.5 at those same trials. He went 31-3-1 overall in two years at Albany State, winning Division II national championships in 1966 and 1967 at 123 pounds. Looking for every advantage, Rick cut down to the 115-pound weight class two weeks later for the 1966 university tournament-NCAA Division I championships. He competed at 115 pounds in 1967 as well, moving to the 123-pound weight class in 1968.[4]

PORTLAND STATE'S "LITTLE GUYS" spearhead their team's drive for its first NCAA College Division title. In 13 duals these five, plus 152-pounder Clarence Seal (not pictured), have won 61 matches—22 by pin—while losing only 13. Left to right: Rich Green, 137 (11-2); Koji Watanabe, 130 (11-2); Rich Sanders, 123 (13-0); Masaru Yatabe, 145 (11-1-1), and Freeman Garrison, 160 (5-6). Seal is 10-2.

The best PSU Vikings. They would be joined by 152 pound Chuck Seal in 1967.

Sanders: In the Moment

Portland State entered the 1966 College Division (NCAA D-II) national tournament with high hopes. Portland State's results were respectable yet underwhelming. The team finished third—Cal Poly won the championship with 55 points; Wilkes, 51 points; and the PSU Vikings with 47 points. Sanders, Yatabe, Green, Garrison, and Siebenthal each finished third in their respective weight classes. It was a semi-final bust for PSU. Yatabe, Green, and Sanders lost in the semis. If Sanders and one other Viking wrestler had advanced to the finals, PSU would likely have garnered the nine points it needed to overtake Cal Poly for the team championship. Moreover, if Sanders would have wrestled at 115 instead of 123, he might have met the eventual champion, Michael Remer, who won the 115-pound championship for Cal Poly 2-1 in overtime. That team point swing could have given PSU its first D-II championship. Speculation and the "what ifs" never measure up to reality and the "try, try, again" adage. Sanders and Yatabe moved on to the NCAA Division I tournament held two weeks later to test their skills at the highest level of collegiate wrestling.[5]

The most engaging sporting event in the world is the annual NCAA Division I wrestling championships. The emotion of the fans and the energy of the wrestling culture is unequaled. The wrestling fan base is purebred, wrestlers and wrestling families infusing the crowd. It's high octane and intimate. Past glory is part of the fabric. Commitment to the sport is welded, brazened parts strengthening the whole. The modern event is so well run even FILA patterns its international events similarly.

The 1966 NCAA Division I Championships were held at Iowa State University in Ames, Iowa March 24th through the 26th. The tournament guide featured a photograph of Yojiro Uetake, the winner of the 1965 championship's Outstanding Wrestler Award, on the cover.[6] It wasn't Uetake's first such award; he'd claimed the prestigious OW award for his performance in the 1964 national tournament as well. Uetake, a Japanese High School Champion, matriculated at Oklahoma State University to wrestle for Coach Myron Roderick at 130 pounds. Uetake finished at OSU undefeated and with three national championships under his belt. He was two years older and two weight classes heavier than Sanders in college.

In his own weight class, Sanders had to contend with Tadaaki Hatta, the 1965 national champion at 115 pounds. For his first D-I tournament, Rick was seeded fourth at 115 pounds based on his 1965 NAIA Championship, his 1966 Division II tournament results, and his undefeated dual meet season record—Hatta was seeded first.

Similar to Yojiro, Hatta was from Japan and wrestled for Oklahoma State University. Tadaaki Hatta followed his brother, Masaaki Hatta, to OSU through the Japanese/American pipeline established by Cowboy coach Myron Roderick and Ichiro Hatta, the boys' father. Ichiro Hatta was himself a freestyle wrestling Olympian in 1932, and he went on to become the Olympic wrestling coach for Japan at the Berlin Olympics in 1936. Ichiro had a reputation for unusual coaching methods. He would wake up wrestlers at odd hours of the night and have them wrestle, just in case the situation demanded it. Odd, but not unfounded: looking back, Mike McKeel, PSU heavyweight, remembers wrestling a consolation match at the 1967 NCAA D-I nationals at 3:00 a.m.[7] Thanks to his unusual dedication, Ichiro Haata helped establish the Japanese Amateur Wrestling Association and still later became a leading Japanese politician, helping bring the 1964 Olympics to Japan, where Yojiro Uetake won the gold medal in the bantamweight division for his country.

While Yojiro Uetake and Tadaaki Hatta had the opportunity to train together, so too did Rick and his PSU teammate Masaru Yatabe. Masaru had been a high school teammate of Uetake back in Japan. Though according to Yatabe, he and Sanders did not drill much together, he no doubt briefed Rick on what to expect from a Japanese-trained wrestler.

The 1966 nationals was Sanders' first Division I tournament, and he made an impact.

Sanders met Al Ogdie of Minnesota State in the first round, pinning Ogdie in 5:42. Next up for Rick was a familiar foe from Oregon State: Ron Iwasaki, seeded fifth. Rick prevailed in a 12-3 decision. The penultimate match was with number one seed Tadaaki Hatta, last year's champion.

Between Hatta and Uetake, Coach Roderick was clearly successful in recruiting outside the U.S. The Japanese/American pipeline was quickly helping Oklahoma State build its winning legacy. Hatta's match was highly anticipated—and so, garnered more attention to the reputation Sanders was building. He pinned Hatta in 5:31, faster than unseeded Ogdie.[8]

Rick's final match was with third seed Ernie Gillum from tournament host, Iowa State. Sanders was able to prevail 9-2, despite Gillum's home crowd support, winning his first D-I championship. Both Sanders and Yatabe became All-Americans, and Masaru placed fifth. Portland State finished eighth as a team on the strength of Sanders' and Yatabe's individual performances. Oklahoma State won the 1966 championship with 79 points; Iowa State placed second with 70, one point ahead of the University of Oklahoma Sooners. With the win, Rick became only the third West Coast national champion of all time. *Amateur Wrestling News* capsulated a review of the finals:

115 Rich Sanders, Portland State sophomore, and Ernie Gillum, Iowa State senior. Sanders kept Gillum on the run through the first period but was unable to take him down inside the circle. He scored a predicament from top position in the second period but Gillum slipped out for a reverse. Sanders escaped and took Gillum down with 8 seconds to go. Gillum was injured but was

Sanders: In the Moment

1966 NATIONAL COLLEGIATE CHAMPIONS, left to right, FRONT: Richard Sanders, 115, Portland State; Mike Caruso, 123, Lehigh; YoJiro Uetake, 130, Oklahoma State; Gene Davis, 137, Oklahoma State; Bill Blacksmith, 145, Lock Haven; Dick Cook, 152, Michigan State. BACK: Gregg Ruth, 160, Oklahoma; Dave Reinbolt, 167, Ohio State; Tom Peckham, 177, Iowa State; Bill Harlow.

Sanders and Lock Haven's Bill Blacksmith were the only D-I champions from D-II schools.

able to continue after treatment. Sanders reversed in the third period and controlled all the way, using an Olympic leg lift effectively. In the semi-finals, Sanders pinned Tadaaki Hatta, Oklahoma State's defending champion. Final score 9-2, Sanders.[9]

Following the college season, the 1966 AAU Nationals were held at Pershing Municipal Auditorium on April 5th-9th in Lincoln, Nebraska. Members of the Multnomah Athletic Club were the defending champs, having won the 1965 tournament held at the San Francisco Olympic Club. The AAU Nationals were a proving ground for wrestlers aspiring to become World Team members. AAU National champions, as well as champions of other nationally recognized tournaments, were likely to receive one of 40-45 select invitations for the World Team try-out camp. Invitees were determined by a selection committee.

Chicago's Mayor Daley Youth Foundation won the 1966 AAU national tournament. Sanders was second at 125.5 pounds to Richard Sofman. Sofman was another free spirit two years older than Rick. He was a quick study and always in the competitive mix with contemporaries Rick Sanders, Don Behm, Masaaki Haata, and a young Dan Gable. Sanders may have emulated Sofman's at times anti-establishment ire and beard growth.

Sofman never wrestled in high school. He became interested in the sport at the University of Pennsylvania, an Ivy league school, where he earned an accounting degree while competing for the college team that elected him captain. Sanders and Sofman would wrestle on the same team at the 1967 Pan American Games held in Winnipeg, Canada, where both wrestlers would win gold for the U.S.—Sofman at 114.5 pounds; Sanders at 125.5. Finally, Sofman and Rick would be on the same U.S. World freestyle team to New Delhi, India, switching weight classes: Rick at 114.5 and Sofman at 125.5. Sofman lost to Don Behm in the 1968 U.S. Olympic Trials, and Behm went on to win a silver medal at the Olympics in Mexico City. Sofman went as an alternate. He was interviewed once by the New York Times and offered the following quote which gives a glimpse of his philosophy on life: "I've been disliked and mistreated because of my thinking and habits, but I feel that in sports everybody is an individual. No one has to live a puritan lifestyle just to please coaches. A lot of coaches look down at me and they let their views interfere with what's fair. And it irks me that there are people who use athletics for their own personal hang-up."[10] Sanders' worldview could have been pulled right out of Richie Sofman's playbook.

Sanders, though not highly educated himself, seemed to have deference for those who were—Dr. Howard Westcott, his PSU coach and mentor; his PSU academic advisor Dr. Earle H. MacCannell with whom he had a close relationship, and who gave the eulogy at Rick's funeral; Dr. David Stockner, Rick's half-brother who he visited periodically for respite. Sofman was a college graduate who had already earned a masters degree in business when he and Rick competed against each other in 1966. Sanders was still operating as a clean-cut college undergraduate in 1966 and 67, but he had additional aspirations that began to take hold. Sanders began to read more. Tolkien's *The Hobbit* and *The Lord of the Rings* trilogy was hugely popular on college campuses in 1966 and 1967 according to Strain's *The Long Sixties*.[11] Sanders was captured by Tolkien's stories. A 1967 *Ramparts* magazine article called *The Lord of the Rings* "the favorite book of every hippie." Perhaps stimulated by relationships with his more erudite friends and acquaintances, Sanders viewed reading as a format to expand his own character. Sanders could easily have imagined the diminutive and bearded Sofman as Bilbo Baggins and perhaps himself as Frodo—Hobbit Halflings of renown. The exercise of reading might have expanded his worldview beyond a mat. At the very least, Tolkien's themes dealing with human temptation and power enlightened Sanders' imagination. Rick had challenges in both arenas.

Though runner up at the 1966 AAU national tournament, Rick was given an invitation to the three-week World Team training camp held at the University of Michigan. Five to eight contestants in each weight class were invited. Challenge matches decided spots on the team. Rick prevailed at 114.5 pounds. The 1966 World Championships were held in Toledo, Ohio June 16-22nd. Bill Smith was the freestyle coach; Dale Thomas was the coach for Greco-Roman. Interestingly, Doug Blubaugh, Tom Evans, and Myron Roderick were named assistant coaches, all of whom became integrally related to Sanders' future wrestling career.

The 1966 Amateur Wrestling World Championships were sponsored by FILA, the international governing body for amateur wrestling. The tournament was held under the auspices of the Amateur Athletic Union (AAU), the official FILA representative in the United States. This was only the second time the world championships were held in the Western Hemisphere. The first Western Hemisphere World Championships, held in 1962, were also at Toledo, Ohio.[12]

Participating in the World Championships was an arduous commitment. Wrestlers for the 1966 FILA tournament attended a twenty-day training camp prior to the tournament. Expenses were paid by the AAU. However, it was up to the wrestler to make travel arrangements and take care of expenses prior to reimbursement by the local AAU affiliate, the MAC for Sanders. The impecunious Sanders was well seasoned in stretching the dollars. He commonly cashed travel vouchers for expense money and hitchhiked to tournaments. Living in Oregon, these were often transcontinental hikes for Sanders at a time of two-lane highways. Rick began living out of a duffle bag.

Sanders: In the Moment

The tournament itself was a three-day affair. FILA adopted new rules for officiating at the 1966 tournament, making scoring more transparent. Up until 1966, three officials scored matches as they occurred, revealing their scores and the ultimate winner only after the match was over and having consulted with one another. The old subjective scoring system was controversial, inherently fraudulent and lacking in integrity. It was often unclear as to which wrestlers were true winners until after the post-match referee confab. For example, at the 1965 Worlds held in England, Sanders refused to leave the mat at the end of his match, insisting he was the winner. Coach Smith debated the score with international officials and was ultimately successful in changing the score, allowing Rick to move on. The new rules simply made the scoring public as points were awarded, and was now the same method used by U.S. high schools and colleges. Interviewed after his 1965 World Championship tournament in England and Finland, Sanders, having just finished his freshman year at Portland State, commented, "I have been fortunate in being able to travel and in having the experience of meeting different people of different nationalities. It's been very educational in human relations."[13] Sanders' statement may have been a little "tongue in cheek" about better understanding the devious actions of foreign wrestling officials bending competition outcomes to serve select countries.

FILA-sponsored international tournaments used the black mark scoring system from 1966 forward through Sanders' career. The black mark system was also suspect, however, especially when wrestlers from former Soviet Union collaborating countries met each other in competition. The communist contestant from the Soviet Union, for example, with little chance of winning a medal, might throw the match by allowing a communist Bulgarian an easy win by pin and thereby prevent black marks from accumulating for the winner. This scenario occurred at

Sanders: In the Moment

the 1960 Olympics in Rome. Late in a semifinal match between Stoyanov of Bulgaria and Koridze of the former Soviet Union, with the score tied and both wrestlers facing elimination from gold medal contention if it ended in a draw, Stoyanov suddenly seemed to lose his competitive will. His capitulation allowed Koridze to win and keep the gold medal away from Martinovic of Yugoslavia. Many thought the Bulgarians were loyal to the Soviets to the point of athletic obedience. Yugoslavia, on the other hand, took pride in beating the Soviets. The Soviets denied the fix, but Rene Coulon of France, the president of FILA, was at the match and witnessed the event. The match was stopped immediately. The Bulgarian was disqualified and the Soviet was given one penalty point. Nevertheless, the Soviet Koridze went on to confiscate the gold medal. Soviet and Russian unethical stratagems continued through the next couple decades.[14]

Sanders was awarded the third place medal on a weigh-in. He was the heaviest by a pound in a three-way tie for first place. Photo and caption courtesy of AWN, 1966.

FREE STYLE TEAM, 1966 World Championships (L-R)—KNEELING: Richard Sanders (114.5), Larry Kristoff (Hwt); STANDING: Coach Bill Smith, Manager Elias George, Werner Holzer (154), Jess Lewis (213.5), Bob Douglas (138.5), Dean Lahr (191.5), Len Kauffman (171.5), Fred Powell (125.5). The third place team trophy in the middle.

Sanders: In the Moment

The 1966 U.S. World Team placed a very respectable third. Bobby Douglas at 138.5 pounds, Larry Kristoff at heavyweight, and Rick Sanders in the flyweight 52 kg class (114.5 pounds) all medaled at the 1966 FILA World Championships. Kristoff and Douglas won silver, and Sanders, bronze. Of note, Sanders had an equal number of black marks as Chang Chang-sun of South Korea, who was awarded the gold medal, and Yasuo Katsumura of Japan, who received silver. Rick did not lose a match in the tournament. A round robin final involving the three wrestlers ended in draws. Medals were awarded on the basis of a weigh-in. Rick was the heaviest wrestler by a pound and therefore was awarded the bronze medal for a third-place finish. But for a pound of flesh (or a few drops of sweat), Sanders would have been the first U.S. world champion three years earlier than he ultimately became in 1969.[15]

Bill Smith followed up the tournament with a heartfelt letter to Sanders, in which he said, "I felt as bad as you did when you had to settle for third because the gold medal was deservingly yours. Your showing in the tournament was an inspiration to all the U.S.A. wrestlers and if they can pattern their wrestling after yours, we will have many gold medals in the future." Further, Smith wrote, "Thank you for the cooperation, comradeship and respectability that you demonstrated in the four weeks that we were together. I hope you know that our relationship during the tournament and training camp was most enjoyable to me and it will long be one of the most memorable moments in my life."[16] This from a former wrestler who was a two-time NCAA champion, a winner of three national AAU titles and between the years of 1947-1952 won 128 matches without a loss and won a gold medal at the 1952 Olympics in Helsinki, Finland. Coach Smith was influential. He was a quality mentor for Rick. Smith had the wrestling track record and exemplified the solid character that was meaningful to the impetuous, free-ranging Sanders.

Sanders: In the Moment

Recapping Sanders' 1966 three-month mid-March to mid-June wrestling tournaments campaign (following his 1965-1966 college season!) is something to contemplate. March 11th-12th, he placed third in the NCAA Division II tournament in Mankato, Minnesota. The top four finishers in the Division II tournament could compete in the D-I tournament held March 24th-26th in Ames, Iowa. Sanders became a first-time NCAA D-I champion there. His next action was at the National AAU tournament in Lincoln, Nebraska April 5th-9th. The Lincoln tournament second place finish earned him an invitation to compete for the 1966 World Team. The twenty-day training and selection camp for the World Team was held at the University of Michigan May 22nd through June 12th. Invitees wrestled challenge matches throughout the three-week camp. Sanders filtered through the selection process to represent the U.S. at the 1966 World Championships held in Toledo, Ohio June 16th through the 22nd. Rick placed third at the Worlds on a weigh-in at 114.5 pounds. He just barely missed becoming America's first world champion in 1966—a milestone he would accomplish three years later.

Sanders' wrestling schedule March through June 1966 was remarkable in several respects. The degree of mental toughness necessary to successfully compete at the highest level of wrestling competition over that time period is amazing. Sanders did it all on the road, 1500-2000 miles from his home in Portland, Oregon. He did not have a car and, of course, at that time there were no cell phones. He was challenged to a spartan diet in order to maintain flyweight status at 114.5 pounds. Moreover, he did it on a modicum of financial support.

Sanders flourished in that "wrestler's culture" for the remainder of his life. But he brought more to the culture than the stereotypical ascetic lifestyle. He brought light-heartedness and a fun-loving spirit. He was gifted, he knew it, and he sacrificed and worked hard to sustain it. The mat experience was intoxicating to Sanders. It got in his head. He loved and nurtured his time in the moment. He came from behind, pinned opponents late in matches, decisioned foes by ten-point margins, and did not dwell on the rare losses. Sanders lived life in the now. Each match paid off hope with joy and peace, and it did so naturally, because for Sanders, that was how life worked. His wrestling reflected his life. He was perhaps the greatest "in the moment" wrestler of all time.

The sixties counterculture continued at pace through 1966. The Haight-Ashbury in San Francisco was the first of several enclaves for the movement, certainly the biggest and most popular. "Freaks" was the name of choice for serious counterculturalists. They were disgusted with the war in Vietnam, racial injustice, capitalism, and basically traditional values of American life. The counterculture, according to Christopher Strain's *The Long Sixties*, was identifiable less by what it stood for than by what it stood against.[17]

Anti-Vietnam war rumblings began in 1966 when the *New York Times* published a series of articles showing that President Johnson lied about military targets in North Vietnam. The Johnson administration was also successful in criminalizing LSD in 1966, though it was still readily available. LSD use did somewhat separate the counterculture from the thrills sought by the mere youth culture—who were more into marijuana, a hallucinogen illegal since 1937.

Juxtaposed to war and drug issues, the counterculture explored different forms of religion as well. Many considered Christianity and Judaism repressive. The movement sought peace, love, understanding, and especially rebellion against established traditions. Buddhism, Hinduism, and Native American mysticism were practiced alternatively.

The counterculture movement spread up the West Coast from California, though it seemed to have little negative influence on production of Oregon world class athletes. Larry Mahan, an Oregon-born contemporary of Sanders, won his first of six World All Around Cowboy Championships in 1966. He would ultimately add two bull riding championships at the 1966 Professional Rodeo Cowboys Association National Finals Rodeo. Mahan was also a wrestler, though of a lower caliber than Sanders in the 1961 Oregon State wrestling tournament. He lost in the first round. Sanders, on the other hand, won his first of three state titles that year. The talent pool of Oregon's world-class athletes was rich in the '60s and '70s. Along with Sanders and Mahan, it included distance runner Steve Prefontaine and high jumper Dick Fosbury in track and field, along with two-time Olympian Don Schollander in swimming.[18]

Jess Lewis, former two-time NCAA Division I national champion at heavyweight for the Oregon State Beavers, was a member of the 1966 World Team and 1968 Olympic team with Sanders. Lewis was a two-sport athlete—wrestling and starring in football for the Beavers. His aggressive go-for-broke style mirrored Sanders and manifested in a 76-1 collegiate win/loss record. Lewis played professional football for the Houston Oilers at the conclusion of his wrestling career. When asked to reflect on Sanders, Lewis' opening comment was insightful: "I want to tell you from the get go, Sanders was the toughest guy I've ever met!" Lewis added, "Sanders was good enough to beat the immortal Robin Reed." Reed was an Olympian from Oregon who, wrestling at 134.5 pounds, beat all teammates on the ocean cruise sailing the Atlantic en route to the 1924 Paris Olympics. Once there, Reed went undefeated in the tournament to win the gold. Lewis' perspective is set against some of the best. Lewis remembered Sanders as being a "wild bugger," but confident, his own man, and a lot smarter than people gave him credit for. Lewis wrestled the great Soviet Aleksandr Medved at the 1966 World Championships in Toledo, Ohio. Medved was recognized as "One of the greatest wrestlers in

Sanders: In the Moment

history" by FILA, Wrestling's International Governing Body. Lewis lost to Medved, but suggesting that Sanders was the toughest guy he ever met, inclusive of Medved, is high praise.[19]

Sanders was viewed as tough, but outside observers wondered whether he worked hard enough. He was often irresponsibly over weight at team weigh-ins before a match. The running he did to augment his on-mat training or weight loss was often counterintuitive. Keith Lowrance, who wrestled for Michigan State in the 1960s, posted a Sanders' anecdote online characteristic of Rick's weight loss methods:

> "At the trials for the Pan American team in Minnesota a couple of us were running when we came across Sanders. He was hiding something in the bushes. I asked him what he was doing and he said, 'Keith, you always need a plan for weight cutting.' He went on to say he was driving around his running route hiding cans of beer every two miles. He said that those beers could keep him going for 10 or 12 miles, and at that distance he could lose the 10 plus pounds he needed to make weight the next day. Sanders jumped in his car and went to his next hiding spot."

Four 12-ounce beers in ten miles—imbibing three pounds of "suds" to lose ten pounds of body weight—if true, was it ridiculous or genius? Modern endurance athletes commonly plant power drinks along their training routes. Was Sanders eccentric or ahead of his time? In any case, it was quintessential Sanders. His training regimen was as unorthodox and innovative as his wrestling. Portland State workout partner Bob Bergen reflected on Sanders' work ethic. "Sanders worked out two to three times a day. He just did it at different times." Sanders had a bartending job at the downtown American Tavern Museum. He got off at odd hours. "I occasionally would get a Sanders call after 10:00 P.M. Rick did not like running for conditioning. One night, finding the wrestling room locked, we worked out on a trampoline." Wayne Baughman, who wrestled in a dozen tournaments with Rick, confirmed, "Sanders worked out when no

Sanders: In the Moment

one else did."[20] PSU teammate Mas Yatabe recalled that Rick never went to sleep during most tournaments, but he busied himself with any manner of activity—washing clothes, stringing beads, and more.[21]

Sanders was usually occupied with losing weight. "Sanders could drop ten pounds in a day and it would not affect his performance," high school competitor Jerry Groover reflected.[22] Ron Iwasaki, another Sanders high school and college competitor, observed, "There were times Rick had to be helped on to the scale at weigh-ins, but then he'd gain fifteen to twenty pounds. His capacity/capability to lose weight, then recover, was phenomenal."[23] PSU teammate Ron Calhoun remembered Rick as relentless in the practice room. Marlin Grahn, former PSU coach added, "Sanders always got tougher the longer the match or practice went."[24] Len Kauffman, former PSU coach, reflected, "Sanders was always in good shape; he wrestled all year long and surrounded himself with other good wrestlers."[25] To argue that Sanders was not in condition to compete as a world class athlete, is to say he could not move optimally on the mat throughout the match. Oft teammate Don Behm regarded Sanders sagely: "You had to stay close to Sanders to win. Amazingly strong muscles win, but leverage beats muscle, and movement beats both. Rick had movement."[26]

The ancient game of chess has been used as a metaphor for many activities. Its intellectual aspects mirror the ancient sport of wrestling quite well. Mike McKeel, Sanders' teammate at Portland State, recalled coach Howard Westcott's injunction. "Always have two moves in mind! If the first doesn't work, immediately go to the second. Next move! Next move," was Howard's catchphrase.[27] Wrestling is like chess: one physically oriented; one mentally oriented. The opponents are one-on-one, squaring off directly with nowhere to hide. There are specific opening patterns in chess just as there are often in wrestling. So, too, there are different styles of play: aggressive and sacrificial, quiet and defensive, tactical (short-term combinations), or strategical (long-term positioning). Accomplished chess players enjoy the game in part for the challenge of seeing multiple moves at once. The five pieces in chess have different values, all used in combination and strategically to ultimately capture the king, to wit, pin your opponent—game over in both sports. The pawn, worth one point, is expendable to the greater good of capturing the king. A pawn might be sacrificed to open a line of attack for the knight, bishop, rook, or queen for example. Similarly, a wrestler in control might allow his opponent to escape, giving up a point but providing the opportunity for a two-point takedown. On the other hand, a wrestler's "pawn" move might be to take a stalling call late in a match allowing time to expire and preserving a win. Other wrestling "pawn" moves might be securing riding time or setting up second moves with an arm drag, shuck, snap down, or level change—any feint to create an offensive opening. When competing, a good wrestler always has two moves in mind, just as Westcott instructed.

The knight in chess is the surreptitious piece. The sneaky guy. Worth three points in chess, its attack is oblique. In wrestling, the "knight" move is comparable to gaining the corner in a single leg attack, a snap down setting up an ankle pick, sacrificing a leg to get in close to an opponent, a whizzer to a hip-out, or any move to set up another move.

The bishop in chess is also worth three points, the same value as the knight. Its line of attack is intractable—it stays on its color in a direct line to the piece under attack. In wrestling, the "bishop" move might be considered as the initiation of a pinning combination, a cradle, a half nelson, the audacious double leg takedown, the cross-body ride to a tilt, or a high amplitude throw in Greco.

Sanders: In the Moment

The rook in chess is worth five points. Its increased value is because it can cover all squares on the chess board. In wrestling, the "rook" move is likened to any move that results in back points. It ensures an offensive advantage, swings momentum, and can occur no matter how destitute the situation. In addition, the rook may work defensively, protecting while enhancing the King's position.

The queen in chess is worth nine points, by far the most valuable piece. Its value stems from its versatility of movement. Losing the queen in chess puts the player in a defensive posture for the remainder of the game. The "queen" move in wrestling is inherent. It is the level of confidence the wrestler has on the mat—the positive psychological mindset of the competitor. The 90% that creates a winner. The unequivocal visceral attitude that, no matter what my training has been, my injuries are, my poor homelife has been, how people perceive me, what my win/loss record is or his—it is the holy righteous attitude saying, 'I' can beat that guy!

Finally, there is the king. The king is the truculent one, able to move one square in any direction. Often in danger but rarely believing it to be so. The superego. The king is gladiator on the mat, the competitor, the wrestler—pleasing the crowd and so serving the self. The king conjures the crowd: "Snap down! Snap down!" "Level change!" "Circle! Circle!" "Hips!" "Short time! Short time!" The king literally moves the crowd, so powerful, alerting the kingdom, yet rarely hearing the legions—the fans, coaches, teammates, or parents. In chess, capturing the king is the objective. No matter at what stage of the game, once the king is captured, checkmate, game over. However, unlike chess, in wrestling the "king" move is the pin. It is not winning by decision. A decision is a win by expiration of time-clock. The pin does more. It serves both the individual wrestler and the team. The wrestler's reputation is enhanced when

Sanders: In the Moment

Picture of Cardinal Lincoln High School's chess team, 1962.
Sanders, second row, far right.
Wrestling is like playing chess. Sanders pursued both.

—

conquering by pin, his armor tempered for the next match. The pinner moves forward with temerity; his next opponent moves with caution. Finally, the pin adds maximum team points. But, more importantly, a pinner brings an aura and thereby power to the team, strengthening the kingdom against all pretenders. The king is noble and revered: a pinner.

Sanders was a pinner. Nine of Sanders' eleven Olympic wins were by fall. He was also a student of chess. He played on his Lincoln High School chess team. He played with roommate Sergio Gonzalez at Munich. He played with Don Behm in '72 while they lined up for the opening Olympic parade, and his miniature chess board and pieces were sent home to Portland from Yugoslavia by the U.S. State Department in his final effects after his death in 1972. In a build-up to the Munich Olympics, the *Sunday Oregonian* of August 27, 1972 wrote of Sanders:

Sanders: In the Moment

Another top American contender is Rick Sanders, 27, of Portland, Ore., an independent soul who wears beads to training sessions, sports long hair and a beard and is allowed his own nightowlish training methods. A student of the sport who wrestles as if he were playing chess, Sanders is considered the most skillful technically of the Americans. He wrestles in the 125-pound class."[28]

Gonzalez reflected, "Rick was a chess piece in motion; he didn't overpower with strength; he could innovate in the moment." He had an uncommon ability to put multiple moves together effectively, under pressure, and in a limited area. He studied chess and seemed to use the "game" to take wrestling to another level.[29]

Chapter Six

The Vietnam War continued to escalate in 1967 under the Johnson administration. President Lyndon Baines Johnson was fearful of becoming the first U.S. President to lose a war. Eleven thousand three hundred and sixty-three U.S. soldiers died in the southeast Asian conflict in 1967, the second highest annual total of the nineteen-year war. Still, if you kept yourself in college, you could keep from being called up to serve. Sanders, under the auspices of the avuncular Howard Westcott, was successful in that objective.

Gasoline was only 33 cents a gallon. If you had access to a car, you could patronize the McDonalds where hamburgers were 15 cents and perhaps watch Dustin Hoffman in the 1967 movie hit *The Graduate* at the local drive-in theater. PSU wrestler Bob Bergen lent his '53 Chevy to Rick one evening and didn't see it again for a week! Bob finally asked Sanders if he could return his car. Sanders' comment was, "Oh, did you need it back?" The outdoor theaters were on their way out by the 1970s owing to suburban and exurban sprawl, oppressive real estate taxes, and short viewing seasons. Too bad—never was there a better venue for freedom to flourish. Sanders could mix his love of the outdoors with dreams spawned by big screen technology and the movie industry.

Sanders: In the Moment

The first Super Bowl was played in 1967 at the LA Memorial Coliseum. Green Bay prevailed over Kansas City 35-10. Sanders had his own "super bowl" season on the mat in '67. In just his junior year as a Viking at Portland State, Sanders continued to build on his athletic stardom. Sanders would win two college national championships in 1967, one at the Division II level and one at Division I. Those championships were accented by being named the Outstanding Wrestler at both the Division II and Division I level. Sanders remains the only wrestler to have been awarded the Outstanding Wrestler Award at the NAIA, NCAA Division II, and NCAA Division I tournaments.[1]

The 1966-1967 wrestling season went optimally for the Portland State University Vikings. The institution itself gained university status in 1967. Howard Westcott's grapplers went 17-0 in dual meet competition. Their wins included home and away duals over Dale Thomas' Oregon State Beavers and duals against the University Oregon Ducks coached by Art Keith.

Portland State University's 197-pound Mike McKeel remembers the 1967 team as an "underfunded rag-tag brotherhood of wrestlers. No one even had the same uniform; It was usually a singlet with some green on it. Sanders' shoes usually had about three layers of duct tape, his hair typically hanging in his eyes."[2] The day they faced Cal Poly, a powerhouse, they were sitting around the locker room waiting, fresh off a win against Fresno State the night before. Howard Westcott picked up a discarded *Amateur Wrestling News* and learned Cal Poly was rated #1; PSU was rated #2. Totally unaware of his team's ranking, Howard informed his team. In the mat side face-off, Cal Poly was decked out in perfect uniforms and looked like they could have come out of Esquire magazine.

PSU won 35-12.

Sanders: In the Moment

Sanders started out the season with high expectations based on his NCAA D-I championship over Iowa State's Ernie Gillum and his bronze medal at the 1966 World freestyle championships in Ohio where he was prevented from the gold medal on a weigh-in. But lightweight wrestlers around the country might have noticed the outcome of the 1966 Sanders/Crow Division II match and thought Rick was not infallible. Overspeculation was risky however. Even with the 19-12 loss to Crow, Rick had five other wins in that D-II tournament—three by fall and two eight-point major decisions. Sanders could score points.

Sanders was awarded his second Outstanding Wrestler award at the 1967 D-II National Tournament.

The 1967 NCAA Division II Championships were held March 9th through the 11th at Wilkes Barre, Pennsylvania. Seventy college teams and a total of 246 wrestlers competed. Portland State won the championship with 86 points; Mankato State Minnesota was second with 57 points. The Vikings' first team national championship saw Rick Sanders lead the way in his individual championship at 115 pounds over John Garcia of California Poly. He pinned all his opponents en route to the championship and was awarded the Outstanding Wrestler award—his second such award, the first at the 1965 NAIA level. Moreover, it was the third national championship in Rick's career. Sanders' teammates Masaru Yatabe at 137 pounds and Chuck Seal at 152 pounds were champions as well. Mike McKeel at 197 pounds finished second for Portland State. Freeman Garrison battled to a third-place finish at 145 while Rich Green was fourth in the 130-pound class, and Tony Campbell was fifth at 177. It was a dominant team victory. Warren Crow, who upset Sanders at 123 pounds in the 1966 championship match, won again at 123 pounds. Rick narrowly missed him, choosing to stay at the 115-pound weight class in 1967. Rick's success at 115 pounds in the 1966 D-I national championships convinced him to remain at the lower weight.[3]

The 1967 NCAA Division I national tournament was held at Kent State University in Kent, Ohio March 23rd-25th. Kent State would later become the site of the 1970 Vietnam War unrest that resulted in Ohio State National Guardsmen squelching student protest. But in 1967, Sanders was the news. Rick was picked number one by *Amateur Wrestling News* mid-season at 115 pounds. Ray Sanchez of Wyoming was second; Dave Unik of Ohio University placed third. The *Amateur Wrestling News'* midseason prognostication held up. Sanders, seeded number one, moved through the 115-pound bracket with relative ease. He won by fall over his first three opponents—Grant Stevens, Bloomsburg; Dave Unik, Ohio University; and Glen McMinn, Arizona. Rick met fellow Oregonian Ron Iwasaki in the semis. Ron came through the third round in a referee's decision over fourth seed Warren Crow. Rick stuck to business, beating Iwasaki 8-3 and moving into the finals. The championship was a 19-2 rout over number two seed Jim Anderson of Minnesota. *Amateur Wrestling News* reviewed the match:

> 115- Rick Sanders, defending champion from Portland State, a junior, and Jim Anderson, Minnesota senior. After a scoreless first period Sanders reversed but Anderson escaped. Sanders took him down and into a nearfall and led 7-1 when the period ended. In the final period Sanders had two nearfalls, one predicament, one takedown and riding time. Anderson got away briefly for one point. Final score, Sanders 19-2.[4]

Sanders: In the Moment

1967 NATIONAL COLLEGIATE CHAMPIONS, left to right, FRONT: Jim Kamman, 152, Michigan; Don Hendersoon, 145, USAFA; Dale Anderson, 137, Michigan State; David McGuire, 130, Oklahoma; Mike Caruso, 123, Lehigh; Rich Sanders, 115, Portland State. BACK: Curly Culp, Hwt., Arizona State; Tom Schlendorf, 191, Syracuse; Fred Fozzard, 177, Oklahoma State; George Radman, 167, Michigan State; Vic Marcucci, 160, Iowa State.

Pictured, above: Sanders was awarded his 3rd Outstanding Wrestler award at the 1967 D-I tournament.

—

Pictured, Right: In his profile statement for the 1968 Wrestling Guide, Sanders explained, "My off-mat interests are poetry, trout fishing, and motorcycles.

Sanders: In the Moment

Sanders was one of only four finalists from small colleges wrestling in the D-I tournament finals. Sanders and Masaru Yatabe were from D-II Portland State, Mike Gallego from D-II Fresno State, and Nick Carollo from NAIA Adams State. Sanders was the only D-II finalist of the four to win a championship. Sanders' Outstanding Wrestler award served to place his visage on the cover of the 1968 NCAA D-I annual Wrestling Guide. In his profile statement for the guide, Sanders explained, "My off-mat interests are poetry, trout fishing, and motorcycles." These were seemingly benign interests for the legendary Rick Sanders.[5]

Along the way, Portland State's Masaru Yatabe upset number one seed and returning champion from 1966, Oklahoma State's Gene Davis. As the tournament's fourth seed at 137 pounds, Yatabe had a strong tournament, fighting his way to the championship against Michigan State's Dale Anderson, the number two seed.

The Yatabe/Anderson finale was a classic. Dale Anderson of Michigan State prevailed 3-2 in overtime. The outcome incited Sanders to make inappropriate comments to Anderson as the Spartan left for post-match interviews. An impassioned Sanders' impromptu monologue evolved into a diatribe. Anderson reflected: "Sanders started his rant by explaining to me that I wasn't good enough to even be carrying Yatabe's jock or tying his shoes. He called me a bunch of names that I never heard in (or out of) church and continued to rattle my cage all the way over to the interview." Yatabe, nonplussed by Rick's behavior, remained baffled at the time and also years later when questioned about the occurrence. It was unusual behavior for Sanders. At this point in Rick's career, he had witnessed, on the international scene, myriad officiating improprieties resulting in questionable outcomes. Perhaps he felt Anderson's close overtime win reflected unfairness, given that Yatabe was from Japan and a Division II program. If so, Sanders' complaint should have been directed at officials, not Anderson, who wrestled a masterful final. Perhaps Rick did give the referees an unrecorded earful. Michigan State won the 1967 team championship, and Anderson chronicles the road to victory in his excellent book *A Spartan Journey*.[6]

Portland State's Clarence (Chuck) Seal also had a terrific D-I tournament for coach Howard Westcott's Vikings. Victories in his first two rounds matched him with Jim Kamman, the number two seed from Michigan, in round three. Kamman, the eventual champion at 152 pounds, moved on with a 7-1 victory. Seal battled back in the consolation bracket. Two more victories found Chuck matched against the number five seed, Borchers from Stanford, who he defeated 4-1. Chuck Seal stood third on the awards podium.

Left to right: Coach Westcott, Rick Sanders, Masaru Yatabe, Chuck Seal.
Yatabe was voted PSUs most valuable wrestler and
team captain of the three D-II national champions.
1968.

Sanders: In the Moment

A recognition dinner was held at the downtown Hilton Hotel at the end of the 1967 season. The Portland State University president and the mayor of Portland were in attendance. The guests of honor were members of Portland State's first ever national championship team in any sport, and recognized for its fifth-place finish at the D-I tournament (the highest place ever for Portland athletes at that level). Of the three Division II national champions crowned, Yatabe was voted Most Valuable Wrestler and team captain.

Meanwhile, Howard Westcott was singing the praises of Sanders to the Portland State Administration and the outside world.

"Sanders has given PSU a million dollars' worth of publicity," Westcott said, noting a stack of inquiry letters. "Of course, our other champions, Clarence Seal and Masaru Yatabe, deserve part of the credit. But I have 30 or 40 letters from boys who want to go to Portland State next year. I mean outstanding boys, from as far away as Oklahoma and Pennsylvania. PSU has a tremendous athletic reputation, especially in wrestling, which Sanders helped build."

Furthermore, Rick's personal reputation beamed in the Portland area. He was the idol kids seemed to want to emulate. He was in high demand as a speaker for high school sports banquets. And he reciprocated. "I like working with kids," he explained in a newspaper article. "I will probably go into teaching [...] maybe as wrestling coach at PSU if Dr. Westcott ever retires." Rick's reputation was further enhanced when he was named Oregon's 1967 Athlete of the Year.[8] Sanders would clearly garner the necessary accolades over his career to compete for the eventual vacant Westcott coaching position.

Sanders reclaimed the 125.5-pound championship in the 1967 AAU national tournament over a prestigious field of competitors. Sofman, the 1966 champ, wound up fourth. Masaaki Hatta, older brother to 1965 NCAA national champion, Tadaaki Hatta, was runner-up to Sanders.

Sanders: In the Moment

Clearly, some of Sanders' wrestling style worked on Japanese-trained wrestlers.[9]

The National AAU bronze medalist in 1967 at 125.5 was the inimitable Dan Gable. Sanders was three years older than Gable, more experienced in freestyle, and clearly just as confident. Gable reflected on the first conversation with his future Olympic teammate in *A Wrestling Life*:

> I was standing off by myself getting ready for the semifinals, when all of a sudden I felt a tap on my shoulder. I turned around, and there stood the older Sanders.
>
> "Hey Gable," Sanders said.
>
> "Yeah?"
>
> "You got a baseball bat?"
>
> The odd question threw me off. I was never the kind of wrestler who did much talking, especially with the competition.
>
> "Why?" I asked cautiously.
>
> Sanders quipped, "You better find one and bring it to the semis. You got me next."
>
> This was my introduction to Rick Sanders and freestyle wrestling. Sanders won the match 6 to 0. I gave up four of those points because I exposed my own shoulders. I learned a lot from him that night and started an ever-building relationship.[10]

The Sanders/Gable anecdote is like the metaphorical bully (Sanders) who beats up the new kid (Gable) forcing a friendship so he can come over to the new kid's house to play. That scene played out a few years later as described in an *Amateur Wrestling News* article by David Zang to wit: "Sanders stopped one summer in Gable's hometown. Finding the clean-living prodigy out-of-town, he grabbed Gable's dad, Mack, and went drinking. Then he spent the night in Gable's bed."[11]

Dan Gable did not lose a match during his high school and college careers until the finals of the 1970 NCAA Division I championships at 142 pounds. He was 181-0 when he was decisioned in the final match of his college career by Larry Owings, a sophomore out of the University of Washington. Like Sanders, Owings was from Oregon, and their unorthodox wrestling styles were similar. Gable's training strategy was to physically outwork the competition. It worked quite well, but after the single loss, he began to work more on improving mental strategy. Gable

1967 AAU National Championships. On stand, left to right: Sanders, Masaaki Hatta, Dan Gable, and Richard Sofman. Far left: Bill Smith, two time NCAA champion and 1952 Olympic gold medalist was the honoree handing out trophies. Smith would coach Rick on three world teams.

—

reflected in *A Wrestling Life*, "I started to train smarter while continuing to outwork everyone else." He went on to win a world championship in 1971 following his new training strategy. A year later, Gable won the prestigious Tbilisi tournament in the USSR and was named the most outstanding wrestler of the tournament. He continued to employ his training strategy in preparation for the 1972 Olympics where he won gold for the United States. Remarkably, Gable was not scored upon at the Munich Olympics. Gable funneled his skill into a stellar coaching career, applying his training methodology to others at the University of Iowa where he supervised 15 NCAA Division I team championships. Forty-five Iowa Hawkeye national champion wrestlers were crowned during his coaching tenure.

Lincoln McIlravy won three NCAA championship titles wrestling for Gable. McIlravy was asked about his secret to success by a camper at a kid-wrestling event. The NCAA champion and 2000 Olympic bronze medalist responded, "The secret to success is to train and compete at a level the competition knows nothing about!" Gable's influence was still resonating. Sanders might have added, "and have fun doing it."

Interviewed by Bob Burnett, staff writer for the *Oregonian*, Sanders reflected, "I wrestle because I enjoy it. When it becomes a task instead of a hobby, it will be time to quit." Coincidentally, Thomas Gilman, the 2020 Olympic bronze medalist and 2021 world champion at 125.5 pounds, the same international weight class Sanders wrestled, spoke similarly in post tournament interviews. "I just want to enjoy the process. Once I stop enjoying it, it's time to hang it up."[12]

The National AAU tournaments took place in the spring just a few weeks after the conclusion of the collegiate national tournaments. The 1967 tournament was held again at Lincoln, Nebraska. The outcome of this tournament, combined with successes at college tournaments, played a large role in which wrestlers would get selected for international competition. In 1967, the paramount international tournament for Western Hemisphere wrestlers was the Pan American Games. The selection committee extended invitations to wrestlers interested in competing for a spot on the 1967 Pan American Team after the 1967 National AAU tournament. Sanders accepted an invitation.

Tryouts for the Pan American Team were held July 3rd in Minneapolis, Minnesota at the University of Minnesota's Williams arena. The top three wrestlers in each weight class were given one day of rest and then competed in a round robin to determine the Pan American Team members. As is often the case in Minnesota over the 4th of July, the temperature and humidity had skyrocketed. Bruce Glenn recalls a trip with Rick and Chuck Seal to a convenience store during a break in the competition. Bruce remained outside while Rick and Chuck went into the store. They came out with three small sandwiches and three quarts of beer. Beer was commonly sold either in twelve-ounce bottles or quarts in that era. Rick's theory was that beer runs right through you, quenches thirst, relaxes the muscles, and the sweat comes off faster when you start running again. Bruce wasn't much of a drinker, so he was unable to put a lie to Sanders' theory.[13] Rick was successful in making the team, however, and continued to train in Minneapolis through July 18th. The team left for Canada on July 19th. Competition ensued in Winnipeg, Canada from July 24th through the 27th.

All eight U.S. wrestlers won gold medals at the 1967 Pan American Games—the brush-up to the 1968 Olympics. The U.S. team had 17 falls in 33 matches. Impressive, especially so considering team captain, Wayne Baughman at 191.5 pounds, was handicapped by a shoulder separation and torn rib cartilage acquired in training prior to the tournament. A Canadian sports writer wrote, "You couldn't help but wonder how many more medals the U.S. would have won had their second and third best wrestlers been able to compete. They may have won all the silver and bronze medals as well."

Rick bested Don Behm at the Pan American trials in Minnesota at 125.5 pounds, the first of many epic matches the two would have over the next five years. Behm ultimately made the 1968 Olympic team in a weight class above Sanders, both becoming silver medalists. The Americans won the Pan Am games, though only Wayne Baughman, Larry Kristoff, and Rick Sanders of the 1967 Pan American team would continue on to compete at the 1968 Olympics.[14]

VICTORIOUS 1967 U. S. Pan-American Wrestling Team (L-R)—FRONT: Richard Sofman, 114.5; Richard Sanders, 125.5; Mike Young, 138.5; Gerald Bell, 154; Pat Kelly, 171.5; BACK: Coach Jimmy Miller, Larry Kristoff, Hwt.; Harry Houska, 213.5; Capt. Wayne Baughman (team captain), 191.5; Tom Lumly, manager.

Pictured: the U.S. Pan Am team, 1967. Rick, front row, second from left.
A Canadian sports writer wrote, "You couldn't help but wonder how many more medals the U.S. would have won had their second and third best wrestlers been able to compete."

Sanders: In the Moment

Sanders received a congratulatory letter on August 10th, 1967 from the Mayor of Portland after his Pan American performance. To wit:

Dear Rick,

On behalf of the citizens of our "City of Roses", I wish to extend to you heartiest congratulations upon bringing home a gold medal from the Pan-American Games in Winnipeg recently. This newest achievement adds to an outstanding record of accomplishment, twice winning the NCAA College Division crown for Portland State, along with an NCAA University Division Championship, and a National AAU Title – and indeed, you can be justly proud.

This has been an outstanding year for you, Rick, and I look forward to seeing you win additional laurels for Portland State College and then bringing home still another medal from the Olympics in Mexico City.

All of us take pride in your accomplishments, and you have our sincere best wishes for continued success.

Best regards!

Yours truly,

Terry D. Schrunk

Mayor

Sanders had one additional tournament in the fall of 1967, yet it was a good tune-up for the start of the 1967-1968 Portland State University wrestling season. The U.S. World Team competed at the 1967 World Championships held in New Delhi, India from November 12th-14th. Rick was the 114.5-pound U.S. representative. He had a good tournament and ended with a silver medal, the highest American finisher. Mike Young of Provo, Utah and Larry Kristoff of Carbondale, Illinois won bronze medals. The American team finished fourth, just one half-point behind Iran. Russia claimed the victory; Japan was second.[15]

The 1967 World gold medalist at 114.5 pounds was Shigeo Nakata from Japan, the country of origin for so many of Rick's toughest opponents. Japanese wrestlers, especially at the smaller weights, were quick and technically sound. Nakata was dominant. He had won the Asian Games' gold medal at 125.5 pounds in 1966. The Asian Games is recognized by the International Olympic Committee and is the second largest multidisciplinary sporting event after the Olympics. It is held every four years, similar to the Pan American Games—the exclusive Western Hemisphere competition held each penultimate year leading to the Olympics. Over forty-five countries have competed in the Asian Games. Athletes from all Asian countries are welcome to participate. Shigeo Nakata, born in 1945 at the end of WWII, and the same age as Rick, would meet Sanders again in 1968 at Mexico City to wrestle for the Olympic gold medal.[16]

Chapter Seven

Sanders was witness to much change in 1968, his final collegiate year. The Vietnam conflict, a presidential election, cultural unrest, assassinations, student rebellion, and the Olympics created the American saga of 1968.

Over half a million men (and 11,000 women) were involved in military service in Vietnam by 1968. It was normally a one-year commitment and most servicemen spent their Vietnam time in support services. Yet the enemy threat was omnipresent. Automatic draft deferments went to those in college and graduate school. College enrollments went from two million in 1950 to seven million in 1968. Moreover, matching the half million draftees were a half million conscientious objectors to the war. Fighting the war was left primarily to the poor and working-class men. Until 1968, most of the press about Vietnam came through print media. However, in 1968, broadcast media started to reveal doubts about the war and political untruths about its efficacy. In March of 1968, Lyndon Baines Johnson informed America and the world that he was quitting. He told the nation, "I shall not seek, and I will not accept, the nomination of my party for another term as your President." At 59, Johnson was exhausted. He died six years later.[1]

Sanders: In the Moment

Martin Luther King was assassinated in April of 1968. His philosophy of nonviolent protest, patterned after Mahatma Gandhi's success in opposition to Britain's colonial rule of India, was integral to the civil rights movement. Dr. King was murdered by a white man, James Earl Ray, perhaps in concert with others never identified. The radical Black Panthers, in that same month, ambushed an Oakland City police car, critically wounding an officer after firing over 150 shots at the vehicle. More than one hundred cities experienced violent rioting after King's assassination. And by 1970, the Panthers had killed eleven police officers.

Two months after King's assassination, one-time attorney general and brother to JFK, Bobby Kennedy, was assassinated. Bobby had evolved as a 1968 presidential candidate. Many felt his charisma, youth, and experience could quell the country's cultural upheaval. Kennedy spoke of curing social ills when he said, "Some men see things as they are and say, why; I dream things that never were and say, why not?" The crux of his message was about change. The message harmonized with Rick Sanders' readily morphing world view. Later, Kennedy had just delivered a speech in California when he was shot by a Palestinian infuriated by Kennedy's pro-Israeli stance. The Palestinian-Israeli conflict would be observed by Sanders perhaps even more closely at the Munich Olympics four years later when Palestinian extremists would kidnap and murder eleven Israeli Olympic athletes.

By 1968, the antiwar movement and the counterculture had melded together. The new movement was generated through the combined energy of students on college campuses and their catalyst, the media. The politics of college campuses pushed for change. The organization, Students for a Democratic Society (SDS), for example, called for "replacement of power rooted in possession, privilege, or circumstances, with power rooted in love, reflectiveness, reason, and creativity." The SDS manifesto, known as the Port Huron Statement, was authored largely by Tom Hayden, a University of Michigan student. Hayden and the SDS became involved in the 1968 trial of the Chicago Eight. Hayden was one of the demonstrators at the Chicago Democratic convention arrested by police for allegedly rioting. Out of the Chicago imbroglio, splinter groups such as the Weathermen, later known as the Weather Underground, were spawned. They rallied for the destruction of U.S. imperialism and the formulation of a classless society.[2]

Protests and rioting occurred in Portland in the middle and late sixties. Sanders was not much involved in the politics of social change, but the idea of unrestrained personal freedom emanating from the counterculture movement resonated deeply. Sergio Gonzalez only remembered Rick depressed one time: "Listening to Vice President Spiro Agnew give a pep talk to the 1972 Olympic wrestlers about representing their country—while knowing how hypocritical politics was."[3] Mentioned in the *Amateur Wrestling News* article by David Zang, "friend and former professor Earle MacCannell suggested Sanders was 'actively disinterested' in politics." Friend and teammate Don Behm vaguely recollected Rick giving Tricia Nixon, the President's daughter, a brief but impassioned scolding for her father's Vietnam War Policy at an honorary dinner prior to the 1972 Olympic Games.[4] Sanders' political discussion with Miss Nixon, who was Rick's age, was likely disingenuous. Rick made time for most women that crossed his path.

Rick's womanizing received much publicity in the retrospect on his life. He had a couple long-time girlfriends at Portland State. One coed lived up the hill from campus in an affluent neighborhood. The girl's parents did not approve of Rick's socioeconomic background. A second girl, Dotty, was a significant but short-lasting relationship for Sanders. There were additional relationship hurdles: he had no viable transportation and no financial means; he slept in attics, sometimes under bridges when on the road, or similar abodes when not at his mother's home; and his career plans were sketchy at best. Female college coeds in the 1960s were likely either career oriented themselves or looking for a provider who was career oriented. Ricks' career trajectory was uncertain, finishing high school with a GED and falling behind in college courses.

Sanders was unquestionably a virile guy. He loved women and they were attracted to him. His relationships were part of his self-discovery. Moving through his twenties, he was in need. Moreover, the culture was more accepting of an affaire de Coeur. Intimates suggest Sanders was respectful of women. Yet, he was not unfamiliar with a menage a trois. The notorious "free love" movement advocated freeing sex from its tie to monogamous marriage. Devotees, men and women, strived toward an ideal of unselfish, unpossessive mutual love. "It's a beautiful thing," was common parlance.[5]

To be sure, Sanders had star quality, recognized it, and had sycophant admirers. The Portland International Airport had an over-life-sized photo of Rick on display in their arrival area during his heyday. The fact that an *Oregonian* reporter would ask him in an interview at the Olympics "whether he checked his appetite for women during competition," clearly added credence to and fanned his reputation. The attention stoked his self-focus objective, if not the underlying need. Sanders was adept at attracting women but struggled to find partners who were satisfied with all sides of himself. He was left with a sense of superficiality.

He was often observed to be quiet, a bit removed, and reflective in crowds, and more open and generous in comment among friends. "Rick was tactile if he knew you," said teammate Ron Calhoun. "He was inherently a hugger, touchy, slap you, sort of person."[6] His actions reflect

Sanders: In the Moment

more of an introvert's behavior—personal energy generated by alone time or one-on-one conversation, unlike the extrovert personality that gains energy through interaction with crowds and partying. PSU teammate Mike McKeel remembers: "Sanders was not much of a socializer in college and a bit of a loner."

Wayne Wells observed Rick as if he were homeless–no family support. For Wells, "Rick was not overly respectful, but he never bragged, and it would be an anomaly for him to run someone down"--the Dale Anderson episode nonwithstanding. Len Kauffman agreed; he recalled Sanders as someone who didn't come across as arrogant and didn't have an outsized ego. Marlin Grahn and Mas Yatabe resolutely believed success did not change him. Sanders, despite his eccentricities and his reputation, never let fame go to his head.

The 1967-1968 Portland State wrestling campaign sallied forth on the strength of Sanders, wrestling up at 123 pounds and even more often at 130. Masaru Yatabe competed at 137 pounds, and Chuck Seal at 145. Howard Westcott's grapplers accrued a winning dual meet record of 13-4. Two of the four losses were to in-state nemesis Oregon State. The loss to the Beavers on January 6th 1968 ended a thirty dual match win streak for the Vikings. Sanders and teammates were victorious over perennial power Cal Poly, however. They weathered a three-point loss to the University of Washington. The Huskies were building a program on the likes of 1968-1969 Oregon freshman recruit Larry Owings.

Amateur Wrestling News Midseason All-American Squad picked Rick as number one at 123 pounds. Dwayne Keller, a state of Washington recruit and a sophomore wrestling for Oklahoma State, was picked number two. Gary Burger of the Navy was third. Previous to the 1968 tournament, the NCAA did not allow freshmen to wrestle varsity at the D-I level. An NCAA investigation was conducted into Sanders' eligibility since he had wrestled at the NAIA national championships as a freshman in 1965. The outcome of the investigation allowed him to wrestle as a senior at the 1968 Division I tournament.[9]

The U.S. Amateur Wrestling Foundation's selection for 1967 Man of the Year found Sanders finishing third. His two national championships, the 1967 Outstanding Wrestler award, and his stellar win/loss record garnered three first place votes. Voting was held by a nationwide panel of coaches, competitors, and officials spanning all phases of amateur wrestling. Michigan State coach of the 1967 National Champion Spartans, Grady Peninger, won the award with four first place votes. Cliff Keen of rival Michigan was second. Oklahoma coach, Tommy Evans, was fourth. Coincidentally, Evans would coach Sanders during the upcoming 1968 Olympic campaign.[10]

Rick wrestled through the dual meet college season undefeated. Though his style of wrestling was unorthodox, he appeared at the time clean-cut with short hair and no facial hair. Academics were not top priority, and he lacked credits to graduate in the spring. Sanders was at a crossroads similar to when he finished his high school career. What next? He loved Oregon and indulged in its nature and the free spirit of its people. In the moment, that was enough. He took a poetry class in his final year. The 1968 PSU yearbook describes Sanders:

Frodo Lives.

PSC's favorite little man, Rick Sanders can often be seen dreaming in the haze of smoke, pizza, and coffee vapors at Montagues coffee shop. Here he can retreat into a relaxed degree of anonymity and escape those who pretend to recognize him as a wrestling celebrity.

He can be seen gazing out the window, slouched in the back row of an advanced poetry writing class, developing another facet of his little-known personality.

Sanders: In the Moment

It is Rick's wrestling prowess that has resulted to a large degree in national recognition for Portland State as a citadel of winning wrestlers. Indeed, success becomes a by-word when it's Sanders' turn on the mat.

Walking down the hall, he wears on his letterman jacket a little button. It says in Elvish script "Be Happy." He is, after all, the wrestler who reads *The Lord of the Rings*, in the locker room before his match.[11]

J.R.R. Tolkien in *The Hobbit* and *The Lord of the Rings* trilogy created a world of magic, fantasy, and make-believe whose archetypes and epic battles between good and evil reverberated through the sixties' counterculture. It's not difficult to see how Sanders' single parent, cloistered adolescence in downtown Portland would create in him a proclivity toward magic, fantasy, and make-believe. What you haven't experienced of the world is left to the imagination. According to Christopher Strain in *The Long Sixties*, "The relaxed priorities of happy, hedonistic, beauty-loving Hobbits—with their second breakfasts, pipe weed, and smoke rings—appealed to many longhairs." Sanders' evolving "good-times" personality fit perfectly with the prototype halfling Hobbit Frodo. Sanders melded quickly into the Hobbit-esque character while reading Tolkien's masterpieces in the steam room. His appearance, benevolence, and aspirations were patterned after Tolkien's Hobbit characters. The Hobbit homeland of the Shire was easily recognized in Portland—"The Rose City." Sanders seemed to have found the means to begin expanding his character beyond just the jock. He took license to stretch his personal freedoms within the historically conservative wrestling culture. What could be wrong with mixing a little hair growth, pipe weed, and wine in the athletic arena? With altruistic intentions, Rick would begin his own quest, one to change wrestling norms. Tolkien speaks for Frodo, the hobbit and Gandalf, his wizard and coach in *The

Sanders: In the Moment

Fellowship of the Ring. "I wish it need not have happened in my time," said Frodo. "So do I," said Gadalf, "And so do all who live to see such times. But that is not for them to decide. All we have to decide is what to do with the time that is given us." Sanders did much in the time he was given.

The 1967-1968 post season began with the college division (or NCAA D-II) tournament in Mankato, Minnesota March 15th-16th. Portland State was the defending champion. Sanders and Yatabe repeated as champions: Rick at 123 pounds; Masaru at 137 pounds. Chuck Seal was runner-up at 145 pounds. Despite their combined efforts, it wasn't enough. Even though Portland State won the 1968 dual 20 to 11, Cal Poly's tournament team was too much for the Vikings. Cal Poly won the championship with 91 points to Portland's 62. Rick was awarded the Outstanding Wrestler Award for the tournament, his second Outstanding Wrestler Award at the D-II National tournament level and fourth overall. He won the OW award at the NAIA level in 1965 and at the D-I level in 1967. Sanders' level of confidence in the post season was well in place.[12]

Don Bartling, South Dakota State University library archivist and wrestling fan, recalled Sanders from the 1968 Division II tournament at Mankato. "I was sitting in the crowd when Sanders and a teammate happened to sit down next to me." The 93-year-old Bartling explains, "Wrestlers sat in the crowd at that time until their match approached. They would go down to mat-side and warm up. I listened in on their conversation." Sanders explained that he had been visualizing how he might be able to pin his first-round opponent using only his legs. Rick observed that his opponent was a 16th round seed and probably wasn't too good, therefore trying his newly conceived pinning combination would not be too risky. Bartling watched intently as Sanders pinned his first round opponent in 4:37 and, as visualized, used only his legs.[13]

Sanders: In the Moment

Sanders may have used a scissors move similar to what fellow Oregonian Robin Reed demonstrated back in the 1920s. Or it may have been some variation of what Rick previously termed a "reverse double grapevine and head lock." Sergio Gonzalez explained, "Elite athletes often used visualization to practice moves in their minds against multiple defense moves by opponents." Sanders pinned his final three tournament opponents in conventional style, the finals match ending in 4:20.

Bartling became a Sanders fan. He chronicled all of Rick's matches using published results listed in *Amateur Wrestling News* at the time. It is difficult to know how broad and deep Sanders' fan following was. Much of the media coverage for wrestling focused on the Midwest, especially on the remarkable win record of Iowa State University phenom, Dan Gable. However, Sanders' profile continued to build throughout his career, especially with T.V. media coverage at the 1972 Munich Olympics.

Following the Division II championships, the 1968 NCAA Division I championships were held at Penn State University, March 21st-23rd. Sanders, Yatabe, and Seal competed in the tournament for Portland State. Sanders breezed through the first two rounds, defeating Harry Weinhofer of Penn State and Tom Bentz of Iowa, both by fall. Rick met Gary Wallman of Iowa State in the quarter round and won his closest match, 8 to zero, en route to the championship. He moved on and met Tim McCall of Indiana in the semis, winning 12-2.[14]

Meanwhile, Dwayne Keller, seeded third from Oklahoma State, was working his way through the lower half of the bracket. Keller was a Myron Roderick recruit out of Kennewick, Washington and the Pacific Northwest. Dwayne's twin, Darrell Keller, was also an elite college wrestler and an eventual NCAA champion. Sanders wrestled Darrell a couple times in high school, winning both matches. Dwayne was a sophomore, while Sanders was a senior and returning champion. Keller

Sanders: In the Moment

swept through the first two rounds, easily defeating Ron Vallance of UCLA 12-5 and Scott Patten of the Army by fall. His quarter final match against Ted Parker of Indiana was a one point 5-4 win, and his semi-final match against Bill DeSario of SUNY Cortland was a close 3-2 win.[15]

The championship match was a thriller, though mostly due to the potential for an upset. Otherwise, there was little scoring, an atypical match for Sanders. Rick took Keller down in the first period for a two-point lead, then rode Keller for the rest of the period, accumulating riding time, but was unable to score back-points adding to his lead.

The second period decided the match. Sanders took the down position. Then "It" happened. As described by Howard Westcott to the Portland *Oregonian*:

> "This is no sour grapes," Westcott emphasized, "but Rick was taking Keller just the way he planned and actually was ahead, 3-0, if you consider riding time. Then it happened—Sanders was attempting to escape early in the second round. The kid made a good move." Westcott said of Keller, who lifted Sanders into the air and spun him to the mat head-first.
>
> "Rick hit hard on the side of his head, and it was just like his injury before the World Championships. The disk in his neck slips, pinching a nerve. His eyes went glassy and it was obvious he wasn't his old self."
>
> "The remarkable thing is," marveled Westcott, "that even in that condition and not having the full use of his right hand because it went numb, Rick almost won on instinct." "He didn't lose (4-2) until the last 10 seconds. The score was tied and he went for a takedown but Keller reversed and that was it."[16]

With the match over, Oklahoma State fans flooded the mat, celebrating Keller. Sanders was discarded to the edge of the mat. His demeanor was unexpected. In the moment, at the conclusion of the match, pondering the celebration, Sanders' reaction was more of euphoric wonder, not loss. He seemed circumspect, intrigued by the novelty of losing. He did it so rarely.

Sergio Gonzalez, a junior engineering major at UCLA, and the first wrestler from UCLA to ever wrestle in the finals, lost a close championship match with Ken Melchior of Lock Haven just before Sanders' loss to Keller. Gonzalez reflected about both losses as described in Mike Chapman's *Legends of the Mat*: "I was really down in the dumps after the NCAA finals and remember walking by Rick's room at the hotel where we were staying. I heard laughter from inside the room and looked in. Rick was sitting on the bed having a beer and there were lots of other people in there, all having a good time. I remember thinking that he sure wasn't taking it very hard, losing his last match in college." Gonzalez continued, "Later, I heard from Rick that he hurt his neck in the match and lost all his strength in his arm. But he never used that as an excuse, it's just something that came out when we were talking a couple of years later."[17]

Keller felt like his ability to ride was the winning factor against Sanders, crediting Sanders as much better than he on his feet. That analysis is contrary to what teammate Mas Yatabe surmised, however. Yatabe saw Sanders as much more a scrambler on the mat than a takedown technician. Keller's ride throughout the match was smothering. Others have speculated that Sanders did not take Keller seriously, having beaten his brother Darrell in the past, and that Sanders stayed out all night before the championships drinking and carousing. Both points well taken, but Sanders rarely slept at tournaments; his energy level ran high continuously. He kept busy, for example, washing work-out clothes, both his and teammates. He may have had a beer or two, and he wasn't opposed to the opinions of those who thought he was a drinker. It was all part of the web he wove, just like most of the hippie lore affixed after his college career. The problem was more likely that he spent much of the night pounding the pavement in a rubber suit and twenty pounds of sweats trying to make weight.

Keller was a great wrestler. He was awarded the 1968 Outstanding Wrestler award largely in recognition of his triumph over Sanders. Dwayne Keller finished his college career at 64-1. Impressive. His win over Sanders was Rick's second loss as a collegian. Sanders did not make excuses. He would rally as champions do. Wrestling was his playground. Occasionally it's a rainy day.

Portland State's fortune at the 1968 University level (Division I) wrestling championships took another hiccup two weight classes later at 137 pounds when Masaru Yatabe met Dale Anderson from Michigan State for the championship. For the second year in a row, the two met in the championship round, and again, as in the 1967 championship match, the referee called Yatabe for stalling with less than five seconds left, giving Anderson the tie and taking the match to overtime. Even Anderson labeled the call serendipitous. Nevertheless, Anderson, taking advantage, prevailed in the overtime period. Whether Sanders saw the match or not, he did not repeat his inappropriate chastisement of the year before. Anderson became a notable two-time Division I national champion and three-time All-American.[18]

Finally, Portland State's 145 pounder, Chuck Seal's 1968 University level (Division I) tournament ended with a first-round loss. His opponent subsequently lost in the second round, ending Seal's opportunity to compete in the consolation bracket. Seal had another year of eligibility and returned in 1969, where he won a championship at the NCAA D-II level. Seal would wrestle in the 1969 NCAA D-I tournament two weeks later, earning a sixth-place finish and All-American status at the championships held at Brigham Young University in Provo, Utah.

Sanders: In the Moment

In 1996, the Division II National Wrestling Hall of Fame inducted four wrestlers into their inaugural hall of fame class. Masaru Yatabe, Chuck Seal, and Rick Sanders from Portland State and Larry Kristoff of the University of Illinois, Carbondale were selected. The synergy developed by the three Portland State wrestlers was appropriately recognized three decades after their time on the mat in the late 1960s.[19]

The Portland State University Viking Wrestling team finished the 1967-1968 season in sixth place at the D-I tournament, one back from their 1966-1967 campaign. They tied with Lock Haven and their D-II rival, Cal Poly. Oklahoma State snuck out a win over Iowa State by three points. The Iowa State Cyclones could really have used a Sanders' victory over Keller. Though it was Sanders' and Yatabe's last collegiate season, both were honored as selectees for the annual East-West College All Stars match.

The annual East-West College All Stars match was held in Stillwater, Oklahoma on April 6th, two weeks after the D-I nationals. The All Stars meet was held annually for a number of years but was discontinued in 2020 for reconsideration as to how it might be revitalized to meet the unique needs of college wrestlers, coaches, and fans. The executive committee of the national coaches' association selected wrestlers for the tournament. The dividing line was the Mississippi River. Every wrestler received an engraved commemorative watch for participating. Sanders participated in the 1967 All Stars match as a member of the West squad. In '67, Rick wrestled to a 2-2 draw with Bob Fehrs of Michigan. In that same East-West dual, Lee Ehler, a senior for UCLA, wrestled and beat NCAA 152 pound champion Jim Kamman of Michigan 8-7. Sanders became fast friends with Ehler over the course of his stay in Stillwater, and the acquaintance would result in a few road trips in the future, including after the Pan American Trials, where Sanders, Ehler, and Sergio

Sanders: In the Moment

Gonzalez would file into Sergio's cramped 1960's VW bug for the long, winding trip back up to the West Coast.[20]

Sanders admitted, "The highest honor I ever received, only a few people know about. At the East-West dual meet in Stillwater, Oklahoma, I was elected team captain by the other wrestlers on the West squad. Those men are the best college wrestlers in the country. I was really proud." Sanders' sentiment reflects a degree of reconciliation in how the public, and especially his peers, viewed him. He wanted to be understood as having leadership quality—not just as an athlete—but one who was worthy of respect. Perhaps, before the team captain selection, Rick felt

WEST ALL-STARS (L-R)—FRONT: Dale Bahr, 145, Iowa State; Pete Nord, 130, Colorado; Wayne Wells, 152, Oklahoma; Masaru Yatabe, 137, Portland State; Tommy Green, 115, Oklahoma State. BACK: Coach Howard Westcott, Portland State; Mike Gallego, 167, Fresno State; Reg Wicks, 160, Iowa State; Fred Fozzard, 177, Oklahoma State; Nick Carollo, 191, Adams State; Rick Sanders, 123, Portland State. Not in picture: Coach Tom Evans, Oklahoma; Curley Culp, Hwt., Arizona State.

Over 6700 roaring fans attended the 1968 East/West
All Stars dual. Sanders pictured in the top row, far right,
wearing a neck brace.

misgivings about how peers thought of him. On the other hand, Sanders clearly held his teammates in high regard, and that speaks well of him.

Sanders' neck stinger abated sufficiently to allow his participation in the 1968 East-West All Stars Dual. Over 6,700 roaring fans attended Gallagher Hall on the Oklahoma State University campus. He and Masaru Yatabe were honored as participants for the West squad. Tommy Evans, Oklahoma's esteemed coach and former two-time Olympian and silver medalist, coached the West team, assisted by Portland's Howard Westcott. Evans would coach Rick later in the year as head coach of the 1968 Olympic freestyle wrestling team headed to Mexico City. Evans' and Westcott's coaching styles could not have been more different. Evans was a task master, though amenable to innovation; Westcott was completely laissez faire. Of course, coaching at such an event was largely gratuitous. It was an honor to be selected to coach a team comprised exclusively of All-Americans. The East was coached by the Navy's coach, Ed Perry and assisted by Grady Peninger, coach of Michigan State's 1967 championship team.[21]

Also wrestling for the West was Fred Fozzard, an Oregonian who was recruited by Myron Roderick and wrestled collegiately for Oklahoma State. Fozzard was a national champion in 1967 but finished third in 1968.

Wayne Wells also wrestled with Sanders for the West team All Stars that April 6th day. Wells was a classic overachiever. He was undaunted in pursuit of worthy objectives. Yet, he accomplished his goals with humility and without fanfare. Wells, coached by Tommy Evans at the University of Oklahoma, had finished his college career two weeks earlier with a 14-4 championship over John Kent of Navy. Wells was unscored upon at the '68 Nationals until the finals with Kent. Wells was stingy at the East-West

Sanders: In the Moment

All Star dual. Kent, returning to Stillwater as a member of the East squad in 1968, was caught in the Wells' whirlwind, losing 6-0.

Rick wrestled a close match for the West team. He met Ted Parker from Indiana. Parker lost to Dwayne Keller 5-4 in the semis at the national tournament two weeks earlier. Sanders fell behind early but rallied for a 6-4 victory. As reported by *Amateur Wrestling News*:

> Rick Sanders, of Portland State 123, who lost his NCAA crown this year to sophomore Dwayne Keller, Oklahoma State, had a tough match with Ted Parker, Indiana State, coming back from a 4-0 deficit to edge the 4-I champion 6-4 with a second period ride, a reverse, takedown and predicament at the bell. Parker had taken the lead with a single leg pick-up that he converted into a predicament in the first period.

Masaru Yatabe met his old nemesis, Dale Anderson from Michigan State at 137 pounds. Anderson won the last two meetings in overtime achieving national championships. It was another exciting and close match. This time, Yatabe won out in a squeaker 7-6. *Amateur Wrestling News* reported:

> In the highlight bout of the night Masaru Yatabe, Portland State's 2-time runner up to Dale Anderson, Michigan State, in the 1967 and 1968 137-pound finals, built up an early lead on three takedowns and then held off a late challenge by the Spartan champion to win 7-6. The huge crowd booed the referee as Yatabe was denied two edge-of-the-mat takedowns in the last period that would have put him safely ahead.[22]

The Anderson/Yatabe championship matches were all classics. Both athletes had great respect for one another. Anderson joined an Athletes In Action cultural exchange trip to Japan after his college career and actually stayed at the home of Yatabe's parents. The international sport of wrestling draws countries and families together.[23]

Fred Fozzard, the third Oregonian taking the mat that afternoon, met Gary Cook from East Stroudsburg State. Cook lost in the semis at nationals at 191 pounds, as did Fozzard at 177 pounds. Cook cut to 177 pounds as an All Star for the East to meet Fozzard. Fred prevailed with a 3-1 win. The West claimed the victory, 23-11, though there were no losers among the twenty-two who competed. In the words of the indomitable Teddy Roosevelt, himself a one-time wrestler,

> "It is not the critic who counts; not the man who points out how the strong man stumbles, or where the doer of deeds could have done them better. The credit belongs to the man who is actually in the arena... who at the worst, if he fails, at least fails while daring greatly, so that his place shall never be with those cold and timid souls who neither know victory nor defeat."

Thus ended the collegiate wrestling careers for three remarkable Oregonians. Sanders established quite a winning legacy as a Portland State Viking. He had a record of 103 wins against two losses. In that run, Rick had a 65 consecutive win streak, of which 48 were pins. In addition, he won five national championships—one NAIA as a freshman, two College D-II crowns, and two University D-I championships. He became the only collegian to win Outstanding Wrestler awards in three divisions, twice at the College D-II level. The PSU Vikings moved up to Division II wrestling from the NAIA level after the 1965 season. In Sanders' next three college seasons, the Vikings, a D-II team wrestling at the D-I Nationals, placed 8th, 5th and 6th. That remarkable record is a part of the Rick Sanders legacy. Sanders was named Oregon's Outstanding Amateur Athlete (Hayward Award) in 1967.[24] Thirty years later, Sanders was elected to Portland State's 1997 inaugural Athletic Hall of Fame class despite never graduating from PSU. His intent was to complete his degree, but at the time, he still had international goals to meet. The 1968 Mexico City Olympic trials were just weeks away, and another attempt at an elusive world title would be available in 1969. Rick could focus on freestyle, the international form of wrestling, after finishing his collegiate career, where folkstyle was used exclusively.

Sanders may have needed the 1968 Olympic challenge to distract him from the disheartening loss to Keller. Not only did his college career end on a sour note, but his adoring fans who filled the Portland area arenas to watch him perform through high school and college would no longer be providing the ego strokes that he seemed to need. Nevertheless, Rick, an integral member of wrestling's international elite culture, moved on boldly. The same group of athletes, with slight variations, competed at the freestyle events over the next few years. Tournaments were sponsored by the AAU, the U.S. Olympic Committee, FILA, and eventually the United States Wrestling Federation. Since it was a tight knit group of similarly elite athletes, Rick may have felt the need to adjust his persona to stand out. From 1968 to 1972, anecdotes about Sanders continued to proliferate at a steady pace. The change was noticeable. Close friend and wrestling great Bobby Douglas commented on the change when Sanders showed up for the Olympic trials camp in summer 1972. "Something was different, something had changed," Douglas said in a David Zang article for *Amateur Wrestling News*. "I couldn't put my finger on it, but I knew it wasn't the same Rick Sanders that I was very close to."[25]

Much is made of Sanders' counterculture lifestyle reflective of the hippies and beat generation of the 1960s. However, most, if not all of that reputation manifested after his college career. He remained short-haired and un-bearded until the 1970s. His reputation for liquor, womanizing, and pot smoking evolved after his college career. Teammate Mas Yatabe recalled that Sanders always lived with his mother during college and would walk to school; not the best environment for drinking, especially when Anita did not touch alcohol and had divorced two alcoholic husbands. Nor would it have been the best of playgrounds for womanizing or dope. Post college was a transformational period for Rick. Friend and Olympic teammate, Don Behm, reflected: "Rick was fun loving. He could be a chatter-box and easy to get to know. Never a recluse, he loved life, and was not profane. He shared and cared, and was a true hippie." However, Behm added, "Rick was needy. He pushed the rules because he loved the attention he got for it."[26]

Sanders seemed to be soul searching after his college career. Rick worked at wrestling camps in between tournaments but was seldom a marque clinician. Bobby Douglas commented in his biography, "Rick was a scrapper and a fighter. He would find a way to beat you. He was one tough son of a bitch." However, "Rick had terrible technique."[27] Masaru Yatabe observed the same deficit; a deficit that did not augur well for a successful coaching career. Moreover, Sanders did not have the necessary academic credentials to coach. He was not a successful academician, and his preoccupation with domestic and international wrestling tournaments precluded any attention he might have given to completing his college degree.

Rick was at a point in his wrestling career where the end was in sight and the future loomed uncertain. Jack Mezirow, an American sociology professor from Columbia University, describes Sanders' post-college change as an example of transformational adult learning.[28] In short, the theory describes how new adults become critically reflective of their own assumptions. Transformative adult learning suggests that the adult challenges their preconceived assumptions, established habits, and points of view, which they formerly accepted without question. Personal reflection is necessary to weigh the perspective of alternative world views. The individual must not accept the ideas of society uncritically, yet must still continue to build the body of knowledge that personally makes sense. Sanders, at this life juncture, needed to be in discourse. His sociology professor and advisor, Dr. Earle H. MacCannell, was a confidant for Sanders. Their close relationship suggests that Sanders may have discussed his future career possibilities with Dr. MacCannell. It was becoming clear to Rick that, at twenty-three years old, he would need to find a way of life outside his mother's home.

Wayne Wells, Rick's World Team and Olympic teammate observed, "Rick didn't have a soul in this world except (Bobby) Douglas." Olympic teammate Ben Peterson observed, "Off the mat, Rick lost. He was a troubled man in the midst of America's hippie movement. He had no moorings for his life."[29] Rick's typical good-natured bantering did not hide from friends and teammates a deeper longing for direction.

This type of transformation of perspective happens infrequently, and often is the result of a disorienting dilemma. Could finishing his college wrestling career have forced Rick to critically reassess his life perspective? He lived heart and soul to wrestle. Concluding that life-run with the loss to Keller in his final college match may have disoriented him. Perhaps the inherent discipline of being an elite athlete assumed a changed value for him. Rick may have felt disjointed and unmoored after college, prompting a change into his new flashy '60s lifestyle.

Chapter Eight

Sanders kept to his familiar haunts after exhausting his college eligibility. Westcott was quite willing to accommodate his star as a volunteer coach for the new set of Viking mat-men. Rick doubled practice time at the Multnomah Athletic Club, as was his pattern. 1968 was an Olympic year, and consequently there were no world championships to prepare for. Rick did not participate in the 1968 National AAU tournament either. The tournament was held again in Lincoln, Nebraska April 11th-16th. The top twenty-two AAU wrestlers qualified for the final freestyle Olympic trials in Ames at Iowa State, May 9th-14th. Champion collegiate wrestlers and wrestlers who prevailed at Olympic Regional Qualifying tournaments would join them.

One of those qualifying was Sanders' MAC workout partner, Larry Owings. Owings was a high school senior and a two-time Oregon high school champion. He wanted to compete at the Ames tournament but had no money to get there. Owings describes the experience in *Wrestlers at the Trials* by James Moffatt: "Fortunately for me, one of my workout partners was Rick Sanders. He was the one who made it possible for me to wrestle in the final trials. One day Rick walked into the gym and to my surprise handed me a round-trip plane ticket to Iowa. He told me not to ask any questions, just be there." Sanders' benevolence was probably conducted surreptitiously due to the Olympics strict adherence to amateurism. Olympic athletes could not accept financial aid from certain sources. Owings competed at Ames where he was defeated handily in the first round by Dan Gable. A second-round defeat had Owings headed back to Portland, a much more seasoned wrestler. He would become downright salty by the 1970 NCAA Championship rematch with Gable.

The two finalists at each weight from the Ames tournament advanced to the training and selection camp at Adams State College in Alamosa, Colorado in September for final team selections. In addition to the two finalists in each weight, the Olympic Wrestling Committee voted to invite five freestyle wrestlers who were prevented from participating at Ames by injuries but were expected to be cleared for final challenges.[1] Sanders was selected at 114.5 pounds more on the basis of his silver medal performance at the 1967 World Games than his collegiate record. The other exempted invitees to Alamosa were James Hansen of the Air Force at 125.5 pounds; Inter-Service winner Mike Young of Provo, Utah, 125.5 or 138.5 at the discretion of the coaches; a third-place finisher in the 1967 World Games at 138.5 and NCAA champion at 152, Wayne Wells, University of Oklahoma, 154; and Pat Kelly, Chicago, 171.5, a Pan American champion. Only the Sanders' and Wells' exemptions by the Olympic Wrestling Committee proved fortuitous to the 1968 Olympic freestyle wrestling team makeup.[2]

Several familiar competitors who ultimately made the Mexico City Olympic Team did participate in the spring AAU—Don Behm at 125.5 pounds, Bobby Douglas at 154 pounds, Tom Peckham at 191.5 pounds, Wayne Baughman at 191.5 pounds, Henk Schenk at 213.5, Jess Lewis at 213.5, and Larry Kristoff at heavyweight. Wayne Wells needed a medical waiver to participate in the 1968 Olympic trials, as did Sanders. Rick's waiver was associated with the neck injury received in the D-I championship match with Keller. The medical waivers allowed Sanders and Wells to compete in the Olympic trials at Alamosa, but they needed to win an extra two matches. Both were successful in that challenge.[3]

The Amateur Athletic Union (AAU), the national governing body for U.S. wrestling at the international level at that time, selected Adams State College in Alamosa, Colorado as the Olympic training site for U.S. wrestlers. The elevation at Alamosa mirrored that of Mexico City. The decreased oxygen levels thought to exist at elevation seemed to affect performance. For example, American 400-meter runner, Lou Jones, while competing at the 1955 Pan American Games held at Mexico City, collapsed unconscious at the end of the race. He did win the race and set a new world record, but it's clear the elevation strongly impacted him. Billy Mills, the American gold medal winner in the 10,000 meters in 1960, claimed that he could not catch his breath in the thin air of Mexico City. His performance was off by a half minute. Almost all of the 16 countries participating in the '55 Games expressed misgivings about detrimental effects experienced by their athletes. The culprit was largely felt to be the thin air at the altitude of Mexico City. It was believed, however, that some athletes could compete at elite levels at elevation while others could not. Therefore, the U.S. Olympic committee decided to hold trial competitions at elevation. Presumably, those athletes who performed well at trials would also compete optimally at Mexico City in 1968. The International Olympic Committee granted an extra two weeks of training to allow athletes to acclimate to the effects of altitude. A six-week wrestling trials camp ensued at Alamosa.[4]

Sanders, starting at the bottom of the challenge process, beat Greg Johnson of Michigan State 10-1 and 15-0. However, Sanders' trials match with two-time NCAA finalist Sergio Gonzalez from UCLA was suspect.

Sanders: In the Moment

Gonzalez put Sanders on his back early in the first meeting, but the pin was not called. Sanders was ultimately declared the winner in a close 7-3 match. Rick won the second match with a fall in 5:22, claiming the Olympic flyweight spot at 114.5 pounds. Gonzalez found Sanders magnanimous in victory. "Before I left camp, I ran into Rick," said Gonzalez. "He shook my hand and said, 'You know, if that was an international match, I would have been called for being pinned." Sergio and Rick became close friends over the next four years leading up to the '72 Munich Olympics, where both made the Olympic team.[5]

Sergio Gonzalez is a slightly built man with an indomitable cheerful optimism—the quintessential compadre for Sanders. Gonzalez was a two-time NCAA D-I All-American with runner up finishes in 1968 and 1969. Sergio's overtime loss in the 1969 championship was to John Miller of Oregon, a workout partner at the MAC with Sanders. Gonzalez had stellar success on the international wrestling circuit, however. After college, when most wrestlers get heavier, Gonzalez got lighter. He went from 115-pound collegiate weight to the 105.5-pound international weight class. He continued to train with those making the team and improved his skill set. Gonzalez was a close friend and confidant of Sanders, having competed against him, trained with him, traveled with him, and recreated together. Sergio Gonzalez was Rick's Samwise Gamgee from Tolkien's *Lord of the Rings*.[6]

Gonzalez recalled the time Rick and Lee Ehrler asked if he could ride with them back to the West Coast after the Pan American trials at Midwest City, Oklahoma. Sergio's Volkswagen broke down en route. The three travelers had little repair money. Sanders' fast talking convinced the mechanic they were international athletes and could be relied on to send the money. This was before the ubiquitous use of credit cards. The repairs were made, the teammates drove home, and the payment was mailed.

Working through adversity seemed to create a bond between Rick and Sergio.[7]

Alamosa was selected as the 1968 Olympic training camp for its mountain elevation but also its low humidity. Wayne Wells commented that the low humidity was much more a challenge than the elevation. The dry air caused nosebleeds for several wrestlers.[8] The U.S. invited countries around the world to train at the U.S. facilities if they so desired. Athletes from West Germany, Norway, India, and Sweden were among those who trained in the American West. The U.S. Track and Field athletes, guided by legendary Oregon coach Bill Bowerman, found themselves at a place called Echo Summit.[9]

Echo Summit was carved from the wilderness at a site ten miles west of South Lake Tahoe in the El Dorado National Forest. It sits at 7,377 feet in elevation, less than a dozen feet different from Mexico City—mother nature could not have birthed twin sites much better. The track and field event venues were excavated and prepared specifically for the two hundred plus track athletes vying for medals as U.S. Olympians at Mexico City. Ponderosa pine trees remained in the middle of the track, obscuring full view for any race beyond 200 meters. The field events were conducted on the infield. Sanders' fellow Oregonian, high jumper Dick Fosbury from Oregon State, described Echo Summit as "a magical place, a fantasy." He qualified for Mexico City, clearing 7'-3", setting the American record and the top height in the world for 1968. The thin air and Don Gordon's new foam Port-a-pits, in use that day, served to introduce a new high jump style—the Fosbury Flop—to the world. Fosbury would go on to a gold medal performance at Mexico City.[10] The U.S. track and field team would win a total of 24 medals at Mexico City, twelve of them gold. The U.S. wrestling team, on the other hand, was looking for an improvement in their medal count from the 1964 Tokyo Olympics where they were limited to Daniel Brand's bronze medal.

The 1968 Olympic wrestling team was formalized by September 23rd and was officially entered into the Olympic Games the following day. Several of the defeated Olympic squad members stayed on and worked out with the team. Other wrestlers were invited to the training camp for the purpose of providing a training squad. Among them were John Miller, University of Oregon; Dan Gable, Iowa State; and Buck Deadrich, California.

1968 U. S. OLYMPIC FREESTYLE TEAM, that took fourth in the Mexico City Games—Left to right, STANDING: Manager Manuel Gorriaran, Larry Kristoff (Hwt.), Jess Lewis (213.5), Jim Peckham (191.5), Steve Combs (171.5), Coach Tommy Evans. FRONT: Richard Sanders (114.5), Donald Behm (125.5), Captain Bobby Douglas (138.5), Wayne Wells (154).

Sanders and Behm, front left, won Olympic silver in 1968.

Sanders: In the Moment

The Olympians left for Denver on October 5th. Wrestlers would go through medical indoctrination at Denver and leave for Mexico City on October 8th. They had ten days to acclimate and train at Mexico City prior to the opening competition.[11]

Mexico City Olympic teammates Rick Sanders and Wayne Wells were subject to the coaching style and philosophy of head coach Tommy Evans in preparation for the 1968 Olympics at Mexico City. Wells was familiar with Evans' coaching style; he competed for Evans collegiately for the University of Oklahoma Sooners. Sanders, however, was in for a surprise.

Evans was tough. He was a two-time NCAA champion and twice was awarded the tournament's Outstanding Wrestler award. His post-college record included membership on the 1952 Olympic team in Helsinki, Finland where he won a silver medal. He returned to the Olympics at Melbourne, Australia in 1956, competing in both freestyle and Greco-Roman styles. Evans succeeded legendary coach Porter Robertson at Oklahoma in 1960. Evans directed his Sooner wrestlers to a national championship in his rookie year as a college coach. His team won a second national championship two years later. His overall coaching record was 140-40-2—an accomplishment even more notable in an environment that included perennial power Oklahoma State. Wells, coached by Evans, reflected, "His coaching philosophy was to never let up, continue to pound, be relentless. Evans coached the pin as the ultimate tactic on the mat."[12] Another former Oklahoma NCAA champion and subsequent long-time wrestling coach at the United States Air Force Academy, Wayne Baughman said of Evans, "He was one of my heroes. He was a leader by example. He took guys with less talent, like myself, and turned them into champions."[13] Sanders was relentless in action and a veritable pinner. He should have meshed well with coach Evans. But he was unorthodox in competition and practice style. Rick and Tommy would clash at Alamosa.

Alamosa, Colorado is a town of less than 10,000, located in southern Colorado in the San Luis Valley. Adams State College in Alamosa provided facilities for practice.[14] Adams State was a premier NAIA school for both wrestling and cross country. Its history of 64 College National Championships at the NAIA and Division II level is a testament in part to the advantage of high-elevation training. Endurance athletes often train at high elevation in an effort to improve the body's ability to oxygenate the blood and increase muscle performance. Wrestling is not by definition an aerobic sport, since a typical match does not last beyond seven or eight minutes. Nevertheless, practicing at elevation would prove beneficial in the later stages of a challenging match or in overtime periods. Adding to this physiological benefit is the potential psychological benefit that an athlete training at mountain elevations has over an opponent training nearer sea level. In the ebb and flow of a match, the wrestler who trained at elevation has the added confidence knowing that his stamina will match or exceed the competition.

Rick, having found himself in his customary impecunious situation at the 1968 Olympic training camp, secured a part-time job at a local bar. Coach Evans held two practices a day. He worked his wrestlers hard. Rick was habitually late for practice, probably due to the bar work, which put him at odds with Tommy Evans. Evans began to call Sanders "Snipe" in reference to the elusive bird hunted at night during the fowl's most active hours. Rick was amused by the nickname and liked the reference. Sanders would show up for practice in a jock strap, his duffle bag under his arm, and proceed to get dressed while other team members were involved in warmups. Evans threatened Sanders to be on time or he would be off the team.[15]

Sanders: In the Moment

The following morning Rick was again late for practice. Wayne Wells describes the scene: "After morning workouts, the team went out to the football field for wind sprints at noon. Everyone was tired from morning practice. The team did twelve one-hundred-yard sprints. I couldn't have done another. Sanders had on twenty pounds of sweats—hoodie, rubber suit, gloves, and cap. He ran them thirty yards behind the team. After the last one, Sanders head-plants. He doesn't move. Evans tells Sanders to get up. Rick doesn't move. Tommy repeats the demand three or four times, then nudges him with his foot, 'get up or you're going home!' Sanders half-turns his head and says, 'Just blow the whistle coach.' Evans tweets the whistle, Sanders explodes up and sprints the hundred yards. Rick ran five more hundred-yard sprints to Evans' whistle and was never late for practice again."[16]

Don Behm, "In a way, Rick was a young kid and the things he did were attention-getting devices." Behm went on to a career in education. Reflecting on Sanders at the 1968 Olympic training camp in Alamosa, Colorado with coach Evans, and in light of his experience as a long-time educator, Don surmised, "Rick was oppositional defiant. Evans was always on Rick's case. The more Evans pushed, the more Rick pushed the rules, because he loved the attention he got for it."[17]

Evans had a successful history employing wind sprint workouts. Leading up to the 1964 NCAA championships, Oklahoma lost six of their last eight duals. They were not expected to accomplish much at the national tournament. Evans decided to at least make sure his team was ready for competition. Two weeks prior to the NCAAs, he had his team run morning wind sprints, three miles of them each morning, in addition to normal afternoon practice. His wrestlers sprinted one hundred yards then jogged fifty to recover, repeating until they reached three miles. The payoff was a second place Sooner finish at the NCAAs, runner-up to

Oklahoma State and twelve points ahead of Iowa State, who they had beaten the year before for the national championship. Sanders and the rest of the Mexico City bound Olympic wrestling team hoped for similar payoff dividends.[18]

The International Olympic Committee awarded the 1968 Olympic Games site to Mexico City in 1963. Detroit was second in the voting and had made a strong bid, but concern over racial tension in the United States in the early '60s and in Detroit specifically affected that bid negatively. Moreover, Avery Brundage, president of the International Olympic Committee (IOC) from 1952-1972, considered the Mexico City nomination as a means of expanding the Olympic movement in Latin America. Mexico City had previously hosted the Pan American Games in 1955 to great fanfare. The country was experiencing impressive economic growth as a result of their oil exports and the burgeoning U.S. auto industry that occurred after World War II. Several stellar sports venues had been built to accommodate the 1955 Pan American Games. The Olympic Committee felt it was time for a Latin American country to receive the bid. Mexico became the first.[19]

Avery Brundage is the only American to have served as the President of the International Olympic Committee, and he did so for twenty years. Brundage ruled the IOC during both of Sanders' Olympic tournaments. Brundage was a controversial figure. He was successful as an amateur athlete and as a multi-millionaire civil engineer and construction magnate. Brundage competed in the 1912 Olympics in the pentathlon and decathlon. His teammate, the legendary Jim Thorpe, won both events. Avery placed sixth in the pentathlon, dropping out of the decathlon. Thorpe's medals were later revoked on disclosure that he had previously played semi-professional baseball. Brundage remained involved in

Sanders: In the Moment

Sanders, pictured at the The Mexico City Olympics site,
1968, held at 7000 feet elevation.

amateur athletics his entire life. He was President of the Amateur Athletic Union (AAU) for ten years before his IOC membership began in 1936. As a member of the United States Olympic Committee, he helped found the Pan American Games—the Western Hemisphere sporting event held the year prior to the Olympics—first held in Buenos Aires, Argentina in 1951.[20]

Brundage became controversial for his intransigence on the issues of amateurism and keeping commercialism and politics out of the Olympics. He wrote, "The athlete should compete for love of the game itself without thought of reward or payment of any kind." Athletes could not benefit in any financial way from their status as a sports figure. Doing so risked loss of their amateur status and opportunity to compete at the Olympic Games. Legendary American star athletes such as Mildred "Babe" Didrikson and even Brundage's own teammate, Jim Thorpe, lost Olympic eligibility under the sanction. Sanders struggled to find sufficient funds for travel and day-to-day existence as an amateur athlete. Elite sports stars of Sanders' status today are frequently worth millions. Wrestlers still lag behind financially for their international success. Olympic gold medal winners today are recognized by U.S.A. Wrestling by awards up to $250,000. Those amounts might be augmented by athlete endorsement of commercial products. Amateur wrestling's popularity is not broad based, however, and therefore the financial rewards are relatively minimal and narrowly bestowed. Interestingly, Sanders' 1972 Olympic medal, if given in 2021, would have been worth $22,500 from the U.S. Olympic and Paralympic Committee; probably enough to avoid needing to hitchhike to Greece from Germany after the Games.[21]

The political phenomenon known as the Cold War that began after World War II made policing politics and commercialism difficult for Brundage and the IOC. The Soviet Union, for example, recognized the propaganda effect sports played in marketing communism as a superior form of world-wide government. They trained and supported their athletes under the guise of state-wide physical fitness programs adjunct to military training or factory work. On the other hand, capitalist countries such as the United States profited by advertising products through print and television used in conjunction with the Olympics. Television was first used at the 1960 Olympics. T.V. was worth $10 million to the IOC in 1968 and worth over $4.5 billion at Tokyo in 2020. Further, Brundage and the IOC spent considerable energy dealing with political unrest both within and between countries. Political elites, threatening to boycott, used the international marque event to showcase particular grievances—racism, wars, international threats, etc.[22]

No one argued that Avery Brundage did not take charge at Mexico City. It was the fourth Summer Olympic Games conducted under his chairmanship. Brundage held the line on amateurism. The infamous Rule 26, which prohibited payment to competing Olympians, was changed in 1960 to allow some expense money to flow to athletes. Monetary contributions could not extend beyond a period of thirty days however, and it was only at subsistence level. Brundage could work with that flexibility. His larger concern was with keeping politics out of the Mexico City Olympics. 1968 was a challenging time of cultural rebellion and change around the world. Racial and economic inequality fostered dozens of riots in the United States as well as in France, in Cuba, and elsewhere.

Much of the world spotlight was focused on the August 1968 Democratic National Convention riots in the United States. They were a cauldron of interconnected social gripes including the Vietnam War, racial injustice, and the youth movement, all of which were exacerbated by the recent assassinations of Martin Luther King Jr. and Senator Robert Kennedy.[23]

The focus on U.S. domestic conflict was so intense, student riots in Mexico City seemed only to rise to second page news. Nevertheless, dozens of Mexican University students were murdered in a peaceful protest that turned violent just two weeks prior to the opening of the Mexico City Olympics. The protest by university students decrying economic and social injustice was brutally squelched by police and military forces. Moreover, the government quashed press coverage of the event. The incident occurred as some 10,000 protestors, including students from two universities, amassed at the historic Plaza de las Tres Culturas in the Tlatelolco district of Mexico City on the evening of October 2nd. Protests, initiated by student activists and attended by as many as 200,000, had occurred periodically in the weeks prior to the Olympic Games opening ceremonies. But on that October 2nd evening, government troops surrounded the plaza, preventing the demonstrators from escaping. The presence of helicopters and gunfire initiated an hour-long barrage of shooting in which an estimated 300 people were killed. Others were arrested, incarcerated, and tortured. The event became known as the Massacre at Tlatelolco. Despite the carnage and the horror of the event, the Olympics began on schedule on October 12, 1968. Ironically, the motto adopted for the '68 Olympics, "Ante los Ojos del Mundo" or, "Before the Eyes of the World," was prominently on display.[24]

One theory concerning the Massacre at Tlatelolco was that students wanted to use the Olympics as a stage presenting their concerns to the rest of the world. Similarly, the Black Power movement in the United States attempted to capitalize on the 1968 Olympics to further their cause. The objective, according to spokesperson Harry Edwards, was for black athletes to boycott the Olympics, thereby creating solidarity with the black race and drawing attention to the inimical racism existing in American society.

Edwards' effort piggybacked on a worldwide boycott movement by Olympic member countries disgruntled by the IOC admitting South Africa back into the Games, despite continuing their apartheid government. Edwards was a sociology professor and track coach from San Jose State University. He was a former 6'8" black athlete of some renown—discus in track and basketball. He felt saturated by the abuse American blacks suffered at the foot of white society. Moreover, he was an orator of some ability. Using those personal assets, Edwards served as the catalyst for a potential Olympic boycott.[25]

In Edwards' view, black athletes were treated disparately from white athletes when the Games were over; therefore, they should proselytize that point by not participating in the Games. The Black Power salute, the raised fist, was commonly used throughout 1968 in pamphlets, posters, athletic events, and myriad demonstrations. It was often accompanied by the black beret and black sunglasses. The caricature was meant to intimidate. The time of peaceful demonstration was at an end. Black society could only ascend separate from white society. "The Revolution has come. It's time to pick up the gun. Off the pigs," was one familiar chant.[26]

Edwards' aspirations were serendipitously bolstered by the presence of two world class athletes on the San Jose State track team that he coached: sprinter Tommie Smith and 400-meter runner Lee Evans. These two athletes had world-class speed and Olympic potential. In the lead-up year to the Olympics, Edwards was able to generate boycott-style protests at several track meets, including that of the prestigious New York Athletic Club, the University of Texas El Paso, and the University of Washington. But the protests did not create the needed solidarity Edwards hoped for. Black athletes could not be convinced en masse that the boycott was commensurate with the personal sacrifice made to compete on the world stage at the Olympics.[27]

The call for a general boycott had failed. Harry Edwards explained, of the twenty-six black athletes, roughly half were unwilling to boycott. A final meeting was held by black athletes to decide on what personal demonstrations they might employ to protest given the chance. There was no consensus, though most meeting attendees were in favor of some form of personal demonstration protesting against racism in the United States. The iconic Tommie Smith and John Carlos Black Power salute that ultimately occurred and became symbolic of the 1968 Olympic Games was a hastily comprised and executed demonstration, though not without some forethought.

The opportunity presented itself when both men finished in medal position in the 200-meter finals—Smith won; Carlos just edged out for silver by Peter Norman of Australia. Carlos had approached Smith just prior to the semi-final heats briefly discussing potential ideas. They agreed to do something on the medal stand but would work out the details later. It evolved that only ten minutes separated the end of the 200-meter final and the presentation of the awards on the medal stand. Smith's wife brought the black gloves. Smith wore the right glove, later explained to symbolize power in black America; Carlos wore the left glove, representing the unity of black America.

The protest has stood the test of time. In a moment, the image of the Mexico City Olympics became co-opted by the United States, the apolitical Olympic policy subverted. The U.S. Olympic Committee apologized to the International Olympic Committee and banned Smith and Carlos from the Olympic Village. The ensuing decades found both athletes struggling to achieve in their chosen careers. However, the general reaction to their demonstration has largely turned sympathetic over time.

Bobby Douglas, the only black wrestler on the 1968 Olympic team, wanted no part of the boycott. Douglas' biography describes this period as a very scary time for him. He received intimidating phone calls pressuring him to boycott the games. "I'm not interested," Douglas told the callers. "I've trained my whole life for this opportunity and I'm planning on winning a gold medal." Douglas attended a meeting of the black athletes participating in the 1968 Olympics. Former 1936 Olympian and four-time gold medalist, Jesse Owens, addressed the group. He encouraged black athletes not to boycott the Games. Owens was booed by many of the attendees. He was called an Uncle Tom. Yet Douglas believed in the purpose of the Olympics and the message presented by Owens. Bobby was elected captain by members of the Olympic wrestling team. He stated, "The Olympic athletes all took an oath to compete honestly and fairly, and to compete in the spirit of the Olympic Games." The Olympics was not the place to be staging protests. In the final analysis as suggested by Kevin Witherspoon in *Before the Eyes of the World—Mexico and the 1968 Olympic Games*, "These Games united politics, culture, diplomacy, and athletics as no Olympics before or since."[28]

The Mexico City Olympics began October 12th, 1968. The games were ceremoniously opened by a female athlete—Norma Enriqueta Basilio, a twenty-year-old 400-meter runner. She became the first woman to have the honor. Her selection was in part meant to show that Mexico was not a sexist country and that women were making strides toward equality.

An estimated 135,000 tourists attended the Games with some 80,000 spectators packing the Olympic stadium. The much-discussed concern over altitude effect became readily apparent during the first event, the

10,000 meters. Several competitors dropped out, and only a few remaining runners were in contention at the end of the race. Those athletes medaling in the event all lived and trained at high elevations. However, world records were being set in almost every event at lower distances and shorter duration.[29]

Americans captured much of the bounty in track and field. American Jim Hines set a world record in the 100 meters. American discus thrower, Al Oerter, still competitive at age thirty-two, broke the world record by five feet and in doing so became the first American to win gold medals at four consecutive Olympic Games. American sprinter, Wyomia Tyus, won the 100 meters in world-record time. American Bob Beaman smashed the long jump world record by nearly two feet. New optical equipment installed to measure long jump distances was only programmed to measure distances to 28 feet. Officials needed a tape measure to record Beamon's 29 feet 2.5 inch world record. Amazingly, through the entire track and field program, world records and Olympic records were matched or set in all events except the 5,000- and 10,000-meter runs.[30]

Dick Fosbury, Oregon State high jumper, not only had on display his unorthodox backwards style of jumping, but entertained the crowd with his rituals of staring at the bar and rocking back and forth from one foot to the other while continuously clenching and unclenching his fists—rituals practiced by many elite high jumpers today. Fosbury, like Sanders at Munich, had a reputation for not practicing—preferring to save his effort and training effect for competition. Fosbury spent his off-hours at Mexico City with U.S. javelin thrower, Gary Stenslund, touring the local beer gardens along with local women in Stenslund's VW bus.[31]

The Mexico City Olympics was the first to install widespread drug testing. Bulgarian Greco-Roman wrestler Hristo Traikov was banned from the Olympics when he tested positive for an illegal substance. His trainer had given him ammonia, an illegal substance, during a match with American Greco-Roman wrestler, David Hazewinkel.[32]

Don Behm was tested after his hard-fought win against Russian opponent Ali Aliyev. Interestingly, Behm was tested again a year later after his win against a Russian wrestler at the 1969 World Championships in Argentina. The Soviets' athletic prowess and a suspicioned corollary to performance enhancing drugs was beginning to draw the attention of international governing bodies.

Athletes questioned what made the list of banned substances versus those deemed as nonperformance enhancing. One article noted, "The sprinter who fancies a double scotch to steel himself for the big occasion must not imbibe, though he can pep himself up with caffeine from a cup of strong black coffee."

Moreover, female athletes from Eastern Bloc countries, beginning in the 1960s, came under suspicion for performance enhancing drugs when they began to break world records and demolish the competition. "It has since been revealed that female athletes from East Germany, Russia, and elsewhere were routinely forced to take steroids and male hormones, with tragic consequences for many such athletes later in life," wrote Kevin Witherspoon in *Before The Eyes of the World*. While no athletes failed the tests in Mexico City, several prominent athletes either withdrew from qualifying tournaments or retired at the announcement that they would be tested.[33]

Gender testing was implemented for the first time as well. American Babe Didrikson, for example, who won two gold medals in the 1932 Olympics and excelled in multiple sports, was often thought to be lesbian or was accused of being male. Stella Walsh, an elite athlete of the 1920s and '30s who competed both as an American and Polish athlete, held the world record in the 100 meters for a time. An autopsy conducted after her death in 1980 revealed intersex organs. The condition results from a chromosomal anomaly known as mosaicism—a genetic mutation characterized by physical symptoms that may include a flattened face, small ears, shorter height (though Walsh was 5'9"), and eyes that tend to slant up.[34]

The 1968 Olympics also continued to deal with the issue of maintaining amateurism. Sports equipment companies were allowed to provide necessary sporting equipment to athletes but not to the extent that it would improve an athlete's financial position. Athletes referred to the dilemma as shamateurism.[35]

Shoe companies made tremendous strides in marketing their products at the Olympics. Hundreds of pairs of Adidas and Puma brand track shoes were given away at the Games. The rival companies were owned by members of the same European family. Holding a stiff line on the principle of amateurism, Avery Brundage demanded that the logos of athletic equipment manufacturers be removed or painted over. Not to be deterred, American sprinters and Black Power protesters, Tommy Smith and John Carlos, while executing their historic medal stand black glove demonstration, were careful to set their shoes with logos to the camera at the side of the awards stand. Puma was rumored to pay athletes clandestinely who medaled wearing Pumas up to five thousand dollars in reward for profiling their company's shoes. Bob Seagram, U.S. gold medal pole vaulter who initially retired from competition after Mexico City, received such a reward directly from Armin Dassler, president of Puma, prior to returning to the States.[36]

Did the '68 Olympic Black Power demonstration by Tommie Smith and John Carlos have an effect on Ricky Sanders, who according to former PSU professor Earle MacCannell was "actively disinterested in politics?" According to teammate Wayne Wells, "It didn't make a damn bit of difference to Sanders."[37] Further, Sergio Gonzalez characterized Rick as a peaceful warrior. "He was a free spirit who lived life to the fullest. He lived in the now. He promoted peace wherever he went, promoting harmony with his fellow man."

Sanders seemed to pick and choose among the smorgasbord of issues emanating from the '60s decade. He took notice of music, hairstyles and dress, cannabis, free love and harmony—even some popular literature such as *Tolkien's Hobbit* and *Lord of the Rings*. However, the weightier issues such as the Vietnam War, race relations, gender equity, and national and international politics did not resonate to any significant degree. Perhaps growing up underprivileged and largely responsible for developing a worldview seldom influenced by parents or other adults left him unimpassioned by the more complex issues of the day. Rick tasted the desserts, but left the main entrées for later. Sanders' primary focus at the Olympics was wrestling.

Sanders received a first-round bye at the 1968 Olympic Games. He won his next four rounds by pin. He scored falls over the wrestlers from Yugoslavia, the Dominican Republic, Iran, and India. Under the

Sanders at the 1968 Olympics.

vagaries of the black mark system of scoring, any competitor accruing six black marks or more was out of the tournament.

Rick entered the sixth round of wrestling with zero black marks. Only three competitors remained after five rounds. His opponent, Shigeo Nakata, the eventual gold medal winner from Japan, entered the sixth round with three and a half black marks. Nakata, through the first five rounds, had pinned only one opponent. Bazaryn Damdinsharav of Mongolia entered the sixth round with five black marks. Since there were only three of the competitors left, the sixth round became the medal round and black marks from the first five rounds were not carried forward.[38]

Olympic Flyweight medal stand, 1968.
Sanders, left; Nakata, center; Damdinsharav, right.
—

Just as at the Indian World Championships the year before, Rick lost to Nakata on points. A loss on points garners three black marks for the loser, and one black mark for the winner. Rick decisioned Damdinsharav, accruing an additional black mark for a total of four. Nakata pinned

Sanders: In the Moment

Sukhbaatar and therefore received zero black marks, finishing the round robin with one black mark and earning the gold medal. Sanders won the silver with four black marks, and Damdinsharav the bronze with seven.

Amateur Wrestling News reported:

Rick Sanders and Donald Behm won silver medals for the United States in 1968 Olympic freestyle wrestling and all but one member of the team scored points to give the United States fourth position in the team race.

Other U.S. place winners were Wayne Wells, fourth at 154; Thomas Peckham, fourth at 191.5; heavyweight Larry Kristoff, fifth; Jess Lewis sixth at 213.5, and Steve Combs, who tied for sixth at 171.5. The team record was 24-9-4 with eight falls, four of them by Sanders. The only U.S. wrestler who failed to place was Captain Bobby Douglas, 138.5, who was injured in his first bout and was unable to continue.[39]

Bobby Douglas roomed with Sanders at Mexico City, perhaps inopportunely. Sanders snored, which made sleeping and rest problematic for anyone rooming with him. Bobby, a friend and team captain, made the sacrifice. In addition, during the acclimation period leading up to competition, Sanders suggested Douglas try eating goat at a café in Mexico City. Douglas explains in his biography by Craig Sesker, "I had never eaten goat in my life. Rick was the one who wanted to try it, and he never even got sick. I got food poisoning, and I was sick for three days. It was very close to the competition, and it affected me." The goat meat made Douglas nauseous and dehydrated, sapping his strength for the upcoming competition.

Douglas' Olympic journey ended in a first-round injury default to an Iranian wrestler when Bobby blew out his Achilles tendon and was forced to default to his opponent. "I got caught in an ankle lace and the guy was turning me. I didn't know how to defend it," Douglas said. "That's how I

Sanders: In the Moment

got injured." Douglas felt he was in the best shape of his life for the 1968 Olympic tournament. Perhaps the food poisoning precipitated by Sanders' suggestion was the catalyst for Douglas' unfortunate finish. Sanders, who had a reputation of being able to eat almost anything without ill effect, should have, if anything, dissuaded Douglas from eating unfamiliar food under the circumstances when Mexico had the reputation for visitors incurring Montezuma's Revenge. The Iranian wrestler ended up with a bronze medal.[40]

Olympic freestyle coach Tommy Evans paid tribute to the 1968 team, and especially Bobby Douglas in *Amateur Wrestling News*, to wit: "The loss of Bobby Douglas was a real tragedy. He was our captain, our leader, hardest worker, most respected man, a heck of a fine gentleman and a great help to me. I will always remember this Olympiad more than the two I competed in. I got to know our wrestlers' personalities and to like them very much. I felt a close personal relationship with each one and enjoyed discovering the manner in which each could be motivated."[41]

Sanders did not gain much press after the 1968 Olympics. Any record of his personal reflection on his performance is scant, perhaps given the lack of T.V. coverage. ABC broadcast the 1968 Olympic Games but failed to show any footage of either freestyle or Greco-Roman wrestling. American athletes accumulated 48 total medals at the XIX Olympiad, two of those by wrestlers Don Behm and Rick Sanders. The wrestling medal tally was only slightly better than the 1964 Olympics when middleweight American, Dan Brand, won bronze for the only medal.[42]

Oregon Governor Tom McCall took the time to post a commendation letter to Sanders after the 1968 Mexico City Olympics.[43]

Dear Rick:

Sanders: In the Moment

I wish to once again commend you for the outstanding accomplishments at Mexico City which earned for you the Olympic Silver Medal.

The State of Oregon is justly proud of the name you have made for yourself, Rick; and, on behalf of all Oregonians, I wish you the very best of luck and happiness in the years to come.

Sincerely

Governor, Tom McCall

That November 26, 1968 letter was addressed in care of the Portland Chamber of Commerce Convention Breakfast in Portland, Oregon. Sanders, though a world class athlete representing the United States of America, had no permanent address.

Mexico City was the first Olympics held in Latin America. Coincidentally, Sanders would return to Latin America the following year for the 1969 World Wrestling Championships in Mar del Plata, Argentina. There he would add to his winning legacy.[44]

Sanders was again prominent in the 1968 Man of the Year balloting by the U.S. Amateur Wrestling Foundation. Rick wound up third in voting by a nationwide panel of coaches, competitors, and officials involved in amateur wrestling. Oklahoma and Olympic coach Tommy Evans was selected Man of the Year with 124 points and five first place votes. Oklahoma State coach Myron Roderick received three first place votes and 83 points as runner-up. Rick just edged out Olympic teammate Don Behm, each with one first place vote, but Sanders with 63 points to Behm's 60. Wayne Wells and Dan Gable were also in the top ten.[45]

Sanders' performance at the '68 Olympic Games was admirable. He had just completed his college career and had adjusted quickly from folkstyle to the international freestyle form of wrestling. His Olympic silver medal finish was a harbinger of future success.

Sanders: In the Moment

At twenty-three, there were more Olympic Games to come—in 1972 and perhaps even a third in 1976. There were also world championships on the horizon.

The 1969 worlds would be held in Argentina. Sanders could anticipate another international wrestling quest in Latin America—perhaps this time earning gold.

Chapter Nine

Shelby Steele of Stanford's Hoover Institute—a scholarly conservative think-tank—suggests the 1960s "was arguably the most fundamentally transformative decade in American history." Steele describes the time period succinctly in *Shame: How America's Past Sins Have Polarized Our Country*. "By 1968 you could question virtually anything," according to Steele. "You could question your religion; the 'relevance' of a college education; the value of monogamy in marriage; the draconian laws against drug use; a college curriculum grounded solely in Western Civilization; the military draft; capitalism; the taboos against interracial marriage and homosexuality; or the view of pregnancy as an absolute commandment to give birth."[1] Sanders probably never really felt the exigency of counterculture issues. Nevertheless, he was exposed organically, especially living on the West Coast, and assimilated his world view in a way pleasing to himself. Rick's challenge became moving between differing degrees of the culture as he crossed the nation and world attending wrestling tournaments.

The state of Michigan has always been a wrestling hotbed as well as a cauldron for political activism. In 1969, both Michigan State and the University of Michigan had top ten finishes at the NCAA D-I

Championships. Michigan was also a hotbed of political unrest in 1969. Several radical splinter groups emerged from the University of Michigan Students for a more Democratic Society (SDS). The Weathermen, largely sons and daughters of the upper-class, were committed to Marxist philosophy and a classless society. The end of U.S. imperialism was a goal that merited extreme measures, and to that end, some 250 bombings were attempted around the country between September 1969 and May 1970. Targets included ROTC buildings, induction centers, draft board offices, and other Vietnam-linked government buildings. The Weathermen were involved in Dr. Timothy Leary's escape from a California prison and resettlement in Tunisia as a guest of the Black Panthers and Eldridge Cleaver. Dr. Leary, the esoteric champion of LSD, was incarcerated for a simple marijuana possession. The aura of change was in the air, whether through violence or through transcendentalism spawned by political radicals or advocates of drug use and alternative religions. Sanders, immersed in the West Coast culture, felt like he had license to experiment. For ease of commitment and ubiquitous availability, he dipped into marijuana use, perhaps the least toxic of the new age offerings.[2]

The top three muscle cars manufactured by the American Auto Industry in 1969 were the Dodge Challenger, the Plymouth Barracuda, and the Plymouth Road Runner—all Chrysler products. Between 1966 and 1973, U.S. auto manufacturers had to recall over 30 million American cars and trucks because of serious defects. The Japanese auto industry gained market share during this time by adopting American technology and improving on it. Ten years later, the U.S. Government bailed Chrysler out of bankruptcy to preserve jobs for auto workers and to shore up its position against foreign competition. Toyota sells the most cars in the U.S. today. The average cost of a new car in 1969 was $3,400, while a gallon of gas was $.35. Rick's part time, minimum wage bar and restaurant work at $1.30 per hour could not have impressed even the most avaricious car salesman. His paramount identification card was not a driver's license, but his AAU card,[3] which he used to great effect as he worked his way through qualifying tournaments to make the annual world championships team.

Sanders' focus for the 1969 wrestling campaign was to make the United States World Team, scheduled to compete at Mar del Plata, Argentina. The world championships held at Yokohama, Japan in 1961 are generally considered by U.S. authorities to be the first official world championship. Previous to 1961, tournaments, ostensibly named world championships, were held irregularly with sporadic attendance, with contested weight classes, and varying wrestling styles. Rick made every world team since his first effort in 1965, when the team competed in freestyle at Manchester, England and Greco-Roman style at Tampere, Finland. The 1968 Olympics removed the need for world team competition until 1969.[4]

The 1969 world team trials were held in New York at the prestigious New York Athletic Club February 18th-28th. Select wrestlers were invited to compete with challenge matches beginning on February 22nd. Of the 45 wrestlers invited, 36 accepted. Food and housing were covered in New York City, but wrestlers needed to cover travel expenses to the Big Apple. Sanders, as usual, traveled and competed under the auspices of the Multnomah Athletic Club (MAC). Sanders decided to move up a weight class from his 114.5 pound Olympic flyweight class and compete for the bantamweight 125.5 pound spot, similar to the weight at which he finished his college career. World Team Coach, Bill Farrell, asked that all wrestlers report to the trials in condition for wrestle-off matches.[5]

Don Behm foiled Rick's plan to compete at 125.5 pounds. In the first of several classic trials wrestle-offs over their careers, Behm prevailed in the best of three wins. The pair actually wrestled four matches that included one draw. Not to be undone, Sanders moved back down in weight class and challenged himself to make the team at 114.5 pounds.

The timing of the World Team Championships fell in the middle of the collegiate season. Nevertheless, most of the nation's experienced international wrestlers were available to compete for a spot on the team. Also accepting invitations and competing at the 114.5-pound weight class were Richard Sofman, Mark Piven, John Hansen, and John Rice. Once the field of competitors was reduced to four through challenge matches, a round robin was used to determine the world team member at the weight class. Rick was able to outwrestle Sofman for the right to represent the U.S. in Argentina. Richard Sofman went as an alternate.[6]

The challenge matches for the 1969 world team were nine-minutes long. Over the weekend trials, Sanders wrestled eight nine-minute matches against world class competitors to make the team. His competitive resolve was extraordinary. Moreover, Behm may have unwittingly set Rick up for success at the 1969 World Championships by forcing Sanders to the lower weight class.

Those qualifying for the team had all expenses paid from New York to Argentina and from Argentina to their homes. The team was scheduled to leave for Argentina February 28th. March was the tourist season in Argentina, and a separate tour to see other South American countries was planned for those team members interested. Though Rick was generally available for sight-seeing, the MAC was unavailable for financial support.

Members of the 1969 U.S. World Team included Dale Kestel, Michigan Wrestling Club at 105; Rick Sanders, MAC at 115; Don Behm, MDYF at 125; Mike Young, Provo, Utah at 137; Bob Douglas, AIA at 154; Wayne Wells, University of Oklahoma at 163; Fred Fozzard, Oklahoma State at 180; Henk Schenk, Army at 198; Larry Kristoff,

Rick Sanders (bottom right,) Don Behm (bottom center,) and Fred Fozzard (bottom left) medaled at Mar del Plata. Sanders and Fozzard became the first U.S. World Champions in 1969 at Mar del Plata, Argentina.

—

MDYF at 220; and Rocky Rasley, Oregon State at Unlimited. Three alternates went along as well. They included Richard Sofman, NYAC at either 115 or 125; Tom Huff, Air Force at 137; and Jerry Bell, NYAC at 154. Four of the ten team members were Oregonians. They included Sanders, Fozzard, Schenk, and Rasley. Sanders, Young, Sofman, and Kristoff were repeat World Team members from the 1967 freestyle team to New Delhi, India.[7]

The 1969 World Team coach was Bill Farrell. Farrell brought a diverse background to coaching at the international level. He won more than 300 matches as an athlete for the prestigious New York Athletic Club. In that run, he won the Canadian nationals and was sixth in the 1962 worlds. Farrell then coached the NYAC from 1960-1972. Simultaneous with wrestling and coaching, he generated a multimillion-dollar sporting goods company. He sold Resilite wrestling mats, Universal weight machines, and Tiger wrestling shoes. Tiger shoes were manufactured in Japan, and Farrell had exclusive rights to sell the brand nationwide. The Tigers brand eventually became ASICS. Farrell at one point filed a lawsuit against Nike founder Phil Knight for selling Tigers along the West Coast.[8]

Farrell's rugged good looks garnered him a spot as the first Marlborough Man, advertising that brand of cigarettes nationwide; in Knight's excellent memoir, *Shoe Dog*, the author rather contemptuously refers to Farrell only as the Marlborough Man. After legal matters were settled, Knight had the national market for running shoes, and Farrell, the wrestling shoe market.[9]

Farrell brought the experience of his international business dealings to international wrestling. He was savvy to some of the underhandedness of foreign competition. Farrell's resume commanded respect, yet he coached with a steady, unpretentious demeanor, and his teams excelled.

Sanders: In the Moment

Though the Mar del Plata, Argentina venue was not as bad as New Delhi, India, Wayne Wells remembered it as "not very nice." For example, "There was one set of scales for all contestants. Usually, there is a scale for each weight class." Further, "The scale was not accurate."

Sanders was struggling to make weight by the second day. One hour to weigh-in, Rick blurted, "Fuck this; I'm done." Coach Farrell and Bobby Douglas grabbed Sanders, saying, "You're not quitting!" Rick began fighting with them and swearing. Douglas and Farrell tried to put clothes on him, but he went limp. Eventually, as though dressing a corpse, they got him ready. But he wouldn't walk. They tried taking him up some stairs to a mezzanine where he could run and sweat to lose the weight. He balked at the bottom of the stairs. Farrell and Douglas had to support him under the arms to get up the stairs.

Rick was working against a mental conundrum. He was characteristically stoked to compete and bring his phenomenal talent to bear, but mentally exhausted from the drudgery of dieting, dehydration, and weight loss. Those watching laughed, but, barely jogging, Rick worked to make the weight. It was a herculean effort. Douglas recalls Sanders climbing onto the scale. Rick was still two ounces over. "A Russian was standing behind Rick in line at weigh-ins," Douglas said. "The Russian reached over and lifted Rick's butt cheek up. The weigh-in official didn't see it, and the scale dropped to 114.5 and Rick made weight."[10] Making the 114.5 weight class for his maturing body was extraordinary, but more impressive than that, Rick wrestled his final matches with an egregiously dislocated thumb.

Wells remembers Sanders waiting to wrestle after the weigh-in, sitting at the top of a flight of seats in the arena drinking a liter of orange pop. He wrestled a half hour later. He took an injury time out during one round and had his hand taped. Rick had been put on his back and was three points down. He came back and pinned his opponent. Taking the wrap off, Wells asked how he was. "Fuck, I think I dislocated my thumb!" Sanders replied. It was lying against his forearm.[11] Sanders was tough, and his pain tolerance extreme.

Jerry Barker, assistant wrestling coach at North Carolina State University in the 1970s, offered a glimpse of the physical toll on college wrestlers over a season. His essay was published in the January 28th, 1970 issue of *Amateur Wrestling News* under the heading The Average Wrestling Season:

> Want to hear some silly statistics about an average wrestling season? If so, listen to these.
>
> Between November and mid-March each year, the average college wrestler will take 195 pills (wheat germ oil, salt, vitamin C, etc.), lose 216 pounds of sweat, suffer 3 hurt knees, groins, or ankles, 2 black eyes, 9 mat burns, 1 painful neck, 18 bruises and cuts, and 3 uncategorized injuries. He will spend 215 hours directly involved in being a member of the wrestling team. For example, 75 hours will be spent at hard practice, 80 hours on trips, 10 hours for weigh-ins and pre-game meals, 25 hours dressing for practice, and 25 hours more showering and dressing after practice. He will do at least 1700 sit-ups, 1650 push-ups, 140 minutes of bridging, wrestle 72 8-minute matches (576 minutes or 9 ½ hours), perform over 600 20-second-execution drills, and hear his coach blow a whistle 1679 times. Some of the wrestlers will smoke 788 fewer cigarettes than during a comparable period of time off-season. Eating habits will change. The average wrestler will eat 170 less slices of bread and toast than he would consume off-season, pass up 163 slices of pie and cake, 39 donuts and 47 pancakes, have 105 fewer servings of potatoes, and sit down to much smaller meals at Thanksgiving and Christmas than normal citizens. (Some of this agony will be forgotten when he "inhales" the pre-match meals, totaling 10 steaks, 12 baked potatoes, 34 glasses of tea, and 24 slices of toast and honey.)
>
> All this goes to make up the average wrestler with an average seasonal record of 5-5-1. OH! The sacrifices to earn the 11-0 record: but then he's the CHAMPION![15]

Sanders: In the Moment

Of course, Sanders was not an average wrestler. Nor did he confine his season to merely five months. On the rare possibility that Portland State offered a post weigh-in/pre-match steak meal, Sanders no doubt inhaled his share of the beef. More likely though is the scenario of a desperate attempt to lose a pre-match extra pound of sweat. Sanders, a smoker, may have smoked less during the season, but if so, he admittedly curtailed his habit to create a better image for young fans. Smoking, at best, provided the oral fixation sacrificed to the requisite Spartan diet. His ADHD tendencies seemed to require the calming effect of nicotine.

Ricky Sanders possessed many outstanding attributes that added up to his status as a world class athlete: competitiveness, superb balance and coordination, perseverance, willingness to sacrifice, and extraordinary durability.

Sanders never missed a match due to injury or illness. The record is void of any missed matches throughout his twelve-year wrestling career. His half-brother, David Stockner, remembers a family medicine physician working on Rick's knees, but Rick suffered no episodes of orthopedic surgery or prolonged periods of convalescence.[12] Rick incurred the neck stinger in his 1968 championship with Dwayne Keller but was able to wrestle in the East/West All Stars match a month later. Wayne Wells said, in his characteristic succinctness, "Sanders had the damndest composition of anyone ever known."

Sanders continued on—despite the injury! He pinned his first four foes and scored a 7-4 victory over Mohammad Ghrbani of Iran in the finals, becoming America's first world champion. He could go from Whimpey to Popeye with one can of spinach. But getting him to open the can at the 1969 world championships took Coach Farrell and "big brother" Bobby Douglas. Thanks to Sanders, the team placed second, the highest finish yet for the U.S. at the world championships.[13]

Sanders: In the Moment

Mike Gallego, an NCAA D-I national champion from Division II Fresno State and 1971 World Team member at 163 pounds, kept a daily reminder for years of Sanders' victory over the Iranian Ghrbani. Saudi Arabia's decades-long antipathy for Iran, and Iran's notable pride in wrestling as its national sport, compelled Saudi production and distribution of a postage stamp with the picture of Sanders holding Ghrbani in a less than flattering spladle position about to be pinned. The Iranian's body is so folded in half, it appears the unfortunate Ghrbani is about to rest his chin on his butt. Gallego kept an enlarged picture of the stamp on his dental practice's wall for forty years, amused, if not intrigued, as were his patients, on the complexity of the hold.[14] It was not uncommon for Rick to sacrifice a single leg on a takedown and then move to a spladle. It was, however, rare for Sanders to convert a wrestling move into a political move.

The United States freestyle wrestling team finished second at the 1969 World Championships. Russia won the tournament. Six of ten U.S. wrestlers medaled at the '69 Worlds. Oregonian Fred Fozzard won the 180.5 weight class when a Bulgarian and Russian wrestler were disqualified for cheating. Sanders and Fozzard are recognized as the first to win world titles for the United States. Also placing for the U.S. were silver medalists Don Behm at 125.5, Wayne Wells at 163, and Larry Kristoff at 220 pounds. Henk Schenk won bronze in the 198-pound weight class.[16]

Wrestling continued to evolve in the United States. The Amateur Athletic Union (AAU), as the governing body for wrestling, came under fire for not representing the sport adequately. The AAU was held in contempt by several major Olympic sports including track and field, gymnastics, and swimming. In addition, while preaching a philosophy of amateurism, they often required Olympic champions to compete at barnstorming events around the world post-Olympics. The AAU received a percentage of gate receipts at these events to finance its organization. The AAU mandated Jesse Owens, for example, to race in several European countries after the 1936 Olympics where he had become a four-time gold medalist. Owens refused to comply, preferring to return to the United States reuniting with his wife and young child and to take advantage of business opportunities available to him. He was suspended from competition by the AAU in retaliation.[17]

In another example, Don Schollander, the four-time gold medal American swimmer at the 1964 Tokyo Olympics, experienced similar avaricious treatment by the AAU. American companies wanted to use the Schollander name and acclaim to promote their products. That was all well and good, but any financial proceeds needed to funnel to the AAU, not to the athlete. Schollander's beneficent neighbors, recognizing the AAU's mandate, passed the hat around collecting $1000 and presented it to the Olympian as a congratulatory gesture. When the AAU found out about the gift, they ordered it be returned or donated to the AAU. Such actions were monitored, and especially in the case of high-profile athletes, to the end that amateurism at the Olympics might be preserved.[18]

Such disquieting actions by the AAU precipitated retaliation. Gymnastics and swimming began organizing to replace the AAU with their own governing bodies. U.S. Wrestling began its break with the AAU in 1968 by forming the United States Wrestling Federation (USWF). In a multi-year, litigious process, the USWF—later becoming USA Wrestling—replaced the AAU. Myron Roderick was elevated from the coaching ranks on August 6th, 1969 to become the first executive director of the USWF.[19]

Sanders: In the Moment

Pictured, right: Sanders dislocated his thumb in the early rounds of the 1969 World Championships, but he continued nevertheless.

Above: Saudi Arabia produced a postage stamp of Sanders pinning an Iranian opponent reflecting Saudi antipathy for Iran.

Sanders: In the Moment

Roderick was a good choice for the directorship. Roderick became head coach of the Oklahoma State Cowboys at age 21 and in thirteen years compiled a 140 and 10 dual meet record with a streak of 84 straight victories. Oklahoma State won seven NCAA Championships in his thirteen years as coach. He was a three-time NCAA champion and a 1956 Olympian. He was a fierce competitor, losing only one match at the Olympics to finish fourth. Roderick's loss was to Japanese wrestler Shozo Sasahara, the eventual gold medal winner. Many considered Sasahara to be the tournament's best wrestler. In addition, Roderick became acquainted with Ichiro Hatta of Japan while competing at Melbourne. Hatta was president of the Japanese Wrestling Federation. As mentioned, the friendship augured a pipeline of outstanding Japanese wrestlers to the Oklahoma State wrestling room over the succeeding thirteen years. He was just thirty-four when he took the new executive level position. His fidelity to the sport was unquestioned.[20] Roderick's experience as a competitor, international recruiter of Japanese wrestlers, and successful college coach held measure for his selection as the inaugural executive director. Unfortunately, the new director would prove damaging to Sanders in the long run. For the moment, however, Sanders rode a wave of popularity after becoming the first world champion.

Amateur Wrestling News reported, "Rick Sanders, the pint-sized world champion from Portland, nipped a long-time coach, Dave McCluskey of Iowa, for third place in 1969 Man of the Year balloting." This was the third consecutive third-place finish for Rick on Man of the Year balloting. His achievement as the first-ever U.S. freestyle world champion factored heavily into the voting. It was the U.S. Wrestling Foundation's eighth annual award. Voting by a nationwide panel of coaches, competitors, and officials picked Dan Gable as 1969 Man of the

Sanders: In the Moment

Year over Michigan coach Cliff Keen 94-86, with Gable receiving four first place votes, and Keen with three. Rick received one first place vote. Though such awards did not seem outwardly to have much meaning to Sanders, they probably would have filled a void missing in his life. It was not the medal or certificate that mattered, rather it was the degree of notice he felt from fans and especially teammates that was meaningful to Rick. He couldn't get enough. It was almost as if he wanted the favorite child status. He was honored to have been named captain of the West team of college all-stars, a group of his peers. Yet, he was not a likely consideration for such honors, given the esoteric nature of his character and demeanor. He didn't act seriously, thus, he wasn't taken seriously.[21]

Rick needed the attention of fans. He seemed to be fully captivated by wrestling while in the moment of the match. But once that stimulation was over, he was bored. Wrestling motivated him to periods of contentment, however brief they may have been. The adoration of fans and the acceptance of teammates likely bolstered his self-esteem.

Abraham Maslow, an American psychologist, promulgated a theory of human motivation in 1943 that helps to explain human behavior in terms of basic needs. Maslow speaks of five human needs that arrange themselves in hierarchies of prepotency. In other words, the appearance of one need usually rests on the satisfaction of the prior satisfaction of another more prepotent need.[22] Basic needs begin with physiological needs: The most prepotent of all needs—Hunger—is the primary physiological need, and once satisfied, other, higher needs emerge. Sanders' experience of starving to make weight, for example, would affect him differently than someone who has never starved. He knew, like most lightweight wrestlers know, how little food is necessary to remain physically viable. Most Americans are only experiencing appetite rather than hunger when they say, "I am hungry." It is assured that Rick's physiological need was sufficiently satisfied since he didn't need much in the way of food to motivate him to be a wrestler in the first place.

According to his half-brother, Dave Stockner, "Rick was born with a rusty spoon in his mouth." Rick's experience growing up poor in a single-parent home accustomed him to meager physiological needs. Therefore, he may be advanced to the next level in the needs hierarchy—safety needs.

Safety needs may serve as the most exclusive organizer of behavior. Practically everything looks less important than safety once physiological needs are met. Danger, illness, unpredictable environment, and adult quarreling are stimuli that impact the safety need. Sanders grew up in a culture that largely affected his safety needs. His first Portland housing, accompanied by only his mother, was on skid row. However, he adapted and became accustomed to it. He moved to three new communities by the time he was twelve. Uprooting a child's environment is highly traumatic. Sanders moved from the rural community of Oakridge to the inner-city neighborhood of Portland, a major metropolitan city. Sanders lived the majority of his peripatetic life in situations unfamiliar to him, from distant tournament sites, to condemned inner city housing, to overnight stays in cars and under bridges. The unpredictability of his lodging was predictable; as such, it felt natural and safe. Finally, the impact of the divorce of Sanders' parents and the subsequent abandonment of his father seemed to be reconciled in Rick's mind. There is no record of comment about either event by Rick. Sanders was seasoned to the calamities of life. The rhythm to his life that provided the necessary measure of safety was the daily routine of wrestling practice all year long.

If both the physiological and safety needs are fairly well gratified, then there will emerge the love, affection and the belonging needs. Rick had a family. Anita, Rick's mother, was affectionate and proud of her son's accomplishments, according to his half-sister Kay Hirons.[23] Hirons had an intimacy with him that allowed her to understand his need for fan adoration. But she was rarely available, living in distant California. Rick's half-brother, Dave Stockner, followed Rick's accomplishments religiously, creating an archive of newspaper clippings that document his extraordinary career.[24] But Stockner was a decade older with a family of his own four boys. Likewise, Patricia Rogers, Sanders' full sister, was four years older, married, and on her own during much of his career. Love and affection were sorely lacking in Rick's adult life. Perhaps that is why, at twenty-seven years old, in an era when most people married in their early twenties, Rick turned to what most would call womanizing.

Sanders was once kicked out of an Athletes In Action sponsored wrestling camp in southern California for allegedly bringing women and booze into the dorm. Did Sanders not understand the inappropriateness of such an action, or did he so desperately need the companionship? An *Oregonian* reporter wrote, "He liked girls and gave himself in spirited pursuit." When asked by another reporter if he checked his appetite for women during competition, Sanders responded while staring at a passing bosom, "I don't put them on a schedule." David Zang, in an article written for *Amateur Wrestling News*, recalled Sanders' funeral when two women, each believing themselves to be the love of his life, stepped forward to place a rose on the Olympic flag covering his casket.[25] Characteristically, like several areas of his life, Rick overshot the goal and remained needy.

Maslow points out, however, that love is not synonymous with sex. Sex is more a physiological need. The love needs involve both giving and receiving love. And at the same time, Rick could not risk sacrificing his one safe arena—wrestling—by entering into a long-term committed relationship. He belonged to the culture, and it supported him through friendships with the likes of Sergio Gonzalez, Don Behm, and Bobby

Douglas. Rick's family members were pursuing their own lives. They rarely saw him wrestle in high school or college. There was never a family member at a national AAU tournament, World Team or Olympic trials tournament, international or Olympic competition. Rick got affection and belongingness reinforcement, however brief, from those of the wrestling culture and from immersing himself in the moment of the match.

Most people in our society have a need or a desire for a stable, firmly based, high evaluation of themselves. They need it for self-respect or self-esteem and for the esteem of others. Esteem needs is the fourth prepotent need. It must be based upon real capacity, achievement, and respect from others. It is the desire for confidence at a level that supports personal independence and freedom. Secondly, esteem needs are the desire for reputation or prestige, recognition, attention, importance, or appreciation. Rick felt inadequate in this dimension. That is why he insisted to an interviewer that it would be time to give up wrestling when it was no longer enjoyable. He wrestled just for fun, but he was multidimensional—loved poetry, fishing, and motorcycles. But wrestling was always Rick's fallback position to fulfill esteem needs. He was a GED high school graduate and could never quite finish his degree at Portland State. So, unable to hang his hat on academic accomplishments that many use to satisfy esteem needs, he leaned into his wrestling talent instead.

But what a man can be, he must be. This fifth need is termed self-actualization. When Rick was in the moment on the mat, his restlessness was allayed. He was in a zone that actualized his full potential. He could exercise his remarkable physical talents but also engage his phenomenal mental creativity. He was able to improvise moves under duress, with time running out, and in that glorious moment for him, when fans were watching. When the match was over, he had to rely on his intellectual acumen to maintain acceptance with his peer group, most of whom were well-educated, bright, and mindful of their career goals. Rick was just developing that part of his character. He was reading more. Reading fostered learning, knowledge acquisition, maturity, and a larger world view. Sanders was just discovering these things. As a result, like many similarly situated, he masked his off-mat insecurity among his peers with adolescent behavior.

Basic needs are very often unconscious. Most members of society who are normal are partially satisfied in all their basic needs and partially unsatisfied at the same time. In 1969, Sanders was at his zenith in terms of wrestling acuity. He was, as the first World Champion, self-actualized. But self-actualization is often short lived. For Rick, the glow may have been over by the time he stepped off the mat. The lower-level needs had crumbled, leaving Sanders destitute to restore them in some other forum. The remaining three years of his life was a quest to reattain that self-actualization through some rocky terrain, and newly appointed USWF President, Myron Roderick, did not do Sanders any favors.

Chapter Ten

Most of the cultural revolution seemed to foment first on the West Coast, proximate to Sanders' environs. The Black Panthers embellished their profile in 1970 through the aid of Angela Davis, whose sawed off shotgun was used by Black Panther perpetrators to kidnap California Marin County Superior Court Judge Harold Haley. Judge Haley was presiding over the trial of Panther George Jackson when Jackson's brother, Jonathan, stormed into the courtroom with an automatic weapon in an escape attempt. Hostages, as well as Jonathan, were killed by police in the melee that ensued. Judge Haley was killed with Davis' shotgun, the barrel duct taped to Judge Haley's neck. George Jackson was returned to prison where he incited further prison riots, murdering several correction officers before he too was killed by a prison guard. Angela Davis was acquitted of involvement, later becoming an adjunct professor in the California system of higher education and an advocate for prison reform. The era's escalating violence at home and worldwide would continue. Sanders would learn of Ohio's Kent State shootings and the Munich hostage crisis in coming years.[1]

The macabre twenty-seven club found its genesis in 1970 as well. Two original members died in 1970 at age 27. Jimi Hendrix died in

London from a combination of drugs and alcohol that caused him to aspirate vomit while he was sleeping. He suffocated. Many view Hendrix as the greatest guitar instrumentalist in the history of Rock and Roll. Hendrix had an amazing, albeit brief, four-year career. Sixteen days later, rock singer and performer Janis Joplin died in California of a heroin overdose. Bisexual and burning the candle at both ends, Joplin was at the head of the counterculture wave. Her music continues to give pause. Sanders would also die at twenty-seven. Not a musician, but clearly one who appreciated human form and movement, the wrestling mat his canvas.[2] Similar to those in the fine arts, Sanders experimented with marijuana for its transcendent qualities.

Coincidentally, Rick Sanders at 5'4" and NBA basketball great Kareem Abdul Jabbar, at 7'2", shared a common fetish for marijuana. Both athletes, during the height of their respective careers, were apprehended by Canadian authorities and fined for marijuana possession. Jabbar suggested that his marijuana use was to relieve the nausea associated with his migraine headaches. However, he admits in his autobiography, *Giant Steps*, that he started smoking weed in high school. He states further, "Drugs are an open secret on all strata of American society: Stockbrokers are smoking pot after hours; lawyers are snorting cocaine… doctors are shooting heroin and hospital morphine…. When an athlete gets caught doing drugs, however, all hell breaks loose. Athletes are supposed to be America's heroes… we are role models for future grandeur. This is nonsense…. Each man and woman, from the most known to the least, should have the confidence and the strength to create and live by his or her own beliefs and not be led blindly by others who may not be qualified for the job." Sanders clearly shared Jabbar's world view on personal freedom. Moreover, Sanders' history of marijuana use from sometime in 1969 to the end of his life suggests an attitude in concert with Jabbar.[3]

The NBA selected Jabbar for Rookie of the Year in 1970. He went on to become a six-time NBA Champion with the Milwaukee Bucks and Los Angeles Lakers. He was voted Most Valuable Player six times during his twenty-year NBA career. Kareem attributed his long career to working out in martial arts, doing yoga, and practicing meditation prior to games. He continued to do notable work after basketball, writing books and promoting humanitarian causes. President Obama, in 2016, bestowed the Presidential Medal of Freedom on the former All-Pro center.

Unabashed by his marijuana use, Sanders returned to the AAU tournament in 1970 after a two-year hiatus. The 1970 USWF national tournament (formerly the AAU Tournament) was held April 17th and 18th in Lincoln, Nebraska. The central U.S. location was thought to be accessible to more competitors. The Multnomah Athletic Club finished second to the venerable New York Athletic Club. The NYAC would win nine of the ten national tournaments during the '70s.[4]

Familiar faces were in the 125.5-pound bracket. Masaaki Hatta faced off with Rick in the championship—same result as in 1967. Sanders won his fourth AAU national championship. Johnny Miller, also wrestling out of Portland's Multnomah Athletic Club, and a workout partner of Rick's, was third. Miller lost a close one to Sanders at Lincoln, Rick prevailing 1-0. Miller wrestled for the University of Oregon Ducks and was a three-time NCAA Division I All-American, capturing the 1969 NCAA D-I national championship at 115 pounds over Sergio Gonzalez of UCLA. Dan Gable, a 1967 competitor in Sanders 125.5-pound weight class, was up two weight classes by 1970 and won the championship at 149.5 pounds.[5]

Sanders: In the Moment

Sanders' competition at the Lincoln tournament held unique interest. Rick pinned Sigeki Mitera in the fourth round. Mitera was wrestling for a club from Japan in the open tournament. The Japanese wrestling program subscribed to the practice of competing internationally to improve the caliber of their wrestlers. As seen, cultural exchange trips took place beginning in high school and continued through college. These exchanges developed further with exhibition matches between Japanese World Team wrestlers and U.S. world class wrestlers. They were held at various locations around the country. Sanders met Hideaki Yanagida of Japan, his future Olympic competitor, for the first time in exhibition matches held at Chattanooga, Tennessee and at LSU in Baton Rouge, Louisiana in 1970.[6]

Masaaki Hatta was a 1962 NCAA Division I National Champion from Oklahoma State. He is the older brother of Tadaaki Hatta, whom Rick defeated on the quest for his first Division I National Championship in 1966. Sanders' 1966 third-round win by fall over the younger Hatta, himself a returning national champion at the Iowa State NCAA Division I championships, legitimized Rick as a wrestling phenom. Sanders captured the 1970 Lincoln tournament with a 9-4 decision over Masaaki Hatta who now wrestled for the Michigan Wrestling Club.[7]

The results from the Lincoln tournament were used to screen contestants for the 1970 World Team. Two hundred and fifteen wrestlers competed at the Lincoln tournament. The top fifty freestyle wrestlers were invited to the 1970 World Team tryout camp, held at Wisconsin State College in Superior, Wisconsin in June. The final selection for the World Team headed to Canada was scheduled for July. However, challenge matches began only two to three days after their arrival in Wisconsin. Winners at Lincoln did not wrestle until the winner of the challenge matches emerged. Sanders won an invitation to Wisconsin by winning the Lincoln tournament wrestling in the 125.5-pound weight class. He would wait to see who emerged from the Wisconsin challenge matches, then try his luck at another World Championship tournament run.[8]

Invitees to the World Team tryouts in Superior, Wisconsin at 125.5 pounds included Don Behm of the Mayor Daley Youth Foundation Club, James Hanson of Air Force, Gary Wallman of Iowa State, and Chris Sones of the University of Iowa. Don Behm emerged as the challenger to Sanders for the 125.5-pound World Team spot on the 1970 team headed to Edmonton, Canada. *Amateur Wrestling News* reported, "Sanders and Don Behm wrestled six times in camp before Sanders won the last two matches and the opportunity to represent the U.S. at the 1970 Worlds."[9]

Bill Farrell was the 1969 U.S. World Team coach in Argentina when Sanders won the championship at 114.5 pounds. Farrell had promised Rick, at the 1969 Worlds, that he would never have to make the 114.5-pound weight again. But Farrell, now the 1970 World Team coach, felt that with Sanders at 114.5 and Behm at 125.5, the U.S. would have a good shot at defeating Russia for a team title. Farrell convinced Rick that he should make 114.5 again, and he unselfishly agreed, knowing that he would forfeit his right to compete at 125.5. Sanders went about making weight in Edmonton, Canada. As the championships approached, it became apparent that Rick just could not make 114.5 despite herculean efforts. He relinquished his 125.5 spot to Behm, who was called back.

Farrell wrote in a letter to *Amateur Wrestling News*, "To know that you could medal at one weight in a World Championships yet undertake a very difficult weight reduction program just to help the team speaks much for the individual. I thought I could teach Rick how to alter his lifestyle but as it turns out he taught me much about selflessness and sacrifice."[10]

Perhaps Rick's greatest sacrifice with respect to the 1970 World Championships was the lost opportunity to face Hideaki Yanagida of Japan. Yanagida won the 125.5-pound gold medal for Japan. Don Behm

Sanders: In the Moment

Sanders (bottom row, 3rd from right) forfeited his spot at 125.5 for the good of the team and in hopes of cutting weight to wrestle at 114.5.
He was unsuccessful in the attempt.

---

did well in the tournament until the 5th round when he suffered an ankle injury and was forced to default. Bobby Douglas represented the U.S. at 149.5 pounds. He defeated Dan Gable 1-0 and 2-0 at the Wisconsin challenge matches. The Douglas/Gable matches were so close that five more were wrestled before Douglas was definitely selected. Unfortunately, Douglas sustained a concussion in Canada during tournament action and spent eight hours in the hospital. He returned to wrestle to a draw with defending champion Movahed of Iran. Douglas did not lose a match but ended with a third-place bronze medal. Fred Fozzard, who like Sanders was a returning 1969 World Champion, injured a knee in training camp and managed a fifth-place finish at 180.5 pounds. Wayne Wells had a stellar tournament and became the third U.S. World Champion, winning the 163-pound title. As explained in *Encyclopedia of American Wrestling* by Mike Chapman: "Wells did not have a close match as he posted five straight wins in Edmonton, Canada. He was leading his

Sanders: In the Moment

Soviet foe Nodar Khorguashvili 5-0 in the finals when the Soviet withdrew, citing an injury to his shoulder. In the opening round, Wells defeated France's 1967 World Champion, Daniel Robin 4-1. The gold medal climaxed a steady climb by the determined Wells. He had placed fourth in the Olympics in 1968 and second in the 1969 World Championships." He was the only gold medal winner at the 1970 Worlds.[11]

The U.S. freestyle team finished second at the World tournament for the second year in a row. Russia won over the U.S. by ten points. Along with Wells' gold, the team won two silvers—Bill Harlow at 198 and Larry Kristoff at 220, and two bronze medals—Mike Young at 136.5 and Bobby Douglas at 149.5. Greg Wojciechowski was 4th at heavyweight, John Morley was 5th at 114.5—the weight Sanders attempted to make after conceding his 125.5 team spot to Don Behm, and Joe Orta was 7th at 105.5.[12]

Sanders represented the team well in Canada as an alternate and workout partner. He was still clean-shaven, but by that time was routinely indulging in marijuana use, which got him in trouble shortly after the tournament. On his return trip to the United States, Canadian authorities found Rick in possession of marijuana at the border.

The maximum Canadian penalty in 1960 for possession of small amounts of pot was six months in prison and a $1,000 fine. However, by 1970, officials dramatically increased the penalty in response to the increased use of the drug. The maximum penalty beginning in 1968 was 14 years to life in prison. Luckily, Rick was sent home with a nominal fine, probably in recognition of his status on an international sports team competing in Canada. But the die was cast. The newly formed United States Wrestling Foundation took notice of the misstep. Though the matter had been reconciled by payment of a fine, Sanders rubbed up against

Myron Roderick and the newly sanctioned and conservative USWF. Sanders would become a pariah among the wrestling culture for the remainder of his career.

Marijuana, or more properly cannabis, has been used for centuries for its medicinal and recreational effects. It was not outlawed in the United States until 1936, shortly after the repeal of the Eighteenth Amendment in 1933 which made consumption of alcohol legal again in the United States. At the beginning of the twentieth century, marijuana was used by Mexican arrivals as an inexpensive relaxant. At that time, marijuana was being used legally, cocaine was still in Coca-Cola, heroin and hypodermic kits were available through Sears, and no drug was illegal.[13]

By 1850, marijuana had been added to the U.S. Pharmacopia for uses such as appetite stimulation, treatment of opioid withdrawal, and suppression of nausea and vomiting. American pharmaceutical companies Parke-Davis and Eli Lilly marketed cannabis extracts in several products. Today's marijuana is much stronger. According to Kevin Hill, M.D. in his book *The Unbiased Truth About The World's Most Popular Weed*, "The potency of today's marijuana versus the drug of the 1960s (Sanders' era) is generally so great, you might as well be talking about two different drugs."[14]

The Federal Bureau of Narcotics (FBN) was formed in 1930 to oversee narcotics and the ban on alcohol. However, with the repeal of the Eighteenth Amendment bringing an end to prohibition, the FBN lost much of its purpose. Not to be abandoned, the FBN department director, Harry Anslinger, repurposed the agency's mission to a war on drugs. Anslinger demonized marijuana through a highly effective movie entitled *Reefer Madness*. He said marijuana led to insanity and made it more likely that users would commit criminal acts. As a result, all states enacted laws regulating marijuana by 1936. Marijuana use became particularly scandalous during the 1960s counterculture revolution. Users became a major target and low hanging fruit for politicians that continue to be relevant today.[15]

Until the pop culture of the '60s, weed was a relatively latent drug. According to award-winning author Martin Lee in his book *Smoke Signals*, the hippie generation found marijuana readily available, cheap, and the induced euphoria enjoyable. Other users experienced relief from chronic pain, lowered sexual inhibitions, greater focus on the moment, and sense of humor and loquacity accentuated. Sanders manifested all these characteristics under the drug's influence.[16]

Studies suggest that nine percent of adults and 17 percent of adolescents who use marijuana develop an addiction to it.[17] By several reports, Sanders was a heavy user and may have had an addiction. His father was an alcoholic, and Anita was a chain smoker, so Rick may have inherited that proclivity to overuse. Though the drug was illegal, Rick subscribed manifestly to the lyric in his favorite singer/songwriter John Prine's 1971 classic song, *Illegal Smile*:

> Ah, but fortunately I have the key to escape reality
>
> And you may see me tonight with an illegal smile
>
> It don't cost very much, but it lasts a long while
>
> Won't you please tell the man I didn't kill anyone
>
> No, I'm just trying to have me some fun.[18]

Sergio Gonzalez insists that while Sanders smoked marijuana, he did not take LSD or any other controlled drugs. Marijuana helped Rick sleep and relax. Similarly, the strings of bead carvings Sanders had begun creating were a way for him to relax in lieu of smoking. Sanders admitted he didn't want to set a poor example to young wrestling fans, so he attempted to transition to bead carving. Rick gave the bead necklaces out as gifts.[19]

One such fan was seven-year-old Lori Baughman, daughter of Wayne Baughman. She met Rick Sanders for the first time at her father's wrestling clinic at Rus Camilleri's ranch.

"I heard the wrestlers saying, 'Here he is! Rick Sanders is here!'" Lori explains, recalling the moment. She'd been on a swing in the front yard when a car drove in. "When Rick got out of the car, I saw he was clearly a wrestler, but he was closer to my height than my dad's. I think that's why Rick did not intimidate me as the other guys did. I started following him around and asking questions. He was very tolerant of me, and clearly enjoyed mentoring kids. I picked up immediately that there was something controversial about him. I asked my dad why Rick was 'different' ad he laughed and said, 'Rick is Rick, a dope smoking hippy, but we all love him.'"

Lori reflected, "I noticed that Rick would often climb a tree by the house, jump onto the Camilleri's rooftop, and load his little wood pipe with dope. After seeing that a few times, I decided to follow him. Being smaller, it took me a little longer to get up there. I jumped onto the roof just as he was lighting up. He was wide eyed with surprise and not happy to see that I'd joined him. I said, 'What are you doing up here?' and he looked at me like that was a dumb question. 'I'm smoking up here,' he said. When I asked why he didn't smoke on the ground, he said, 'Because some people don't like smoking, and since smoke rises, if I'm up here, it doesn't bother anybody.' I told him his smoke didn't smell like cigarettes; it was slightly better. To this, Rick laughed heartily. Then he said, 'You better get out of here before you get me in trouble. Your dad can kick my ass, and he probably wouldn't want you up here while I'm smoking."

Sanders: In the Moment

Though Sanders might accurately have been labeled a pothead, Rick would have found it difficult to be an intravenous drug user. Former PSU teammate Mike McKeel explained, "It took some courage for Sanders to call one day about fixing a cavity." McKeel still wrestled at the MAC while attending dental school and did some "bushwack" dentistry. Sanders showed up and got in the chair, though he was extremely nervous. When Mike showed him the needle for Novocain, "Rick fainted in the chair." McKeel mused. "It took a cool rag to revive him and complete the filling."[20]

Today, the negative stigma associated with marijuana use is receding in the United States. Recreational and medicinal use has been decriminalized by many government entities. Nevertheless, its use during Sanders' era was illegal. While many prominent figures used—future high-profile athletes and politicians—Kareem Abdul Jabbar (NBA), Ricky Williams (NFL), Presidents Barack Obama and Bill Clinton, et.al.—the culpability rested more with not abiding the law than indulging in the drug.[22]

Sanders was changing. His success in wrestling and the continual disciplined devotion necessary to that success spawned an inimical need to explore alternative lifestyle choices. Or perhaps more simply, his notoriety was beyond his maturity, and it got the best of him. To be sure, Rick acquired an affinity for several of the personal freedoms promulgated by the counterculture of the sixties and early seventies—long hair, free love, and weed. Marijuana use may have allowed Rick medicinal qualities, relieving aches and pains acquired over a decade of daily mat time. Marijuana ameliorated his hyperactivity and enhanced his ability to sleep. Some hospitalized insomniacs are able to sleep well thanks to cannabis, but results are inconsistent. Rick's habitual nocturnal activities, certainly exacerbated by his insomnia, may have been curbed by smoking grass.

Marijuana's effects are highly variable even in small doses. Realms of touch, taste, and smell are magnified under the herb's influence. Quickened mental associations are often accompanied by a tendency to become hyper focused. As a result, many elite athletes of the generation, and perhaps more frequently today, were regular users.[23]

In the music arena, jazz musicians often smoked dope. Louis Armstrong, the trumpet maestro of the Savoy Ballroom in the Harlem neighborhood of Manhattan, liked the sweet smell and taste. It calmed his nerves and lifted his spirits. "It's a thousand times better than whiskey," said Armstrong, who toked up daily. In the 1970s, Oregon lawmakers decriminalized marijuana. Though still not legal, a date with "Mary Jane" would not get you thrown in jail.

Discipline was de rigueur of the U. S. wrestling culture, and Sanders' new Bohemian lifestyle was antithetical to that moral code. But despite the drug's notoriety, possessing marijuana was not nearly as scandalous as possessing long hair. Long hair was the most conspicuous and controversial breach of discipline in wrestling. High school and college teams regulated hair length strictly. Wrestling officials stuck to the 50s hairstyles: off the ears and shirt collar, tight on the sides, no sideburns, and no long beards. Long hair was considered a fad in the 60s and 70s, popularized by rock bands, seen as an insidious influence of the counterculture.

The NCAA Rules Committee ruled that long hair was taboo for wrestlers. It appeared rebellious, unsanitary, and feminine. The rule read: "Contestants shall be clean-shaven, free of mustaches, side-burns trimmed no lower than ear-lobe level and hair trimmed and well-groomed. Because of the body contact involved, this rule has been approved in the interest of health, sanitary and safety measures…" Wrestlers were made to wear headgear that sufficiently enclosed the excess hair if prescribed length wasn't met. Some referees carried tape measures to officiate pre-match inspections.

International rules were much more liberal. Sanders, though not bearded, had hair covering his ears in a photo of champions at the first USWF National Open Freestyle tournament in 1970. Buck Deadrich, the 220-pound champion from California, pushed respectability parameters by sporting a beard. Internationally sponsored U.S. teams held attitudes toward long hair that mirrored domestic rules. The absurdity of hair length rules existed for decades. High school hair length rules were the last to be eliminated. The hair rule was not discarded at the high school level until April 2020 when the National Federation of State High School Associations promulgated their 2020-2021 Wrestling Rule Changes.

The NCAA Rules Committee promulgated the hair rule to the consternation of many wrestlers, coaches, and officials. Though forthright in design, debate over the issue proliferated. A typical reaction was that of David N. Camaione, Ph.D. and Associate Professor of P.E. at Central Connecticut State College at the time:

> "This rule, by evidence of court cases against the NCAA and rejection by athletic conferences, is obviously controversial. I firmly believe in the intent of the rule, but object to the rationale used to justify it. The rule is ill-conceived. Moreover, it violates one's individual rights and is thus discriminatory...
>
> It is my belief that the rule legislates against long hair. I have seen many wrestlers with short dirty hair allowed to compete and have observed long clean hair being asked to be cut. In all fairness the latter is more worthy for competition based on the health concept. As for facial hair—take time to feel the texture of one's mustache or beard and most often you will find the hair soft and unabrasive. For those not clean-shaven, abrasiveness often causes skin irritation for his opponent. But let's not be hypocritical, you have little scientific evidence upon which to base your

claim as the rule is presently stated. Unfortunately, much controversy and harm has been engendered because the rule is philosophically, conceptually, and scientifically unfounded."[24]

Issues related to drug and alcohol use, hair and beard length, and general athlete decorum fell under the purview of wrestling's governing body. In 1969, Myron Roderick was the pioneer of the newly minted United States Wrestling Federation (USWF), the organization developed by those "inside" wrestling to replace the AAU as the governing body for U.S. wrestling at the local and international level. "Roderick was the most successful college wrestling coach at the time and was a fairly easy choice for USWF decision makers to select to fill the executive director position," wrote Werner Holzer in his book, *History of the United States Wrestling /USA Wrestling*. Working out of his garage, Roderick took on his new role at age thirty-four with zeal. He took direction from the USWF Executive Committee whose members were largely from the conservative Midwest.[25]

Unfortunately for Rick Sanders, a convention between the newly inaugurated USWF, the AAU, and FILA, the international wrestling federation, was held simultaneously to the 1970 World Championships in Edmonton in Alberta, Canada. The USWF was trying desperately to gain recognition from FILA to replace the AAU and become the national governing body (NGB) for wrestling at the international level. The USWF did not need any embarrassing events suggesting lack of control at this crucial time. Sanders' drug incident at the border was untimely. Clearly, Sanders was an embarrassment and an undisciplined nonconformist—a burr under the saddle of the former Oklahoma State Cowboy coach.

Another nonconformist was Buck Deadrich, a freestyle and Greco-Roman wrestler who won several national and international tournaments. He and Sanders became friends while wrestling at an AAU tournament in 1968. Both were born in 1945 on the West Coast, Deadrich growing up near Oakland, California. Buck wrestled in the 198 to 220-pound weight classes and was occasionally coached by Bill Smith at the San Francisco Olympic Club. Deadrich became an Olympian competing in Greco-Roman at the 1972 Olympics. Unlike Sanders, Deadrich was a good student, twice becoming an Academic All-American and ultimately obtaining a Master's Degree from the University of California at Berkeley. He later coached at California Lutheran University. Nevertheless, Sanders and Deadrich shared common interests of the era as well—long hair and advocacy of personal freedoms including polyamorous relationships with like-minded women. Largely, they found commonality on all of the things that drew the ire of conservative society.

Deadrich enjoyed relating the following Sanders' anecdote, which reveals the cultural polarization at the time, both in wrestling and in society at large: "Rick was wrestling in the finals of the AAU nationals being held in Stillwater, Oklahoma. Back then, Oklahoma was 'the last and tightest notch in the Bible belt' and people who looked like Sanders—long hair, shaggy beard, peace button on his jacket, etc, were not fully appreciated in Oklahoma. Coincidentally, Rick's opponent in the finals was the great Gene Davis, who was both an Oklahoma State alumnus as well as a clean-cut member of the Athletes in Action-Campus Crusade for Christ wrestling club. Clearly, Gene was coming in as the fan favorite. When it was time for their match, Davis walked out into the spotlight, and the PA announcer said something like 'Now wrestling in the 136.5-pound final, and wrestling for the Lord—Mr. Gene Davis!' The crowd cheered long and loud. As the noise died down a bit, but before the PA announcer could say anything else, Sanders ran out onto the mat, dropped to his knees and shouted, 'And wrestling for the devil… Rick Sanders!' There was a slight, stunned pause, before the crowd rained boos down on Sanders, who promptly pinned Davis in the first period."[26]

Davis would lose to Sanders in competition at a U.S. Wrestling Federation-sponsored event held in Oklahoma in May 1972. They wrestled at 136.5 pounds. But Davis doesn't recall Sanders' center-mat oration to the crowd—"though he may have been preoccupied preparing for the match," Davis admitted. A year earlier, in 1971, both Sanders and Davis would become AAU freestyle national champions. Both were a little heavy, Rick at 136.5 pounds and Gene at 149.5. Davis and Sanders became workout partners in 1972, training for the Munich Olympics. Though total opposites, Davis opined: "We related well. I learned from Rick, and Sanders was open to spiritual matters. He worked out hard." Davis added, "There was nobody on the team like Rick. He was the first wrestling hippie. He genuinely did not care what anyone thought about how he acted!"[27]

Wayne Wells was named *Amateur Wrestling News'* Man of the Year for 1970. Wells was a deserving 1970 Man of the Year. He had won both the newly established U.S. Wrestling Federation and the AAU National Championships and a World Title in Edmonton, Canada at 163 pounds. It was the third ever World Title by an American. He was steel throughout 1970, dominating all competitions. Furthermore, while competing in 1970, Wells was also working his way through the University of Oklahoma Law School. The combination of athletics and academics led to Wells' nomination for the prestigious Sullivan award. "The AAU James E. Sullivan Award annually recognizes the amateur athlete whose outstanding athletic accomplishments are complemented by qualities of leadership, character, and sportsmanship." It has been awarded since 1930. Despite Wells' nomination, the 1970 Sullivan was instead bestowed on another stellar athlete of the era, swimmer Mark Spitz. Twenty years later, another Oklahoma product, John Smith, became the first wrestler to win the Sullivan. Thereafter, wrestling was well recognized by a number of Sullivan recipients. Bruce Baumgartner won a Sullivan in 1995, Rulan Gartner in 2000, Kyle Snyder in 2017, and most recently, Spencer Lee in 2019.[28]

Sanders, unfortunately, did not make the top twenty Man of the Year finishers in 1970, garnering but a few votes. Moreover, the following year, Myron Roderick would be voted Man of the Year for 1971, while Sanders would not tally a single vote.[29]

Sanders' fall from consideration was precipitous. Rick's 1970 World Team sacrifice, forfeiting his spot at 125.5 pounds and trying to make 114.5 for the good of the team, was of little consequence. Already cut to 125.5 pounds, Rick challenged himself to lose another 11 pounds (another 9% of his body weight) in a couple days before competition began in Canada. Who were they that said Sanders didn't work hard? After finishing third in the Man of the Year balloting the previous three years, and sacrificing a spot on the 1970 World Team, ingratitude flourished.

Sanders stayed active throughout 1970 by wrestling in international freestyle events sponsored by the newly formed United States Wrestling Federation.[30] He won the 1970 USWF Freestyle Senior Open Championships at 125.5 pounds. In that tournament, Sanders defeated Yoshiro Fujita, Ron Thrasher, and Dwayne Keller, all wrestling out of Stillwater. Sanders absolved his only D-I collegiate loss by defeating Keller en route to the championship. Rick wrestled independently; the MAC was unavailable for sponsorship. The USWF needed him for exhibition duals with foreign teams for those duals to remain respectable losses in the eyes of U.S. fans. Nevertheless, Sanders was rejected on traveling teams for events abroad. The USWF could not risk Sanders on international tours for the potential consternation he would cause.

Duals with a traveling Russian National team were held in Chattanooga, Tennessee; Oklahoma City, Oklahoma; Waterloo, Iowa; and finished at Evanston, Illinois. United States team members shuffled in and out of the lineup. Rick wrestled three times over the four duals. He lost 2-1 in his first match at Chattanooga against Yagub Mamedov. Rick had a well-publicized journey to the contest in Tennessee. Bob Hurt, columnist for a Portland newspaper reported:

Stewardesses know how to pacify everything from babies to drunks to skyjackers. But joggers? There was nothing in the book about that.

"You'll have to stop that," said the stewardesses to the jogger.

"So what can you do?" he asked. "Throw me off!"

Airliners have learned to bend to the convenience of passengers. They did this time, once the situation was explained.

The passenger was Rick Sanders, assistant wrestling coach at Portland State where he won the world title in 1969 at 125.5 pounds. Sanders was flying to Chattanooga where that night he joined the U.S. team for the first in a series of duals with the Russians.

But flights had been fouled up by weather. Rick left Portland at 7 a.m. He wasn't to make Chattanooga until 6:45 p.m. More concern than the delays was Rick's weight. He had to drop off four pounds to make his limit by 7:30 p.m.

It's a lot easier to lose baggage than pounds on the airlines. Hence, Rick decided on the jogging, figuring apparently it was a little late for Metrecal.

Rick was awakened from a sound sleep Monday at his hotel. In his drowsy condition, he was reluctant to relate the story, particularly the jogging bit. After all, the stewardesses had been nice when the situation was explained.

He passed that part of the episode off with, "I was just a little upset."

But he was highly complimentary of the airlines' cooperation after the abbreviated jogging. With the blessing of the stewardesses, he retired to the restroom and changed into a rubber suit.

Sanders: In the Moment

An area near the kitchen was cleaned. So, there, high in the clouds and looking something like a frogman, Rick Sanders started doing pushups.

Understanding stewardesses even piled blankets on him to help him break a weight-losing sweat.

The plane stopped briefly at Cincinnati. Out hopped Sanders to make the most of the 15-minute layover. He jogged around the field, huffing and puffing his way back into the cabin just before departure.

The pushups were augmented with isometric exercises. Slowly, the pounds melted away.

It was a rush from the airport to the arena for the weigh-in but Rick made it. And the scales told a delightful story. He was right on weight.

Which should make for a happy ending. But, alas, our jogging hero after a day of fighting weather delays, plane connections and stewardesses, was worse for wear. He lost to his Russian foe, Yagub Mamedov, 2-1.

That's why Rick was taking it easy Monday. He figured an afternoon in the sack was better than an afternoon jogging somewhere 25,000 feet over Ohio. He was optimistic about his chances for revenge in Monday's match.

"I'll make him a cosmonaut," boasted Sanders with a laugh.[31]

Sanders was no doubt exhausted by the travel to Chattanooga, but still playful. Wayne Baughman recalled how Sanders focused energies in needless and puzzling ways shocking people. After the Chattanooga, Tennessee wrestling event, contestants were invited to a celebratory barbecue. Sanders indulged liberally in the offered beer. He kept coming back for more and soon appeared drunk. "Rick looked completely wasted after about his tenth beer," said Baughman. Later, needing to use the facilities, Baughman was surprised to witness Sanders surreptitiously

Sanders: In the Moment

Rick worked national camps during the summer.
He had some sense of paying back aspiring
H.S. athletes for their support.

—

pouring the beer down the bathroom sink drain. Sanders was sober as an alley cat at midnight.[32] Was his drinking act a psychological ploy in anticipation of the next exhibition match to come? If so, it seemed to work.

Sanders beat Mamedov the next night in Oklahoma City 9-2. Wrestling the third match at Waterloo, Iowa, (Dan Gable's hometown), Rick won by fall over his opponent. Sanders and Gable recorded the only two pins for the Americans in the four exhibition duals with the Russians. In contrast, the Russians recorded no pins during the tour. Don Behm filled in for Sanders in the final match at Evanston, Illinois, winning 3-1.[33]

Sanders: In the Moment

Rick devoted time post college as a clinician at area high schools and camps around the country. Often, he devoted his time gratis in order to be with young athletes, inspiring them and attempting to impart some of his unorthodox moves and approach to the sport. He was a hero. His friend Bobby Douglas, on occasion, accompanied Rick to these random high school wrestling rooms. The Olympian and future Arizona State and Iowa State coaching legend created a memory for several prep stars. Years later, Bobby Janisse, a top national recruit out of Portland's Jefferson high school, would wrestle for Douglas at ASU.

The "standing room only" crowds at Portland State were largely composed of aspiring high school athletes, and Sanders had some sense of paying them back for their support. Rick worked national camps during the summer as well. He spent time at the Squaw Valley Wrestling Camp in California near where his half-sister Kay lived. He also worked at Russ Houk's camp in Pennsylvania during August of 1970. Russ Houk was a long-time coach of the Bloomsburg College Huskies, an NAIA wrestling power. Sanders was still welcomed at Houk's camp. Despite the blemish to his reputation from the Canadian drug violation, campers were quick to forgive, still awed by Sanders whose career started with an NAIA national championship and Outstanding Wrestler award as a college freshman in 1965.

Chapter Eleven

Oregon's Governor Tom McCall captured the tailwind of the nation's counterculture movement when he appeared on television in January of 1971 and effectively told a national audience to stay out of Oregon. McCall said, "Come visit us again and again, but for heaven's sake, don't come here to live." The McCall advisory was an effort to protect the unique northwest environment. Oregon aimed to preserve the green natural beauty that was Sanders' northwest Shire. Oregon was the first state to pass what was known as the Bottle Bill, an effort to control litter on beaches, waterways, and roadways throughout the state by mandating a ten-cent refund for returned bottles. McCall shut down Boise Cascade, the Salem timber conglomerate, until they agreed to cease their egregious air pollution practices. In the 1970s, nearly one of every eight jobs in Oregon was tied to the timber industry. McCall was undeterred. He quipped, "Industry must come here on our terms, play the game by our environmental rules, and be members of the Oregon family."[1] In view of McCall's protestation, Sanders could stand boldly for simply wearing a beard on a wrestling mat.

The U.S. culture continued unsettled during 1971. The Vietnam War was a huge bone of contention. The historic "March on Washington" in

March of 1971 was marked by 500,000 anti-war protestors. Moreover, racial unrest burgeoned. Members of the Ku Klux Klan were arrested in connection with ten school bus bombings in the South.

President Nixon's "War on Drugs" seemed only to produce inequitable and dubious results, though some events warranted interdiction. For example, a Grateful Dead Concert saw thirty members of the crowd hospitalized after drinking apple cider spiked with LSD. The lead singer of the rock band *The Doors*, Jim Morrison, on the other hand, required no explanations for his drug use. He was found dead in a Paris apartment bathtub at age 27. The popular rocker became the newest member of the 27 club.[2]

Finally, the Oklahoma State Cowboys won the Division I wrestling crown over Iowa State, the 1970 champions, by 28 points. The Portland State Vikings finished 9th in coach Westcott's final season. Don Conway, a former NCAA D-I champion from Oregon State University, would assume Westcott's head coaching position. Sanders continued in the PSU Viking wrestling room as a non-paid assistant.

The U.S. Wrestling Federation in January 1971 named the team for the return visit to wrestle the Russians. The former Soviet Union held their annual tournament in Tbilisi, Georgia, a province of the Soviet Union. Tbilisi was generally considered the toughest tournament in the world. The Soviets often entered multiple wrestlers in each weight class. All of them were high caliber wrestlers competitive on the national stage. This would be the first U.S. team participating in the Tbilisi tournament.

When the Russians wrestled their 1970 exhibition matches in the United States at the invitation of the United States Wrestling Federation, Sanders was one of only two wrestlers to win, once by pin and once by decision. Nevertheless, he was left off the team headed to Russia.

Sanders: In the Moment

Don Behm wrestled at 125.5 and Mike Young at 136.5 for the United States at Tbilisi, the two weight classes that might have been represented by Sanders. Behm became the first American to win a gold medal at Tbilisi. The Americans competed in nine weight classes at the February tournament. The U.S. had no entry at 105.5 pounds. Dan Gable, Wayne Wells, Larry Kristoff, and Chris Taylor won silver. John Morley and Bill Harlow joined Mike Young in winning bronze. Silver and bronze finishes are difficult to assess, however. Tournament rules allowed only one medal per country per weight class. Therefore, while Russians may have had the top five finishers in a weight class, the sixth-place finisher from another country would have received the silver medal. The U.S. garnered a second-place team finish, a tremendous outcome for U.S. wrestling.[3] Sanders' absence from the team is unexplained. He missed valuable international experience against wrestlers who planned to compete in the following year's Munich Olympics. If multiple wrestlers could be entered by a country, why not Sanders?

The USWF held a tournament in Oklahoma City on April 1st-3rd 1971. Sanders did not compete. Rather, he participated, as was his custom, in the AAU-sponsored national tournament held in Tampa, Florida two weeks later April 15th through the 17th. Sanders became a bit pudgy in his last two appearances at the annual AAU tournament. He moved up to the 136.5-pound weight class and won the championship over David Pruzansky.[4] The 1971 championship was his fourth AAU national championship.

The USWF and the AAU continued to compete for the right to sponsor national and international events. At the Edmonton, Alberta World Games conference, FILA established a probationary period for both U.S. wrestling organizations to showcase their superiority in hosting international events. As a result, the organizations found themselves inviting elite athletes from other countries to compete in their open tournaments. For several years, the two U.S. organizations vied for FILA's endorsement as the official governing body to represent the U.S. at international events.

The qualifying tournament for the 1971 Pan American Games was held at Midwest City, Oklahoma in May. Sanders won at 136.5 pounds over David Pruzansky and was to join the team for training camp at the University of South Florida at Tampa in late July. In anticipation of the Games, however, *Amateur Wrestling News* reported, "The only change to the final team was at 136.5 pounds, with David Pruzansky, Passaic, N.J. replacing Richard Sanders, Portland, Oregon." No explanation was given for the change.[5] Sanders had just defeated Pruzansky the month before at the annual national AAU tournament. Why the switch? The Pan Ams were often dominated by the United States. Perhaps the USWF felt Pruzansky would win for the U.S. (he did) and using their prerogative, scrubbed Sanders from the lineup. Was Rick being disciplined for his marijuana violation? Was his wrestling talent now outweighed by his off-mat behavior?

The 1971 Pan American Games and World Championship tournaments were now under the auspices of the U.S. Wrestling Federation, a change from the traditional AAU sponsorship. The U.S. Olympic Committee, back in 1969, nominated coaches for the 1971 Pan American Games and the 1972 Munich Olympics. Of that list of venerable coaches, Bill Farrell was selected as the 1972 Olympic coach and Doug Blubaugh as coach for the Pan American and World Championships teams.

Blubaugh was a long-time assistant coach to Grady Peninger at Michigan State and helped lead the Spartans to a 1967 National Championship. He was a national champion at Oklahoma State in 1957 and a Pan American gold medal winner in 1959. Then in 1960, Blubaugh won an Olympic gold medal in Rome. He was renowned as an athlete and a clinician. He was to cultivate new ground as head coach of teams representing the newly formed United States Wrestling Federation, now recognized intermittently as the official governing body for wrestling in the United States. As a product of Oklahoma State, Blubaugh had the ear of USWF Executive Director, Myron Roderick. Blubaugh could anticipate the auspicious challenge of managing Rick Sanders in the tournaments to come. Rick's success was, to all intents and purposes, tantamount to Blubaugh's good fortune. Was Rick worth the risk?

Training for the 1971 Pan Am games in July at the University of South Florida in Tampa went well. Freestyle team members included Sergio Gonzalez, 105.5; Randall Miller, 114.5; Donald Behm, 125.5; David Pruzansky, 136.5; Dan Gable, 149.5; Wayne Wells, 163; Bob Anderson, 180.5; Russ Hellickson, 198; Dominic Carollo, 220; and Jeff Smith, heavyweight. Of the ten wrestlers on the 1971 Pan Am team, Gonzalez, Gable, and Wells would go on to make the 1972 Olympic team.[6] Ben and John Peterson were at the Tampa training camp as workout partners and would ultimately make the Munich Olympic team as well.

The Pan Am venue at Cali, Columbia left much to be desired. The team arrived August 4th. The venue offered only one mat, and some wrestling sessions lasted 7-8 hours. Thanks to the single mat issue, the first five weight classes were completed before the last five could begin. On several occasions, an official from the International Olympic Committee was desperately needed to facilitate the event in order for it to finish on schedule. The team experienced great difficulty in obtaining satisfactory travel arrangements through the United States Olympic Committee. Many wrestlers paid their way to training camp, and a few experienced difficulties after the games in attempting to return home once they got back to Miami. Several team members worried about the coming World Championships trials, held at Annapolis, Maryland on August 13th through the 15th, unsure whether they would make the tournament in time.

Despite the difficulties, the U. S. Pan Am freestyle team accomplished their objective in winning the 1971 Pan Am Championships. Gonzalez, Behm, Pruzansky, Gable, Hellickson, Corollo, and Smith won gold medals; Wells and Anderson finished with silver. Coach Blubaugh was commended for the job he did. Blubaugh's next challenge was as head coach for the 1971 World Team headed to Bulgaria. He was under the same time crunch returning from Columbia as some of the Pan Am wrestlers who planned to compete at Annapolis.

When Sergio Gonzalez arrived at the U.S. Naval Academy in Annapolis, Maryland to compete for a spot on the freestyle World Team, Rick Sanders was already there. Rick was quite upset because he was prohibited from competing for the World Team. Sanders told Gonzalez the reason he was denied the opportunity to try out was because of a recent incident in Pennsylvania.[7]

Unfortunately, in Pennsylvania in August of 1971, Sanders was arrested a second time on suspicion of being under the influence of drugs or alcohol. Sanders had been working a camp in Pennsylvania prior to the World Team trials. During an off-hour time, he was stopped for allegedly walking naked along a Pennsylvania turnpike with a bottle of wine. Sanders told patrol officers that someone had spiked his coffee with LSD. According to a conversation Don Behm had with former wrestling great, Gene Gibbons, who was privy to the Sanders' episode, Rick was not naked as inflated stories have suggested. Rick was put in the police car, and while the officer stopped at another crime scene en route to the police station, Rick climbed into the squad car's driver seat and drove a short distance. He very quickly ended the stunt with no harm done.[8] However, the "attention getting" objective did not play well with World Team coaches anticipating Rick's participation in the 1971 trials tournament. His second altercation with the law within a year further alienated him from the graces of the newly functioning United States Wrestling Federation.

Rick told Gonzalez it was primarily Roderick that kept him out of the World Team trials. He emphasized that he was found not guilty of any wrongdoing for that incident.[9] Another rumored report said that Rick called Coach Blubaugh to say he may have trouble getting to the trials on time. Blubaugh, uncertain how to respond, consulted with Myron Roderick who suggested offering Sanders an ultimatum. Rick was told to give a phone number where he could be reached night or day so that Blubaugh could monitor his status. Rick offered the requested phone number.[10] Upon hanging up the phone, Roderick suggested calling the number back immediately to confirm its veracity. When no one answered, Sanders was prohibited from the World Team trials, allegedly not for the Pennsylvania incident, but rather because he was untruthful by giving an unreliable phone number. Of course, there were no cell phones at that time, so a landline phone number where Sanders could be reached at any time was a setup for failure. Sanders would, of necessity, be en route to Maryland. Even if Rick was already at Annapolis, his well-known peripatetic nature (perhaps ADHD) would quite obviously frustrate his obligation to wait for a phone call.

Sanders was miffed by Roderick's treatment, so much so that he sought to enjoin the United States Wrestling Federation from denying him an opportunity to try-out for the 1971 World Team. His affidavit read as follows:

Sanders: In the Moment

State of Maryland

County of Anne Arundel

I Richard Sanders, make oath that the following facts are true to the best of my knowledge, information, and belief:

    1. That I duly qualified for the United States Wrestling Federations (USWF) elimination tournament now being held at the Naval Academy to select representatives for the world wrestling championships at Sofia, Bulgaria during the latter part of August, 1971.

    2. That I am being prevented from participating in said elimination tournament by USWF officials including Douglas Blubaugh, Myron Roderick, and Ed Peery, who have decided arbitrarily, without justification and without a hearing, that I could not participate in the elimination tournament, and who have refused to give me any written statement enunciating their decision and reasons, but have instead told me that their counsel would issue me a written statement and reasons in October 1971.

    3. That this action on the part of the USWF is wrongful and unjustified, and if it is permitted to happen and not prevented by the issuance of a temporary injunction entitling me to participate in the elimination tournament now being held at the Naval Academy August 14 and 15, I shall suffer immediate, substantial, and irreparable injury because by the time an adversary hearing can be had, the tournament will be over.

    Richard Sanders

    Notary Public

There is no record that Rick pursued the injunction beyond constructing the affidavit. It was not signed by Rick or formally notarized. Sanders was fast, but events moved even faster, making any attempt at an injunction a moot point. Don Behm went to Sofia, Bulgaria at 125.5 pounds—Sanders' usual freestyle weight class—and won a silver medal at the 1971 World Championships. Former Oklahoma State wrestler Dwayne Keller was at the Annapolis trials, competing at 125.5 pounds. His former coach Myron Roderick would have been pleased to see Keller on the 1971 World Team gaining international experience, especially with the Olympics to come in the following year. Don Behm made short work of that aspiration, defeating Keller 3-1 for the spot.[11]

Bill Farrell was the ideal coach for Sanders, whose unorthodox style and off-mat shenanigans clashed with many. Mike Chapman in his wrestling treatise, *Encyclopedia of American Wrestling* writes: "Farrell was known for his ability to blend individuals with diverse personalities and different techniques into a successful unit obtaining maximum effort from each without conflict."[12] In addition to World Teams, Farrell was also named coach for the 1972 Munich Olympics. Now, in months leading up to the Olympic trials, Sanders had been arrested twice on separate violations. The United States Olympic Committee (USOC) was of the mind to keep Rick from trying out. Farrell and Cy Mitchell, Rick's MAC coach, defended Rick before the committee. It was a challenge. Bill Farrell, who coached Rick on the 1969 and 1970 World Teams, had great rapport with Sanders. He wrote Sanders a heartfelt letter after learning of the Pennsylvania episode:

Dear Richard,   September 15, 1971

In three weeks the USOC will have a wrestling committee meeting. I know that your name will come up as a result of the drug charge this summer. I know also that there will be some and in fact many who will vote not to allow you to try out for the Olympic team. There will be others, fully in the majority who will vote for you providing Cy (Cy Mitchell, Coach at the MAC) and myself can give some assurance that you will give us your cooperation this coming year.

Sanders: In the Moment

Some in the Federation do not want you to wrestle again because of the influence on the young wrestler. For this I cannot disagree. I cannot see any good coming from the knowledge that a world champion drinks and has been arrested two times on drugs. There are some young wrestlers whom this type of thing might influence. I cannot agree that your attitude on these things benefits wrestling.

The incident this summer will be very difficult to explain. There are many who will not believe any explanation. I am more concerned about the future than the past. I spoke for you as did Cy in an AAU meeting before the 1970 World Championships. Some wanted to create problems because they knew you took "pot." We convinced them you would not touch it in camp. Now the problem is much larger. Two arrests in a short period. The latter quite serious even if there is a good explanation.

Quite honestly, though I do not condone drugs or pot in any form. I cannot stop the wrestler from smoking in private as long as he does not create attention because he is taking drugs of some type. I can though prevent this from happening at my camp. To be honest Rick, I am on the spot enough without taking on another responsibility such as a wrestler who admits to drinking, smoking pot and one who has been arrested.

[...] You must stop creating such a bad image. If you want to drink a little, drink in private. Don't tell everyone. If you want to smoke pot, do so in private, don't tell everyone. Stay out of trouble. If you have just one incident between now and June, 1972, there will not be one vote to let you wrestle. Not one. Rick, you have got to stop trying to "shock" everyone. You must stop trying to convince people that you don't care.

Coach Farrell stepped up when Sanders unwittingly needed paternal advice the most. By the letter, Farrell demonstrated care when Rick's urge was to show the culture that Rick Sanders didn't care. Farrell's calm held sway with Rick. Farrell was careful to ally himself and his concern with Cy Mitchell, Sanders' long-time MAC coach. Farrell and Mitchell were integral to Sanders' level of achievement on the international level.

Sanders: In the Moment

Sanders trusted them unequivocally. They treated Rick like an adult when he sensed he was on shaky ground.

The U.S. World Team trials concluded and the team embarked to Bulgaria without Sanders. The Bulgarian World Championships were the largest international wrestling event ever held. Forty-one teams competed. There were 280 participants in freestyle. Dan Gable won a World Championship gold medal, the only U.S. Champion. Don Behm won silver, pinning three, wrestling to a draw against a Russian, and finally losing to the 1970 World Champion Hideaki Yanagida. Russ Hellickson won bronze at 198 pounds for the United States. After finishing second in 1970, the U.S. freestyle team finished fifth in 1971. Rick missed a second chance at facing Yanagida on the international stage—forfeiting his spot on the 1970 team to Behm and kept off the 1971 World Team to Bulgaria by USWF decision makers.[13]

Was Sanders kept from competing to ease the way for a Roderick protégé (Keller)? Was Sanders too much of an embarrassment risk to take abroad for the USWF? Roderick, as executive director of the fledgling organization, was the paramount decision maker. His philosophy, on appointment to the post, was, "We, as an organization, must always make our decisions based upon what will be best for the wrestler and for the sport of wrestling in general." Clearly, Roderick placed more emphasis on the sport than the individual athlete, as far as it concerned Ricky Sanders and the 1971 Pan Ams, the Bulgaria World Championships, the Tbilisi, or the world class competition in advance of the '72 Olympics. Wrestling was Sanders' identity. He was unparalleled on the mat, but he wound up losing to the establishment at Annapolis, not even given a chance.

The neophyte USWF Director, on the other hand, may not have appreciated the perilous predicament Rick had him in. A lawsuit by a resolute Sanders could have buried the impecunious one-year-old United

States Wrestling Federation. Some conjecture is warranted. Certainly, a successful coach does not always make the best rookie administrator, especially if they tend to micromanage. Myron Roderick put a lot of energy into the USWF. The organization continued to battle with the AAU over the next several years for status as the National Governing Body for wrestling in the United States. Roderick's tenure lasted five years when, in 1974, he unexpectedly resigned.[14]

Roderick's leadership philosophy had merit. The USWF continued to evolve into what is today U.S.A. Wrestling. The AAU ultimately lost the National Governing Body battle to the USWF, and Roderick led the early charge. But he was not immune to poor decisions, even when made ostensibly in defense of the greater good. Roderick's vituperative regard for Rick Sanders and the manner in which he prosecuted that unhealthy attitude was cavalier, mean spirited, and pernicious. In short, he seems to have acted as a prejudicial bully. The USWF, Doug Blubaugh, Ed Peery, and Roderick continued to prosper in their respective careers. Sanders, on the other hand, needed to slow down for the times. Rick was a twenty-six-year-old late adolescent, on his own, searching for adulthood. He possessed supreme talent, but was best handled under the likes of an avuncular Bill Smith or Bill Farrell who, perhaps, employed similar methodologies to those used with ADHD athletes of today. Notwithstanding his two arrests, for which he paid fines and reconciled with the State, Sanders was deprived of valuable international experience that could have served the team effort at Munich. To be sure, more egregious was Sanders' exclusion from the family he identified with, flourished in, and found meaning: the culture and the brotherhood of wrestling.

Chapter Twelve

Rick's challenges continued when, in January of 1972, his mother Anita died of a heart attack while visiting her son David Stockner's home. She was a chain smoker and had been suffering from ovarian cancer. At age 63, she was kind, loving, and had many close friends, according to Kay Hirons, Sanders' half-sister. "She loved her part of being a mom and was proud of Rick's accomplishments," Kay explained. Rick's sister Patricia chuckled when she recalled how Rick would practice wrestling moves with Anita on their apartment balcony.

Anita never remarried after the divorce from Melvin. She always resided in downtown Portland in the area known as the Park Blocks. Anita, despite being always self-reliant, never owned a car or learned how to drive. She learned of the national and international exploits of her son largely through a network of friends and acquaintances. Rarely did Anita see Rick compete.[1] He understood. She was on her own, as was he. While Anita was not a church-goer, at graveside, Rick hugged a grieving Patricia, affirming, "It's okay Patricia; Mom believed."

The 1972 Winter Olympics were held in February. Japan hosted its first Winter Olympics at Sapporo. The United States won eight medals, four of those in women's speed skating. Anne Henning won a gold and a bronze in the 500 meters and 1000 meters respectively, and Dianne Holum won gold in the 1500 meters and silver in the 3000 meters. Coincidentally, Ard Schenk of the Netherlands, a three-time gold medal winner in the speed skating sprints, is a cousin to Henk Schenk, the U.S. 220- pound freestyle wrestler at the Summer games in Munich. The Winter and Summer games were held in the same year until 1994 when Lillehammer, Norway began the tradition of hosting the Winter Games on alternating years from the Summer games.

Second wave feminism maintained its momentum from the 1960s with the U.S. Senate passage of the Equal Rights Amendment in February of 1972. The initiative stalled when less than the requisite 38 states ratified the proposed amendment. Passage of the federal legislation remains an issue fifty years later. The movement spawned the passage of Title IX of the Civil Rights law in June of 1972. Title IX, a federal civil rights law passed as part of the education amendments of 1972, prohibits sex-based discrimination in any school or other education program that receives federal money.[2] This legislation would heavily influence U.S. wrestling. To be in compliance with the law, myriad collegiate NCAA wrestling programs were eliminated. A 2003 *New York Times* editorial by celebrated author and longtime wrestling coach John Irving reported a loss of 134 NCAA wrestling programs between 1982 and 2001. Marquette University lost its program as a result of Title IX, though the wrestling program was completely financed by alumni and outside supporters.[3]

The NCAA tournament was held at the University of Maryland in March of 1972. Iowa State, setting a wrestling attendance record of over 10,000 fans in a dual with Oklahoma State in January, won the tournament by 30 points over Michigan State. Reminiscent of Rick Sanders in his unorthodox style, Wade Schalles at 150 pounds of Clarion State was named most outstanding wrestler.[4]

Sanders: In the Moment

The Spring baseball season was delayed in April of 1972 when both the American and National league teams voted to strike. The impasse between owners and players was over pensions. It was the first labor strike by professional baseball players' unions. Salaries were not much of an issue. Player salaries in 1972 averaged $167,000 per year. The average American worker's salary was $11,800; gasoline was 55 cents a gallon. Sanders probably never made $10,000 over his lifetime or thought a thing about it.

Also in July of 1972, the USWF selected Stillwater, Oklahoma as site for the National Amateur Wrestling Hall of Fame. Oklahoma State University donated land and architectural services to advance the $350,000 project. The Hall planned to feature a library of sports books and films, an Honors Court recognizing wrestling's notable figures, and a museum tracing the development of wrestling. The building would also serve as the national headquarters of the USWF—at the time in its third year of existence under Director Myron Roderick.

Rick continued to work out and compete for the Multnomah Athletic Club as well as in the Portland State wrestling room, assisting new head coach Don Conway. The MAC continued to cover travel expenses to freestyle tournaments and duals arranged by the USWF with Russian and Japanese national teams. The USWF was still at odds with the AAU as to who held more sway as the exclusive U.S. representative for international wrestling. Sanders won a 5-1 decision against a Russian opponent at 125.5 at an exhibition dual at Kent State on March 22nd. He went on to Hofstra College two days later and wrestled to a draw with the same Russian.[6]

Rick then traveled back to Stillwater to compete in the annual USWF national tournament. The Japanese national team was in town to compete in the open tournament. Sanders, wrestling at 136.5, was annihilated 14-2 by Abe of Japan. The defeat may have been the most lopsided loss of his

Sanders: In the Moment

TOP U. S. A. WRESTLERS in the U. S. Wrestling Federation National Open Freestyle Championships (L-R)—Joe Cliffe, 105.5, Daley; Robert Dieli, 114.5, Ohio W.C.; Don Behm, 125.5, Daley; Rick Sanders, 136.5, Portland, Ore. BACK: Wayne Wells, 163, Okla. City W.C.; Fred Fozzard, 180.5, Oklahoma City W.C.; Russ Hellickson, 198, Daley; Buck Deadrich, 220, Olympic Club; Jeff Smith, Hwt., Southland W.C. (Dave Maple, 149.5, Northern Ill., not in picture).

Yanagida became Sanders' world class nemesis.

career. But he came back 14-8 to beat Gene Davis for second place. Don Behm, wrestling at 125.5, won a silver at the same tournament, losing a 2-1 decision to Hideaki Yanagida—Japan's two-time World Champion and a favorite for gold at Munich. Over the next week, Yanagida won four exhibition duals. Behm lost 5-0 to Yanagida at Memphis, Sanders' injury defaulted to him at Chattanooga, Dale Brumit was decisioned 12-0 at Birmingham by Yanagida, and finally, Yanagida decisioned Rick again at Baton Rouge 6-3. *The Oregonian* reported results of the LSU match: "Yanagida was very effective with single-leg take downs and built up a 6-1 lead in the first three-minute period. Rick came back strong in the last three minutes, got a two-point "tilt" (rolled his foe into a near pin position) with :16 seconds left and was trying for a win when the clock ran out."[7]

Yanagida became Sanders' world class nemesis. Yanagida was two years younger than Sanders and, at 5'3", about one inch shorter than Rick. He was coached by Yojiro Uetake, a three-time Oklahoma State NCAA D-I champion. Uetake, wrestling for Japan, won gold medals at the 1964 and 1968 Olympics. As Uetake's protégé, Yanagida was talented, quick, and well coached. Uetake said of Yanagida prior to the 1972 Olympics: "I'm sure he's going to win at Munich. He's so tough and quick it's hard for him not to win." High praise from a coach who never lost a match while competing for Oklahoma State. Uetake continued, "People in the United States have never seen a wrestler move like him, really."[8] Sanders had his hands full with Yanagida, who destroyed all those in his path. PSU teammate Masaru Yatabe felt Rick always gave Yanagida and Japanese wrestlers in general too much respect. The lightweight Japanese wrestlers were quick and technically sound, but more harmful to Sanders was that he allowed Yanagida's reputation to get in his head. Yatabe saw Sanders' less than confident approach when wrestling Yanagida.[9]

Sanders: In the Moment

Rick next found himself at the annual national AAU tournament at John Carroll University in Cleveland, Ohio, April 12th-14th. The AAU nationals were still a viable venue for high-level freestyle competition despite the emergence of the USWF. There were many familiar faces at the 1972 tournament including Sergio Gonzalez, Wayne Wells, Wayne Baughman, Buck Deadrich, and Henk Schenk. Rick took second in the 136.5-pound weight class. In his final appearance at the AAU and representing the venerable Multnomah Athletic Club, Rick finished runner-up in 1972 to Tetsu Ikeno who was wrestling for the New York Athletic Club. Sanders wrestled in six AAU national championship matches during his career. He won four and was runner-up twice. He skipped 1968, focusing on the Mexico City Olympics, and 1969, the year he became the first World Champion for the United States at the World Championships in Mar del Plata, Argentina. John Miller, also competing for the MAC, won the 125.5-pound championship. Miller and Sanders would compete weeks later at the Olympic trials.[10]

The private athletic club sponsorship of wrestling was vibrant during Sanders' career. Later on, clubs such as the San Francisco Olympic Club, Portland's Multnomah Athletic Club, Chicago's Mayor Daley Youth Foundation, and the venerable New York Athletic Club began to emphasize more popular sports of a new era. Sanders, among others, learned how to wrestle the international freestyle and Greco-Roman styles at these clubs. The private clubs were integral in developing the competitiveness of Americans on the world stage. Without sponsorship, few wrestlers would have overcome the financial hurdles to compete at distant tournaments. Other entities sponsored wrestlers—colleges, independent wrestling clubs, and Army and Air Force sponsorship. But in Sanders' era, athletic clubs served as the backbone for competition.

By the 1980s, while club emphasis on wrestling began to wane, AAU wrestling would lose support as well. After a significant history of anemic support for wrestling, the AAU would be replaced by The United States Wrestling Federation. FILA no longer debated whether the AAU or USWF should be the representative organization for the United States. Years of wrangling by those committed to improving America's wrestling prowess in international competition would finally come to fruition.[11] The AAU was feeble financial support for tournaments or the individual athlete. The annual AAU national tournament, in its heyday, had a reputation as prestigious as the collegiate national tournaments. However, it was the venerable clubs providing the annual impetus for the AAU National Tournament success, not the AAU itself.

The San Francisco Olympic Club (SFOC), for example, sent twenty-three athletes to the 1924 Olympic Games in Paris. The SFOC acquired a couple golf courses through the years and sponsored the U.S. Open Golf Tournament in 1955, 1966, 1998, and 2012. The SFOC was also the venue for Portland's Multnomah Club to win its only national team wrestling championship. Sanders won his first AAU national championship at that tournament in 1965. SFOC's wrestling program was discontinued as club interest turned more to golf and leisure sports. Moreover, area colleges began to add wrestling teams to their athletic programs—some even provided sponsorship to AAU and USWF freestyle tournaments. Despite their withdrawal from wrestling, the SFOC sports a rich legacy as the patron for many U.S. Olympic and World Team members such as Buck Deadrich, Mike Gallego, Ron Finley, Jim Burke, and Russ Camilleri—all contemporaries of Rick Sanders.[12]

The Mayor Daley Youth Foundation, located in Chicago, was another huge seedbed for U.S. sponsored wrestlers. Mexico City Olympian Werner Holzer, another of Sanders' international teammates, co-founded the MDYF in 1965. When Holzer learned the AAU was not going to finance the 1967 U.S. World Team trip to New Delhi, India, he sought an audience with Chicago Mayor Richard J. Daley who agreed to pay half the required funding. Later, Holzer transcended from an athlete to an advocate in his zealous campaign to form USA Wrestling, the current governing body for amateur wrestling in the U.S. Five MDYF wrestlers competed at the 1968 Mexico City Olympics, including Don Behm and Bobby Douglas, close friends of Sanders. Terry McCann, 1960 Olympic gold medalist, served as a volunteer coach at the MDYF. His teams won eleven national titles during his seven-year tenure. McCann wrestled at 125.5 pounds at the 1960 Rome Olympics, the same weight Sanders wrestled at Mexico City in 1968 and Munich in 1972. Clearly, plenty of U.S. wrestlers gained experience in freestyle and Greco, the international wrestling styles, through the auspices of the MDYF.[13]

Today, the New York Athletic Club is the only private club of the earlier era that continues to sponsor wrestling. The NYAC was founded in 1868. Its members have competed in every Olympics since 1900, except the U.S. boycotted 1980 Olympics. Doug Blubaugh, Bobby Weaver, and Bruce Baumgartner—all Olympic gold medalists—were members while active. Bill Farrell, Sanders' coach at Munich in 1972, was the club's wrestling coach from 1960-1972. Farrell ultimately became president of the NYAC. The club now sponsors both men's and women's wrestling. Active wrestlers include Adeline Gray, Sarah Hildebrandt, and Adam Coon. The women's wrestling coach is former NCAA champion, and Sanders' 1967 NCAA D-I semi-finals opponent, Tadaaki Hatta.[14]

While not all aspiring Olympic wrestlers lived proximate to a MAC-type club or had the good fortune to be members, the buildup to the 1972 Olympic trials was an equitable endeavor. Thirty-five district tournaments were held throughout the United States from January 1st to June 5th.

Every interested wrestler in the country could try out. Moreover, wrestlers could compete at multiple tournaments in order to qualify and move on. Olympic coach Bill Farrell was interested in wrestlers gaining as much freestyle experience as possible through the elimination tournaments. In addition, Coach Farrell arranged a three-and-a-half-day pre-camp for top Olympic prospects. The pre-camp was held May 26th-29th at St. Andrews, Tennessee. Sixty-three of the top Olympic prospects were invited. The United States Olympic Committee sponsored room and board, but wrestlers needed private donations to pay for travel. Farrell, the 1969 and 1970 World Team coach, preferred the shorter mini-camp equivalent to longer camps, as techniques shown could be taken home, digested, and practiced before the next competition, presumably the Olympic trials. His methodology seemed to pay dividends, as nine of the ten ultimate Olympic freestyle wrestlers, including Sanders, attended the mini-camp.[15]

The final team trials were held at Anoka, Minnesota, a suburb of Minneapolis, June 22nd-24th. Anoka High School served as the venue. Four hundred and thirty-three entries competed—294 in freestyle and 139 in Greco-Roman. The top two finishers at district tournaments were eligible to compete in freestyle. In addition, the top two NCAA finalists, the top three USAWA Nationals finalists, the top three USWF Nationals finalists, the top two Armed Forces tournament finalists, the top two NCAA College finalists, the top two NAIA Nationals finalists, the NJCAA champion, and the YMCA national champion were eligible to compete at Anoka.[16]

Dave and Jim Hazewinkel were pleased with the venue selection, as Anoka High School was their alma mater. The Hazewinkel twins competed in Greco-Roman, and both made the Olympic team in that style. It was only necessary to show up at the final trials to compete in Greco-

Roman. The international Greco-Roman style took longer to gel in the United States. Foreign countries emphasize freestyle and Greco-Roman wrestling in their programs. The United States, on the other hand, focuses on folkstyle wrestling in high school and college programs. International freestyle wrestling is more like folkstyle than Greco-Roman. Consequently, fewer U.S. wrestlers compete in Greco-Roman, preferring the more familiar freestyle form.

The Hazewinkels, along with Russell Camilleri, Wayne Baughman, and J. Robinson, were early groundbreakers in Greco-Roman. Steven Fraser would become the first American to win an Olympic gold in Greco, doing so at 198 pounds in 1984 at Los Angeles. Mike Houck followed with a World Championship in 1985 at Kolbotn, Norway, competing at 198 pounds.

Wayne Baughman and J. Robinson had the most success in Greco-Roman wrestling at Munich, making it to the third round before being eliminated. Both men would continue to do great work for American wrestling and establish lasting legacies in the coaching ranks. Four years later, Major Baughman would coach the 1976 Olympic freestyle team at Montreal in a five-medal performance—one gold, three silver, and one bronze.[18]

Representing the United States in freestyle was a more arduous journey in 1972, requiring multiple rounds of competition. The top three place winners in both styles qualified for the final training camps, from which the two U.S. teams were chosen through challenge matches. Sanders, Don Behm, and Donald Fay finished first, second, and third respectively in the first round of tournament action at 125.5 pounds.

The fourth, fifth, and sixth place winners in the Anoka tournament qualified for a pre-camp tournament held July 24th-26th at Williams Arena on the campus of the University of Minnesota in downtown

Sanders: In the Moment

Minneapolis. The winner qualified as the number four candidate for a potential berth on the freestyle team. Seven other wrestlers who missed the qualifying tournament at Anoka for medical reasons were also invited by the Olympic Wrestling Committee to compete in the pre-camp tournament. The number of wrestlers advancing ensured that, if necessary, a replacement wrestler would be ready to compete for the final Olympic team. Moreover, top-flite wrestlers were necessary as workout partners.[19]

The pre-camp competitors at 125.5 pounds were John Miller, Multnomah Athletic Club; Brad Jacot, University of Washington; and James Abbott, Racine, Wisconsin. Abbott emerged to compete in the challenge matches. Donald Fay, from NYAC, then won the best two out of three over Abbott. Don Behm then won handily over Fay in the best of three. Finally, Sanders and Behm met in Williams Arena at the University of Minnesota for the Olympic spot at 125.5 pounds.

Of course, both Behm and Sanders were already Olympians. Each won silver medals at the 1968 Mexico City Olympics—Behm at 125.5 and Sanders at 114.5. Now, however, they were both competing for the 57kg (125.5 pound) bantamweight spot. Behm, speaking with a reporter, admitted, "I've got probably the toughest weight class. Just between Sanders and I, there are ten international medals in the class. No other weight has so many medals." Don added, "Whoever makes one mistake is going to be sitting home. I've wrestled that guy 15 times now, and we're so evenly matched that we've had eight draws. He's beaten me one more time than I've beaten him."[20]

Behm's analysis on the quality of the competition at 125.5 may have been slightly misleading. True that it was perhaps the toughest weight class, but only because he and Sanders were in it. Behm beat Don Fay of the NYAC, the third-place wrestler at the trials, 15-0 and 10-2 to reach Sanders.

Sanders: In the Moment

The Sanders/Behm match was clearly the marquee matchup of the trials. Stan Dziedzic, runner-up to Wayne Wells and future world champion, says the final match between Sanders and Behm was probably the best match he's ever seen. "These two were so highly competitive, it was a fantastic match to watch."[21]

But first, the two gladiators needed to make weight. Behm offers the following anecdote:

"We both hate making weight and we had to be at scratch weight. Both sitting in the steam room, Sanders all of a sudden says, 'Is this a weight losing contest or a wrestling contest?' I knew I was on, having checked before entering the steam room. I assumed Ricky was on or close. But, of course, he always left much to chance. I followed Rick into the steam room knowing he needed attention. We were friends off the mat. When the whistle blew, we're competitors full on. Rick was babbling, I listened. Anyway, we both agree it was about wrestling and not about cutting weight. He says, 'Okay, let's forget about this steam room stuff and not make weight for our match. What are they going to do—take the third-place guy? I don't think so!'

I agree with him.

We leave the steam room and go get something to eat and drink. Coach Farrell was having Bill Weick weigh-in each of the wrestlers. After a while we go over to Weick and he asks, 'When do you fellas want to weigh in?' We tell him, 'In a little while,' and we go have some more to eat and drink. A couple hours later we see Bill and tell him we're ready now.' And take off for the locker room scales. Sanders races into the locker room and jumps on the scales and the needle goes way up past 125. I jump on right after him and the needle does the same. Weick comes walking into the locker room just as I'm jumping off—and headed to the water cooler as Sanders had just done. Weick asks Sanders, 'Did you make weight?' Yep! Says Sanders guzzling down more water. He looks at me and I say, 'Yea he did.' Then he asks me, 'Behm did you make 125?' Yep! I say, and Sanders backs me up. Weick gives us both a funny look and says, 'Okay, let's go wrestle.'"[22]

Sanders: In the Moment

Sanders and Behm were veteran weight loss specialists. There was nothing untoward about their agreement at the '72 trials. They had met their obligation regarding the weight loss sufferfest associated with wrestling. Their mutual decision was a marvelous example of trust and a remarkable friendship steeped in the culture.

Bill Farrell remembers the Sanders/Behm match as, "The hardest-fought of all the challenge matches—very, very close. No one ever backed up or stalled. They could have gone either way. The two of them were amongst the best in the world."[23]

Mark Lieberman, just a teenager at the time, remembers, "While Behm and Sanders were going at it, Dan Gable was wrestling his final wrestle-off on an adjoining mat. Hardly anyone was watching his match, including Dan. Dan would ride on top, control his guy and keep looking at the Sanders/Behm match. It was incredible!"[24]

The matches were three periods of three minutes each, separated by two one-minute rest periods (3-1-3-1-3). Sergio Gonzalez was Rick's corner man. Jeff Callard, a three-time NCAA All-American from Oklahoma, was in Don's corner. Callard was a former high school wrestler from East Lansing, Michigan who had been coached by Behm. Callard remembers the match as extremely close, with both wrestlers working the center of the mat, and both wrestlers working out of several plank positions, avoiding dropping a knee to give up a takedown point. A plank position is simply a pushup position frequently used by lightweight wrestlers to avoid a takedown. Callard, who went on to earn a Ph.D. in engineering, explained that lightweight wrestlers possess greater strength-to-weight ratios than do heavier wrestlers and therefore find themselves more often in the defensive plank position.

In the closing seconds of the match, with the score tied, Sanders exploded for a go-behind, throwing in his legs on Behm's plank position and simultaneously knocking Behm's elbows out. Behm went flat, giving up the takedown point to Rick as time expired.[25]

Stunning in his audacity, execution, and timing, Sanders was going to Munich.

Since Sanders beat Behm at Anoka, he only had to defeat Behm once at the wrestle-offs. Scoring a takedown with seconds left, Sanders decisioned Behm 2-1 to win the 125.5-pound Olympic team berth. Behm surmised, "It was a crowning moment in my career. Even though I lost, I was, and forever will be, part of one of the best wrestling matches ever!"[26]

With the match concluded, the 1972 Olympic Games U.S. freestyle team was set: Sergio Gonzalez at 105.5, Jimmy Carr at 114.5, Rick Sanders at 125.5, Gene Davis at 136.5, Dan Gable at 149.5, Wayne Wells at 163, John Peterson at 180.5, Ben Peterson at 198, Henk Schenk at 220, and Chris Taylor at +220. Coach Farrell asked Behm to join the team as an alternate and chaperone for Sanders. Behm agreed to assume the Olympic challenge.[27]

The 1972 Olympic training camp continued at Williams Arena on the University of Minnesota campus from July 27th until departure for Washington D.C., where athletes coalesced prior to traveling to Munich. The Williams Arena, part of the University of Minnesota's downtown campus, was arranged as the pre-Olympic camp. The university was chosen in part because of its new state-of-the-art athletic facility, offering space for six wrestling mats on which to hold challenge matches. Unfortunately, the new facility was not finished. Williams Arena, with space for only two mats, would suffice.

Coach Farrell held double and triple practices daily during the training pre-camp. The intensity of the practices continued up to the move to Washington, D.C. Farrell noted his philosophy on the need for compulsory team practices prior to the Games. Elite athletes in other sports as well as wrestling were often of a mind to follow their own individual practice routines—either more or less intense than that of team practices. Farrell left nothing to chance regarding the 1972 Olympic team. He was familiar with the months-long training schedules of the Soviet and Eastern European wrestlers. The U.S., by comparison, played catch-up to be on par for international competition, though the Soviets counter-claimed that U.S. collegiate wrestling mirrored the Soviet program.

There was a wide range of practice experience between members of the U.S. team. Jimmy Carr, the 114.5-pound team member, was a seventeen-year-old familiar with high school level practices, though he had already competed in the 1971 World Games and gone undefeated in a European exhibition tour. Dan Gable and the Peterson brothers were heralded as training fanatics, conducting individual workouts in addition to the three-a-days.

Rick, in contrast, had a reputation for not training very hard. It was a claim Rick cared little about—and, in fact, seemed to foster with lifestyle choices and his affinity for personal freedom that bloomed ever more robustly around 1969. However, Sergio Gonzales emphatically disputed the claim. "Rick always tried to give the impression he didn't train very hard. That was just part of his mind games," Sergio recalled.[34] In a David Zang article written for *Amateur Wrestling News*, 1972 Assistant Olympic Training Coach Jim Peckham recalled a day in training camp where wrestlers were scheduled to run stadium steps: "Ricky Sanders did nothing but complain and moan and groan and whine and bitch. But, when the team finished, everyone came down to the field except Sanders and Gonzalez. Ricky and Sergio did it again," said Peckham. "Then Sergio dropped out and Sanders did them again."[35]

The steps leading up to the University of Minnesota Gopher Football Stadium, located across the street from Williams Arena, were Coach

Sanders: In the Moment

Farrell's favorite team workout venue, according to John Peterson, the 180.5- pound team member. John reflected on Sanders' effort at the training camp. "It was very hot at the Minnesota camp. I remember Rick Sanders as a very hard worker. He trained harder than most of us. He taught me all kinds of single leg counters. His lifestyle wasn't the best, but he did have a more serious side. We had some good talks about the Bible and he had some genuine interest in that area. My brother wasn't real happy with him, though, especially the loud boom box that he carried around. Ben would go over and turn it down or off. Minutes later, Rick with this little smirk of a smile on his face, would turn it right back up again."[28]

Jeff Callard remembers Rick because of his free spirit, and admired him. Rick showed Callard how to whittle beads out of sumac wood. Sanders' long hair and beard was an expression of personal freedom that appealed to Callard, who was just finishing his freshman year at the University of Oklahoma. Rick accented his hirsute countenance with wooden bead necklaces, sometimes completed with an adorning pot pipe. Rick admitted to Oregonian reporter Leo Davis, "I carve beads to keep my hands busy so I won't smoke. I wear them as a symbol of triumph, not as a protest."[29]

Rick's easygoing appearance may have contributed to the rumors of his lax training efforts, at least domestically. The hair rule did not apply in international competition, and West Coast wrestlers were often bearded and wore their hair long as was the style of the era. In addition to Sanders, West Coast Olympians Buck Deadrich and Sergio Gonzalez were long haired, bearded, and mustachioed. Gonzalez observed, "Sanders grew the long hair and beard, but had none of the tattoos that adorn many athletes and even high school wrestlers today."[30] According to Callard, Buck and

Sergio got the same treatment as Sanders for brushing up against the hair rule.[31]

Gonzalez' long hair served him well in reserve. At an early morning Olympic weigh-in, the U.S. 105.5 pounder was 100 grams over weight with sixty seconds to go before being forced to forfeit. Coach Farrell instructed manager Bill Wieck to cut Sergio's thick locks. Gonzalez made weight with seconds to spare, albeit still sporting the mustache.[32]

In Sanders' case, the beard was a rather new effect in appearance. Rick was clean shaven earlier in the year when he competed in the USWF national tournament held March 31st-April 1st at Stillwater, Oklahoma. Prior to the USWF nationals, he wrestled in two Russian dual meets, and after nationals, he competed in two duals against the Japanese National team on April 5th and 10th. Rick downplayed the beard, saying to a reporter, "You can't imagine how good it feels not to face a razor every morning of your life."[33] Sanders needed that early morning "good feeling" relief, because coach Farrell's Olympic practices in the Minnesota summer heat and humidity were withering.

Ben Peterson, 1972 Olympian, reflected on the buildup to the '72 Olympics. Brothers John and Ben worked out with already-legendary Dan Gable. Gable would reference a wrestling coaching point by saying, "This is a 'Sanders' technique," before the Petersons knew Sanders. Ben witnessed both the epic Don Behm/Rick Sanders Olympic Trials matches at Anoka and the Behm/Sanders wrestle off at the 1970 World Trials at Superior, Wisconsin. On both occasions, Ben distinctly remembers wondering if he could ever perform at that level; the action was so intense.[36] At the Olympic training camp on the University of Minnesota campus, Gable took the Petersons on a "Sanders workout"—running around trees, hanging on to them, first one arm then the other. Pleasant, unorthodox, freedom-loving movement.

Sanders: In the Moment

John Peterson agreed that Rick's workouts were unorthodox, but effective. Observing Sanders one day running with one foot on the sidewalk and one in the gutter, John asked, "Why are you running like that?" Rick replied, "To give my hips more flexibility."[37] Behm labeled the practice the "Sanders' expansion and contraction theory."[38]

Gene Davis, 1972 Olympian with Sanders, observed, "Rick had super strong legs and could run forever."

Contrasting his style with Gable's, Rick told Leo Davis of the *Oregonian*, "Gable isn't as relaxed as I am—that's something I learned from the Russians. He shoots more, I wait and counter. He wrestles the same way I used to in college—balls out, trying to overpower people. He'll learn, though, and if he stays around, he'll be great."[39] Candid, as well as prescient, Sanders' analysis was spot on. Sanders, as noted, was unorthodox in training as in competition.

When asked by Davis about concerns, Rick responded, "Who am I concerned with? Me, I'm concerned about proper diet, and sleep, and mental attitude. But the guy I'll have to beat finally is that Japanese stud, Yanagida. Every day I go out there assuming this is the day—sooner or later it's gonna be me and him."[40]

Chapter Thirteen

The International Olympic Committee gave the nod to Munich, Germany as host for the 1972 Summer Olympic Games. The 1966 nomination denied Detroit, Michigan the host opportunity. The Motor City was making its seventh bid to host the Games, but once again fell short. Munich, after all, was home to Bavarian Motor Works (BMW), its own high-end automobile manufacturer, but also was home to a major German University, and to Germany's movie industry. In addition, Munich promoters claimed merits such as a beautiful, tranquil landscape, plenty of clean air, and salubrious climate—all somewhat the antithesis of Detroit, Michigan in 1972.[41]

Munich had roughly six years to get ready for the Olympic party. Organizers promised improvements over Mexico City—shorter travel distances for athletes from the Olympic Village to competition venues, forward-looking innovative architecture that included an expansive tent-like glass roof covering several of the competition venues, the most carefree and happy-go-lucky Olympics in history, and the least expansive and expensive Olympics to date. The carefree and happy-go-lucky pitch was an effort to displace the memory of Germany's 1936 Olympics held under the Nazi regime of Adolf Hitler.[42]

The Olympic site was roughly four kilometers (2.4 miles) north of Munich city center. Just the right distance to dissuade the vastly heightened criminality expected. Officials anticipated an inundation of pick pockets, auto thieves, hotel "cat burglars," aggressive prostitutes, vandals, drug dealers, and other hooligans. Athletes were housed in apartments surrounded by a six-and-a-half-foot chain link fence, though no retardant barbed wire topped the easily-scaled fence. Reflective of the era, 3000 apartments were allocated to male athletes, 1800 for females.[43]

German officials wanted to avoid any reminders of the 1936 Nazi-sponsored Olympics, where Hitler stationed armed soldiers directly in public spaces, hoping to propagandize Germany's strength prior to WWII. To that end, security personnel did not carry weapons and were dressed pleasantly, colored in blue, green, and orange pastels. In the interest of presenting a "convivial image" to the world, uniformed forces were stationed well away from the Olympic grounds. After the first two or three days, nighttime patrols were scaled back. Ironically, the effort to make Munich '72 different from Berlin '36 made it easier for Palestinian terrorists to kidnap Israeli athletes and coaches on September 5th, the ninth day of the Olympics. Security posed no threat to the terrorists because security personnel were not on site. The double irony was the Munich slogan—"The Cheerful Games."[44]

The German Olympic Committee was not unaware of potential extremist threats, according to author David Clay Large in his book *Munich 1972*. Several terrorist organizations were active during the era: Germany's own RAF or Bader-Meinhof group, the Irish Republican Army (IRA), the Italian Mafia, a Basque separatist group known as ETA, and finally, Black September—the Palestinian terrorist group that was destined to assassinate eleven Israeli Olympic athletes. In advance of the games, security officials employed a police psychologist, Georg Sieber, to develop a risk analysis on twenty-six terror groups. The Palestinian Black September group was #21. "Threat scenario number 21 involved twelve armed Palestinian commandos scaling the perimeter of the Olympic Village, invading the Israeli team compound, taking a number of hostages, and threatening to kill those hostages unless Arab political prisoners were freed from Israeli jails and the Palestinian commandos flown to safety in some Arab-friendly capital. Even if the Palestinians failed in their primary mission, warned Sieber, they would undoubtedly make a bloody mess of the Munich Games and on no account would they surrender alive." Manfried Schreiber, Munich's police chief, felt Sieber's scenarios too far-fetched. To be sure, they seemed extreme, but, as it turned out, almost exactly true.[45]

The 80-thousand-seat Olympic stadium and adjoining sports complex were covered by the tent-like glass roof, modeling the futuristic theme. Ongoing problems with the roof added to the overall expense of the '72 Games. The Munich Olympics ultimately became the most expensive Olympics yet—three times that of Mexico City. Germany used proceeds from its nationwide T.V. lottery to pay much of the cost. The television rights, paid for by ABC, covered some of the cost as well. Coca Cola won the bid as the official Olympic soft-drink, and that revenue helped pay expenses. Finally, homegrown shoe manufacturers Adidas and Puma, as in Mexico City, threw in some sponsorship money to defray some of Germany's cost in hosting the 1972 Olympic Games.[46]

The Games of the twentieth Olympiad began on August 26th. Seven thousand one hundred thirty-one athletes from 121 teams attended—more than ever before. Five hundred people made up the American delegation.

As in Mexico City, none of Sanders' family was present. Rick roomed with Don Behm and Sergio Gonzalez. In less than a couple of days, their room could only be described, according to Behm, as a "pig-

Sanders: In the Moment

Sanders at Munich ready to wrestle.

sty."[1] People came and went, workout gear hung about the premises drying, and empties littered the common areas. Coaches were unconcerned, focused instead on adhering to schedules and protocol. The evening of the opening ceremony, wrestlers were required to be dressed in U.S. formal wear for the opening march into the Olympic stadium. Unfortunately, Jimmy Carr, the seventeen-year-old 114.5-pound American phenom, was nowhere to be found. Thinking fast, Sanders and Chris Taylor—the U.S. mammoth heavyweight freestyle and Greco wrestler—insisted Behm wear Jimmy's blazer and join the parade. And so, Behm joined Sanders and Gonzalez in what turned out to be the front row of the U.S. delegation. The Three Musketeers took part in the opening ceremonial parade while Jimmy toured Munich with his parents.[2]

Jim Peckham and Bill Weick were assistant coaches with Bill Farrell at Munich. Peckham was a 1956 Olympian in Greco-Roman wrestling. He coached at Emerson College in Boston, Massachusetts and at Harvard. Over a thirty-year career, he coached three world championship teams and was head coach for the Greco-Roman Olympic team at the 1976 Montreal Olympics. Weick was a two-time NCAA national champion and went on to a phenomenal coaching career at multiple levels. His high school teams in Illinois won 749 duals against 112 losses over his career. Weick was on the Olympic coaching staff for freestyle again in 1980, 1984, and 1988, and worked with the Greco-Roman team in 1976.[3]

Russ Houk was team manager for the freestyle team. His myriad duties included managing mail, food, video tapes, projectors, commuter bus schedules, laundry, equipment, dope tests, bout sheets, etc. A successful wrestling coach is intimate with every detail necessary for a successful tournament campaign. That awareness is what Houk contributed at Munich. Houk was wrestling coach at Pennsylvania's Bloomsburg College for fourteen years. In that time, he compiled a dual meet record of 142-34-2. His teams won three NAIA national championships. Just as credible was the success of his summer wrestling camps, begun in 1962, that drew the likes of Wayne Wells, John and Ben Peterson, Dan Gable, Don Behm, Chris Taylor, Wade Schalles, Gray Simons, Stan Dziedzic, and Rick Sanders.[4]

Freestyle wrestling began the first day following the opening ceremony. Matches were held in Ringer-Judo-Halle, the only building newly built for the 1972 Olympics. The busy freestyle competition held Sanders' stereotyped profligate behavior partially in check. Yet, according to a David Zang article written for *Amateur Wrestling News* twenty-five years after Munich, "When Assistant Coach Peckham entered Sanders' room a few days before the first competition, he found empty beer bottles littering the floor and Sanders in bed with two women. 'Ricky, don't cross me on this,' Peckham scolded. 'I want those two women out of here now.' When he returned the next day, he found that Sanders had followed orders exactly. 'If I hadn't seen it, I don't know if I'd believe it,' Peckham said, his head still wagging in disbelief twenty-five years later. 'He was in bed with two more'."[5] While the story may have a measure of authenticity, it didn't happen before freestyle wrestling was completed, according to Don Behm.

As team captain at Munich, Wayne Wells observed, "Frankly, Rick Sanders was doing things in the Village that he'd probably get arrested for. I'd bang on the wall at night in no uncertain terms, telling Rick to get his ass to bed. Shut that music off. He had the girls over there and they were—I'm pretty sure—smoking dope."[6]

It is difficult to understand Sanders' licentious behavior at such a pivotal time in his career, when it could have easily compromised the U.S. freestyle team effort. He may have been exhibiting some form of oppositional defiance related to being banned by the USWF in 1971. On the other hand, perhaps he simply felt at ease in the company of women, and not particularly concerned with the early rounds of competition. Rick was an insomniac, perhaps exacerbated by ADHD. He busied himself in nocturnal activities.

Rick was well aware that his toughest opponent would likely come in the later rounds. That wrestler was Hideaki Yanagida from Japan. He was quite aware of Sanders' ability as well and, like Rick, anticipated the expected match with some trepidation. The two world champions had met twice previously, Yanagida prevailing by Sanders' injury default in their first match and in a second match by a 6-3 decision. The two might have met more often if not for Sanders' decision to forfeit his 125.5-pound spot on the 1970 world team and his exclusion from the 1971 world team trials by the USWF. Perhaps Rick might have figured out how to more effectively handle Yanagida, who had also won the 1970 Asian Games at 57 kgs. Of course, Yanagida would have had the same opportunity vis a vis Sanders, had the two wrestled more frequently. Yet in the words of Myron Roderick summarizing the 1972 Olympic wrestling performance, "Experience—international experience, against the best in the rest of the world—is the answer. The only answer to wrestling success at the international level."[7] Sanders and Roderick could clearly agree on that philosophy.

Coach Farrell was particularly astute with regard to officiating shenanigans that had plagued the American team prior to Sanders' match with Japan's Yanagida. The bias at Munich was perpetrated primarily by the Soviets and Eastern Europeans against the U.S. and Japanese teams. There was no reason to suspect that Japan would collude with other nations to the detriment of the U.S. Japan played by the rules and ethics of international wrestling competition. It was not so with the Soviet Union and communist East Germany.

The opening match between U.S. heavyweight Chris Taylor and Alexander Medved of the former Soviet Union was heavily disputed. Taylor, the obvious aggressor in the match, was nevertheless penalized for stalling. Consequently, Medved won the match by one point. The Turkish referee admitted he called Taylor for passivity, since the American heavyweight weighed twice as much as the former two-time Olympic champion. The ruling was so egregious that FILA banned the referee from further matches at Munich and future international competitions. A draw with Medved would have likely given Tayor the gold medal. Instead, Taylor ended with a bronze.[8] Medved finished with gold—his third Olympic gold medal finish.

Similarly, at 48 kgs, American Sergio Gonzalez was the victim of biased officiating. Coach Farrell was quite vocal and close to combat with officials at least two or three times in Gonzalez' third round match with his East German opponent. At least six different times the ref and the judge called or failed to call points that affected Sergio. Then after a second caution against Gonzalez that tied the score, the German ran for the final 52 seconds of the match without a caution. Sergio was the aggressor throughout the match, but ended with his third draw in a row, giving him six black mark points and eliminating him from further competition. A third-round win would have secured a medal for Gonzalez. Instead, Sergio finished his Olympics never losing a match, but out of the medals.[9]

Sanders, when queried about the result, gritted his teeth in a response that inculpated the politics inherent in the supposedly apolitical Olympics. Rick insisted Gonzalez was the best in the world at his weight, adding, "Two lousy decisions, and Gonzalez is out of it. The Europeans are ganging up on the rest of the world."[10]

Sanders: In the Moment

Millions of viewers tuned in to ABC to watch the Munich Olympics. After not getting one minute of T.V. coverage at the Mexico City Olympics, ABC assured wrestling fans that coverage would improve. ABC sports announcer Frank Gifford and Northwestern University wrestling coach Ken Kraft combined to provide quality comment and analysis as the matches began.[5] Viewers across the country anticipated success from the 1972 team. Sanders, Wayne Wells, and Dan Gable were world champions. Gable won Tbilisi earlier in the year, which was big news in Russia as well as in the U.S. Since college, the press enjoyed covering Gable's success—so much so that it could interfere with his desire to focus on the task at hand.

Sanders was a horse of a completely different color. Sanders was a "gold mine" to the ABC team. Rick's esoteric reputation and colorful mat presence gained popularity for wrestling, a sport not widely understood by the general television audience. Gifford, amused, introduced Sanders to viewers as: "one of the more interesting characters we have ever seen, and certainly a brilliant wrestler. He's kept everyone around here alert—laughing, checking the crowd out, and putting the referee on."

Contrasting himself with Gable, Rick admitted to an *Oregonian* reporter, "I used to work hard all the time. But as you get older (Rick was three years older than Gable) you don't work as hard; you enjoy the techniques. I've built the machinery. I have a wrestler's body. Now I have to find out what I can do with it. Sure, our lifestyles are different; so are our wrestling styles. Most Americans don't have style. Me, I'm a cosmopolite. I can wrestle like a Japanese, a Romanian, or a Russian."[11]

Despite their differences in style, both Gable and Sanders had their fans. Marlin Grahn, future Portland State wrestling coach who attended the Games with a contingent of Oregon wrestlers just finishing a foreign exchange trip to South Africa, noted that whenever Sanders was on the

Sanders: In the Moment

RICK SANDERS, USA 125.5 freestyle wrestler, pinned Hatziidannidis of Greece in the first round of the Olympic Games. (Photo by Don Sayenga)

Rick Sanders, left.
Rick Sanders, USA 125.5 freestlye wrestler, pinned Hatziioannidis of Greece in the first round of the Olympic Games.
Photo by Don Sayenga. Original caption courtesy of Amateur Wrestling News, 1972.

—

mat at Munich, all fans in attendance filled empty seats closest to Rick's match in order to watch the esoteric American.[12]

Sanders met Georgios Hatziioannidis of Greece in the first round of the bantamweight class, 57 kgs. Rick pinned the Greek wrestler in 5:15. A win by fall moved the winning wrestler ahead with zero bad points. A wrestler was out of the tournament after accruing six black marks. This was the same scoring system used at the 1968 Mexico City Olympic Games. Sanders moved ahead after round two, again accruing no black marks. He pinned Nicolae Dumitru of Romania in 5:34. Sanders then met Eduardo Miggiolo of Argentina in round three. Sanders built a 23-0 lead over Eduardo in less than two minutes, pinning the Argentine in 1:32.[13] With amazing efficiency, Rick moved into the fourth round to face Hideaki Yanagida of Japan.

Sanders had accrued zero black marks. Not exactly the result expected from a long-haired, hippie-type, womanizing-wino-slacker, who spends too much time with "Maryjane," but here he was in the fourth round of the Olympics, confident of his chances in a match-up with a two-time world champion. True to form, Sanders let freedom ring.

Sanders: In the Moment

Pictured right: Sanders, characteristically adorned with wooden bead necklace, a beard, and long hair. 1972.

Rick arrived at mat side in the fourth round characteristically adorned with his wooden bead necklace accented with pot pipe. Coach Bill Farrell and Don Behm were in his corner offering strategy, but mostly encouragement. U.S. fans scrabbled to find seats closer to Sanders' action. This was the marquee match-up at the bantamweight class.

Sanders calmly gazed at Yanagida who was waiting with the referee at center mat. Rick removed his adornments and reverently placed them in his duffle bag. The crowd's anticipation was building, but Sanders paid it little mind as he double tied the laces of his black Tiger wrestling shoes. Standing upright, Sanders breathed deeply, as cornerman Don Behm and Coach Farrell simultaneously rubbed Rick's arms, alerting synapses and fast twitch muscle fibers. Sanders appeared unperturbed. He was on a roll—three pins in the first three tournament rounds. Zero black marks accrued, and he hadn't shown any of his new "stuff" yet. Rick heard little of Farrell's goodwill hype. Sanders double slapped his well carved quads, shook his shaggy mane, and moved to center-mat fully animated. This was going to be fun like he'd never had before!

Sanders: In the Moment

Rick gave a nod of acknowledgement to Yanagida, slapped his proffered hand according to custom and steadied for the referee's whistle starting the match. In that moment, Yanagida seemed anxious, as if he wasn't settled into the task at hand. A promising omen. Sanders generally got better the longer the match went.

The whistle blew.

Yanagida darted forward-right to Rick's left. He was quick and small—a couple inches shorter than Sanders. Gaining an angle, Yanagida shot a single. Sanders countered with a whizzer, but the Japanese wrestler had gained the corner and Sanders was not able to get his legs in on the scramble. Two points for Yanagida. After a period of inaction with no improvement by either wrestler, the referee started them on their feet again at center mat.

Sanders stayed undeterred. He knew Yanagida was quick. All the Japanese wrestlers were quick on their feet. Wait till Rick got rolling down on the mat. Back points were Sanders' forte. A different scoreboard picture could be painted with a bit of scrambling artistry.

The whistle blew. Again, Yanagida was quick on the whistle. He moved forward-left again, but this time, changed his level. The Japanese world champion left his crouched position and straightened in a flash that extended to a double leg attack on Rick. Sanders' exposure was not easily defended. Butt on the mat, Rick spent considerable time and energy trying to elevate Yanagida to a position where he could use his tried-and-true or newly developed "stuff." Yanagida edged his body to a position of advantage. Two-point takedown. Yanagida was ahead four to zero. The referee started the pair on their feet again.

With little time remaining in the first period, Yanagida made quick feints both right and left with Sanders in pursuit. The Japanese wrestler seemed to have his man measured. Rick needed momentum.

Sanders: In the Moment

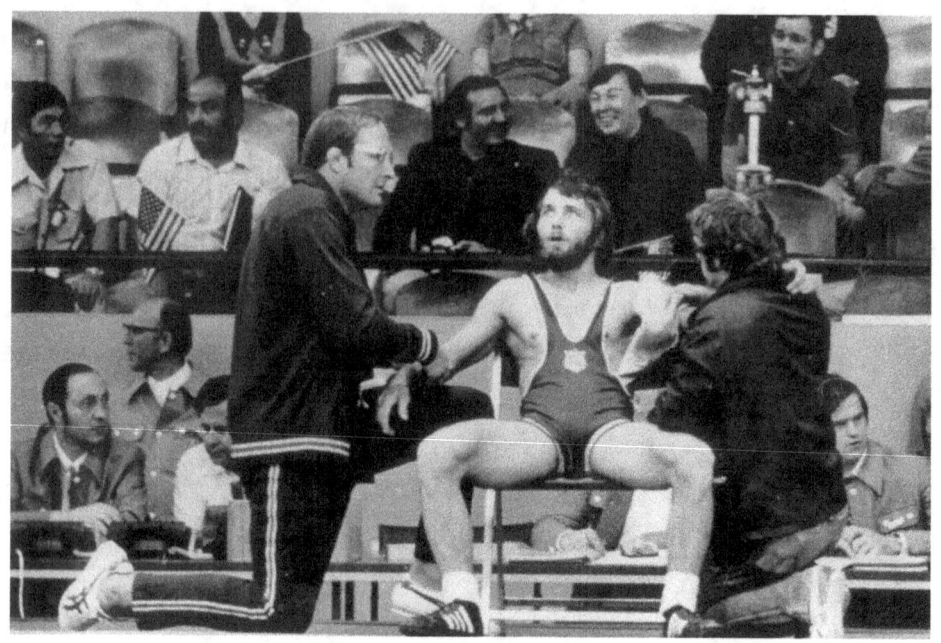

Sanders flanked by Farrell to his right, and Behm, left.
During the match, Sanders appeared tired and befuddled.

The period ended. Both wrestlers went to their corners for a one-minute strategy with coaches. Sanders appeared tired and befuddled. Down four points—Rick had rallied for a comeback against worse odds before. But was it too much this time? Coach Farrell rubbed his arms and offered encouragement, then with a slap on the butt, urged Sanders back to center mat for the final period.

Yanagida was visibly confident. Sanders seemed nonchalant. Yet, on the whistle Sanders took the attack to Yanagida. The Japanese wrestler was difficult to corral, using the edge of the mat effectively to ward off a Sanders tie-up. They went out of bounds several times before Rick scored a two-point takedown that livened up the American fan base. Sanders closed the gap, 4-2.

Sanders: In the Moment

Yanagida was wary of Sanders' ability to use his legs in pinning combinations. Rick found himself unable to pursue his leg advantage as Yangida wisely avoided engagement. The referee called Yanagida for stalling twice, but time was running out, and Sanders remained two points behind.

Then, the unorthodox Sanders employed perhaps his most original quixotic move—he fell to the mat as if injured. Farrell and Behm hurried to his aid, while perplexed officials looked on. The clock stopped, Rick composed himself, and considered the rare predicament he was in. Behm relates the following memory: "Sanders and Yanagida go off the mat. Returning to the center, Rick drops to the mat and falls to his back. The referee stops the match. Farrell and I run to Rick. Farrell confers with the referee. This to make sure the ref does not examine Rick. I lean over Rick, and he winks at me and says, 'I'm ok, I just needed a rest.' Staying on his back another minute, then slowly gets up. I'm rubbing his arm like that was the reason he collapsed. He finished the match behind 4-2. We never talked about the collapse."[14]

The partisan U.S. crowd expected Rick to pull out a win from his magic bag of moves. He was so smooth, his back point totals often seemed to accumulate imperceptibly. But Yanagida was savvy. Ahead in the score, he knew not to engage with Sanders. Yanagida had stalling calls to employ, and he used them effectively to erode the final period. The outcome for Yanagida, the slight pre-match favorite, was seldom in doubt.

Rick's final match with Yanagida was close and well fought by both wrestlers. Both wrestlers received double cautions over the course of the match. For Sanders to receive cautions was uncharacteristic, yet indicative of the respect he had for Yanagida's quickness and overall ability. With two rounds remaining, Sanders was still had a shot at the silver medal on fewer black marks accumulated.

Sanders and Yanagida would never meet on the mat again. Though Yanagida was two years younger than Sanders, he decided to retire from competition after the Munich Olympics. He complained of the pressure he felt to win. He won every tournament he entered at the international level in freestyle at 57 kgs or 125.5 pounds—Olympic gold, two gold medal world championships, and a gold medal at the Asian Games. Yanagida was undefeated while wrestling in the United States, whether at AAU or USWF sponsored tournaments and exhibitions held around the country. Yanagida did not wrestle for an American college or university program like Yojiro Uetake, his coach, or the Hatta brothers Masaaki and Tadaaki did—Yanagida's skills evolved exclusively from Japan's wrestling program that developed after the country's humiliating performance at the 1960 Olympic Games.

Sanders needed to mentally reconstitute himself after the loss to Yanagida who he knew would likely win the remainder of his matches for the gold medal. Rick rallied. He had three remaining matches to win to preserve the silver medal. In the fifth round of competition, Sanders met Prem Nath of India. Rick disposed of Nath by pin in 1:23. Rick met Ivan Shavov of Bulgaria in round six. He decisioned the Bulgarian who likewise had been decisioned by Yanagida. Finally, Sanders met Laszlo Klinga of Hungary in the seventh and final round of competition. Sanders toyed with Klinga in an almost unsportsmanlike exhibition, so out-classing the Hungarian that Assistant Coach Jim Peckham, Rick's cornerman, became quite distressed at Sanders' display. At the break, Peckham implored Rick to forego embarrassment of the Hungarian, arguing further that other American wrestlers might incur further biased officiating from Eastern European referees offended by Sanders' drubbing of Klinga.

Sanders: In the Moment

Rick's passive response inquired whether Peckham wanted him to pin Laszlo. Peckham suggested Sanders simply treat the Hungarian in the spirit of sportsmanship. Rick returned to action and pinned Laszlo Klinga in 6:38.[15] It was the last match of Sanders' career.

Years later, silver medalist John Peterson was conducting Christian mission work in Eastern Europe and ran into Laszlo Klinga, the same Klinga Sanders humiliated in Munich. Peterson asked Klinga whether he had a Bible, to which Laszlo answered, yes, he did. Peterson asked where he was able to get one, and the Hungarian responded, "Rick Sanders gave it to me".[16] Perhaps Sanders was chastened by Coach Peckham's pointed advice. Perhaps he was moved on the occasion, in the spirit of sportsmanship, to seek penance from a higher power than his coach. An Olympic bronze and the Word of God made a pretty good day for Klinga—and a sense of amends for Sanders.

After the freestyle competition, Rick reflected on the Yanagida match; "I just got beat by a better wrestler," he claimed, but added, "Wrestling is just for recreation. It's just a sport with me, not my life."[17] Yet, he assured the fans in public statements that there would be at least one more Olympics for him. Over the seven rounds of competition, Sanders actually accumulated equal black mark totals as Yanagida on double the number of falls. Yanagida accrued four black marks: three decisions (one against Sanders) three pts, two superior decisions one pt, and two pins, zero pts. Four total black marks. Sanders also scored four black marks: one win by decision one pt, five pins zero pts, and one loss by decision (against Yanagida) three pts.

Rick scored the most falls of any wrestler on the U. S. team. Wayne Wells at 74 kgs scored four falls over eight matches, wrestling the most matches of any American. His advancement to the Olympic Games was hampered by having incurred three cracked ribs. The sore ribs made

Sanders: In the Moment

Arguably the best freestyle team ever.
Pictured from let to right:
Bill Farrell, head coach; Don Behm, assistant coach; Ed Lane, trainer; Sergio Gonzales, 105; John Peterson, 180.5; Jimmy Carr, 114.5; Ben Peterson, 198; Rick Sanders, 125.5; Henk Shenk, 220; Gene Davis, 136.5; Chris Taylor, unlimited; Dan Gable, 149.5; Jim Peckham, assistant coach; Wayne Wells, 163; Bill Weick, assistant coach; and Russ Houk, manager.

training difficult. Although not painful in competition, the loss of training affected his conditioning. In the final day of wrestling, Wells had an unusually tough time with Segar of West Germany in the round robin. Wells, who had been elected the U.S. freestyle captain, came back in the final period with four takedowns to break the second-round tie, winning the gold medal.

The freestyle team exceeded performance expectations. Ben Peterson, Wayne Wells, and Dan Gable won gold medals for the U.S. Ben Peterson's gold medal performance was unexpected. Also unexpected was John Peterson's silver medal performance. Sanders was expected to win silver, and he did. Heavyweight Chris Taylor finished with a bronze, though only a hair's breadth from gold. Munich was the best freestyle team performance since the 1960 Rome Olympics, and arguably the best of any non-boycotted Olympics ever.

It would not have surprised the wrestling world if Rick would have taken gold. He lost to Yanagida twice previously, but they were close matches. But while Yanagida was improving himself at the highest echelons of the sport at 1970 and 1971 world championships, Rick was on the shelf serving out disciplinary actions.

Sanders was subject to the inevitable comparison to Dan Gable. David Clay Large makes the comparison succinctly in *Munich 1972*:

> Even before he got to Munich and won the gold medal in his division, Dan Gable had become legendary for his athletic brilliance and fanatical commitment to his sport. In his entire college career, he lost only one match, his last. As a teenage wrestler he kept his weight down by mowing lawns dressed in a wet suit with lead weights attached to his arms and legs. In preparation for the Munich Games, he trained seven hours a day every day for three years straight. In winning his gold medal at Munich he did not surrender a single point, an unprecedented achievement... If American wrestling had a shining poster boy, Gable was it.

Sanders: In the Moment

Rick Sanders was not such an icon; indeed, he might be considered an anti-poster boy. Although a domineering wrestler in his own right, having compiled a high school record in Oregon of 80-1 and winning five national freestyle championships in college, Sanders was famous for not training very hard and for having to go on crash diets to meet his weight before upcoming matches... and then there was his physical appearance and personal style. Put simply, Sanders was a classic Oregon hippie, adorned in long hair, beard, sandals, and love beads. Of course, he smoked his share of weed and drank his share of Ripple. While working as a part-time bartender in Portland, Sanders took part in local anti-Vietnam War rallies... he refused to trim his beliefs—much less his beard and hair—to conform to the image of athletic Americanism that most USOC officials expected to see represented in Munich. And yet, probably all this would have been forgiven if he had only won a gold medal, as he was expected to do. Instead, he came away with a mere silver medal, and for that he was widely vilified in the U.S. press as a slacker whose dissolute lifestyle had contributed to his failure to bring home the gold.[18]

What can be said of Sanders' final international wrestling campaign? He was a world class wrestler. That ability garnered a sizable fanbase. Yet Sanders wanted to be known beyond wrestling—he wanted to be seen as himself. He brought with him "the relaxed priorities of happy, hedonistic, beauty-loving hobbits—with their second breakfasts, pipe weed, and smoke rings" into the wrestling culture, challenging wrestling norms. Rick was on his own quest, much like Frodo Baggins, halfway across the world. Would a silver medal allow him to achieve his goals, let his fans see him in a broader light? In the end, Rick lived according to his nature, simply trying to get back to the Shire of downtown Portland, searching for rest, a pipe, a book, a glass of wine, and a good hearty meal amongst other halflings.

John Peterson compared Rick's wrestling style to 1984 Olympian Dave Schultz: "Both were very relaxed on the mat. They seemed to thoroughly enjoy the experience, where many wrestlers do not." After the freestyle competition, Sanders happened to meet John and Ben Peterson in the U.S. locker room area. Rick asked them pointedly whether he could train with them in preparation for the 1976 Olympic campaign. Their success was in concert with the Gable training philosophy to which Sanders had apparently acquiesced. John Peterson's observation was that "Rick could really push himself in training camp; but lacked conditioning against Yanagida." Further, that "If he would have had better shape, he would have dominated at world events; Rick had no business getting beat by Yanagida."[19]

John Peterson's insight was unique. He was perhaps the teammate of least renown on the 1972 Olympic team. He never made it to the Wisconsin state meet while in high school. Moreover, he decided late to even try wrestling at Wisconsin's Stout State University, an NAIA level school. His best nationals finish was fifth. But he won the 1971 esteemed Midlands tournament at 177 pounds. He gained international experience later that year when he made the 1971 world team to Bulgaria. Finally, competing with top international wrestlers as a member of the 1972 U.S. team at the prestigious Tbilisi tournament in the former Soviet Union, Peterson honed his talent for a run at the 1972 Olympics.[20] He willed himself to train and compete with the best, and he ascended at the Olympics, according to Bill Farrell, "almost by the minute!"[21] Peterson had inherent latent talent discovered through persevering effort and desire, eventually making two Olympic teams at 180.5 pounds. He went from silver in '72 to gold in '76 at Montreal. Peterson was the "book on desire" that Sanders was perhaps ready to read.

Sanders approached Gable similarly, seeking training, and Dan, taking Rick at his word, dropped by Sanders' Munich Olympiad apartment for an early morning run following the freestyle competition. Rick begged off, in no condition to work out, having just returned from an all-night prowl. Though Gable and others learned a lot about freestyle wrestling from Sanders through the years, Rick was late in recognizing the benefit he might have gained from Gable and the Peterson brothers in return. Alas, that morning proved to be the last time Gable saw Sanders.[22]

Sanders' second Olympic silver medal performance was evaluated and commented on by teammates and fans. Sanders, eschewing approbation of any kind, still seemed to be disappointed in the Munich outcome. The 1996 Nike ad, "You don't win silver, You lose gold," though much maligned a couple decades later in advance of the Atlanta Olympics, reflected fan sentiment in 1972 and beyond. The growing focus on sports and hero worship of athletes in the United States had its pernicious side. Sanders was aware of it and countered that powerful influence with his Hobbit-esque lifestyle. His quest envisioned acceptance, tolerance, and change by the wrestling culture. Sanders decided, partially on the encouragement of Gonzalez, to avoid stateside press by touring Europe for a time until focus on the Olympics subsided.[23] The Games and accommodations at the Olympic Village continued until September 11th. Rick transitioned into free spirit mode

Right: Toni was the same age as Sanders. Extroverted and popular, she was a good student and had a degree from San Francisco State College where she pursued an interest in anthropology and archeology.

for the duration.

Rick continued to socialize beyond the freestyle competition. He was a regular at the German beer gardens and enjoyed sharing the ubiquitous marijuana joints within groups of new acquaintances. Sexual liaisons continued as well. On the morning of the start of Greco-Roman wrestling, Sanders woke up in bed with an American woman, Hellene Antoinetta Torres.

"Toni" was a twenty-seven-year-old Californian, the same age as Sanders. She was a graduate of Hayward High School in Hayward, California. Quite extroverted and popular, she was a good student and active as a high school cheerleader. Toni pursued an interest in anthropology and archeology at San Francisco State College where she earned her degree. The occasion of the Munich Olympics allowed her to combine a trip to the Mykonos Island area of Greece—a favorite party destination—while also supporting her long-time boyfriend, U.S. Greco-Roman wrestler Buck Deadrich.[24]

Toni was a child of the sixties. She emerged from the "1967 Summer of Love" wearing tie-dye shirts and fully in concert with the "free love" movement. Sergio Gonzalez observed, "Toni and Buck were together since high school. They had a wonderful understanding of free love between them." [25]

The '60's free love phenomenon's initial goal was to separate the state from sexual matters. Issues like marriage, birth control, and adultery should be left to the individual, unrestricted by governmental entities. Those issues were the concern of the people involved and no one else. The philosophy is often associated with promiscuity, but historically, free love did not advocate multiple sexual partners or short-term sexual relationships. The belief opposed the idea of forced sexual activity in relationships. On the other hand, it advocated for women to use their bodies in any way that they pleased. Free love for women meant sexual freedom on par with men. The movement was largely over by the early seventies. Sexually transmitted diseases (STDs), especially AIDS and HIV, made "free love" less attractive.[26]

Toni and Rick were in a lengthy conversation in Buck's Olympic Village apartment the night before the Greco-Roman competition. Greco teammate Wayne Baughman recalled that Rick's endless chatter annoyed Deadrich, who was trying to sleep as he should have been the night before an Olympic debut. Exasperated, Buck deferred to Sanders in Rick's obvious pursuit of Toni.[26] Rick and Toni shared the rest of the evening in concert with the culture of their era. Perhaps the relationship even flourished as the five-day Greco competition continued. Meaningful relationships with women were elusive for Sanders. Sergio Gonzalez recognized the greater good as "a beautiful thing."[27] But as events evolved, the bright and free-spirited lives of both flower children would end tragically just weeks later.

The twentieth Olympiad continued to cough up U.S. hiccups despite the success of the American freestyle wrestling team and the record number of gold medals (seven) won by American swimmer Mark Spitz.

On the track, American sprinters Eddie Hart and Rey Robinson were late to their quarter-final heats and were disqualified. Both men had equaled the world record time in the 100 meters. The U.S. sprint coach relied on an outdated schedule of events and admitted blame in the disqualifications. The American press and the esteemed sportscaster, Howard Cosell, vilified him for not having had an updated schedule. Later in the Games, Hart, running the anchor on the 4 X 100 sprint relay, was able to expand a lead over Russian anchor Valery Borzov who had captured the 100-meter dash, winning the title of "World's Fastest

Human," a title both Hart and Robinson aspired to claim. The winning U.S. 4 x 100 team set a world record in the race.[28]

American pole vaulter Bob Seagram was flummoxed by officials' last minute banning of Cata Poles—a new brand of pole used by himself and other world class vaulters. The East Germans were instrumental in the ban. Coincidentally, their star, Nordwig, won the gold medal when the field was made to use the old poles. Seagram, the 1968 gold medal winner at Mexico City, got silver.[29]

America's great distance runner from Oregon, Steve Prefontaine, ended out of the medals when he finished fourth in the 5000 meters. Finland's Lasse Viran not only won the 5000, but earlier had won the 10,000. Frank Shorter, winning the marathon, maintained some measure of respect for American distance running. Shorter nursed a bottle of flat Coca Cola—his miracle gold medal elixir—as he scurried through Munich neighborhoods.[30]

American 1500-meter great Jim Ryun's track performance was heartbreaking. The Kansan was the first high schooler to run a mile in under four minutes. He was expected to win gold at Mexico City back in 1968, but ended up winning silver. In the Munich prelims, Ryan got tangled up with another runner and fell on the track with about 500 meters to go. He was unable to recover. American officials protested, demanding a rerun, but to no avail.[31]

The '72 Olympics was the doom year for U.S. basketball, too. Three seconds remained in the game with the Soviets. The U.S. had just gone up 50-49 on a Dave Collins free throw. The Soviets in-bounded the ball and, with one second left, called a time-out. The Soviets insisted they had called a time-out after Collins' second free throw. A second Soviet in-bound pass was allowed with one second on the clock, and time expired. The U.S. stormed the floor in celebration. However, the Soviets protested, claiming three seconds needed to be put back on the clock prior to the inbound pass. Their protest was upheld, and a third in-bound pass was allowed to the Soviets. A Hail Mary pass by the Soviets from the far end of the court to a streaking Soviet player resulted in a layup as time expired. With three seconds remaining in regulation time, the Soviets were allowed three in-bound passes, ultimately winning the gold medal 51-50.[32]

As with freestyle wrestling, Eastern European boxing judges were egregiously biased in their decisions. America's Reginald Jones sent his Russian foe to the canvas three times in his second-round light middleweight-class bout while barely being touched. The Yugoslav judge gave the victory to the Russian. The bias continued so glaringly that several boxing judges were dismissed later in the tournament. Jones was so miffed, he declared he would never box again.[33]

Anabolic steroids began to surface more conspicuously at the Munich Games where testing for drugs was implemented. However, the science to reveal steroid use was not advanced enough in 1972 to offer much detection. American swimmer Rick DeMont was stripped of his swimming gold medal when residue from an asthma prescription he was using showed up in a drug screen. DeMont had declared the asthma drug to U.S. Olympic officials prior to the games, but those officials failed to relay the data to the International Olympic Committee officials. DeMont's success was aborted by the incompetence of U.S. officials, and like Eddie Hart and Rey Robinson, exceptions were not made for U.S. athletes.[34]

Then on September 5th, the same day that began the Greco-Roman competition—the morning Sanders and Toni woke tangled up—came the horrific attack by the Palestinian Black September terrorists on the Israeli compound at the Olympic Village. Eleven Israeli athletes and five of eight Black September Palestinians were ultimately killed in a terribly botched rescue operation conducted by German authorities.[35]

Sanders: In the Moment

What was coined as the "Carefree Olympics" lacked sufficient security to protect athletes from the myriad political interest groups intent on using a scene at the Games to draw world-wide attention to their causes. The six and a half foot tall chain-link fences surrounding the Olympic Village were easily breached. Sanders brought a steady stream of outside acquaintances to his digs inside the Olympic Village at all hours. German patrols were specifically told to not be conspicuous to avoid heightening fear or stifling the goodwill of the Games. Thanks to the lax security, kidnapping the Israeli athletes and coaches was easy work.

The Palestinians' media splash objective worked dynamically. ABC broadcast the actual events worldwide, and T.V. audiences watched, spellbound. The terrorists watched themselves and the attempted rescue on television as events played out.[36]

The Games were halted. Two hostages had been killed in the initial assault, but by evening the remaining hostages and the fedayeen were transported by two helicopters to a remote airport where they were to board a plane traveling to safety in an Arab country.

Events continued to spiral out of control at the airport. German snipers attempted to shoot the Palestinians as the fedayeen leaders inspected the airliner Germany had provided for their escape. The gunfire precipitated the wholesale assassination of the bound Israelis waiting in the helicopters. By the early morning of September 6th, the news reported that all hostages were gone. Five of the eight Palestinians were also killed.[37]

A memorial service was held for the slain Israeli athletes. There was controversy on whether competition should continue. However, under the patronage of Avery Brundage, serving as International Olympic Committee Chairman in his final year, the Games went on. Sanders advocated for their continuance. "Life goes on," he said when asked by one reporter. In a newspaper article, Sanders proved to be a man of keen insight. "When at Munich he was asked if the tragic murders at the Olympic Games horrified him. He replied that he was not shocked by what had happened because he saw it happening every day."[38] In a twenty-five-year-old *Amateur Wrestling News* article, Rick is remembered as one of the few wrestlers who attended the memorial for the slain Israeli athletes held at Olympic Stadium. When Sanders found an angry coach Peckham fuming about man's inhumanity to man, Sanders put his arm around him, kissed him gently on the shoulder and told him: "Coach, you shouldn't talk like that; it's not good for the soul."[39]

Rick's movements after September 11th, the final Olympic ceremony, are clouded. He sent a letter to Dr. Earle MacCannell, his advisor and former sociology professor at PSU, indicating that he was headed to Greece, but that he had been contacted by the Soviets. They wanted him to visit and provide wrestling pointers. Money was short, however, and he wasn't sure how things were going to work out.

Rick adhered to Sergio's suggestion that he stay in Europe a while to avoid the media crowd and fans disappointed by his silver medal performance. The notoriety normally would not have bothered Sanders. Nonetheless, Rick was a naturalist who loved the outdoors and agreed to migrate down to Greece where he would rendezvous with Gonzalez. They would enjoy the Greek Islands—popular party venues for American tourists. Meanwhile, unaware of Rick's detour, friends were planning a homecoming for their favorite son at the American Museum, a bar in downtown Portland where he once worked. A huge green and white sign inside proclaimed: "Welcome Home Party for Silver Medal Winner, Rick Sanders."

As it happened, Buck Deadrich and Toni had made plans to travel Europe after the Games in a Volkswagen van they had purchased for that purpose. Unfortunately, paperwork for the van was canvassed in government red tape, making it unavailable to use as transportation, and beyond that, Buck needed to return to California to complete a test for a graduate course he was taking. Still, he planned to return to Europe, rejoining Toni and hooking up with the party in Greece. Sergio left the Olympic Village for Greece on October 12th. Rick was the last person he said goodbye to before stepping out onto the road. Rick was entertaining yet another lady friend in an apartment and was not completely committed to Greece. Gonzalez remembers an overwhelming feeling of doom at that last meeting he had with Sanders. "I thought little of it. I thought the feeling pertained to me, not Rick." In retrospect, Sergio understood he was picking up the vibe from Sanders.[40] Toni, however, who had stayed in Europe awaiting Buck's return, was excited to visit Greece and anxious to go there since soon, Sergio would be waiting for them. Feeling a sense of urgency, she and Rick decided to hitchhike to Greece.

The route taken suggests the couple left Austria on October 16th, catching a ride from a Yugoslav driver, a Mr. Marijan Grizak of Ljubljana, Yugoslavia and headed to Skopje, Yugoslavia. In the elapsing decades, the country has been renamed Northern Macedonia. Skopje is a couple hundred miles from Greece, their intended destination. The terrain is mountainous and the fall climate unpredictable.

North of Skopje, on a very stormy, windy, rainy day, the land rover in which the three were riding hit a school bus head on while rounding a curve on a mountain highway. According to reports, all three occupants in the vehicle were killed instantly. It was Wednesday, October 18th, 1972. Astonishingly, Sergio Gonzalez was celebrating his birthday on the island of Santorini in the middle of the Aegean Sea. It wasn't until two weeks later, while in Athens, that Gonzalez learned what happened to Rick and Toni.

Sanders: In the Moment

The retrieval of Rick's remains caused a great deal of consternation. Toni's body was cremated and the ashes given to Buck Deadrich and Dennis Bettencourt, Toni's brother, in France where they arranged to meet authorities. A *New York Times* News Services article of October 29, 1972 frames the issue on the return of Rick's remains:

In the last two Olympics, Rick Sanders brought glory to the United States, winning silver medals in free-style wrestling. Eleven days ago he was killed in a car-bus crash in Yugoslavia.

"All this time and we still haven't been able to bury Rick." Said Dr. Howard Westcott, wrestling coach at Portland State University, where Sanders was a star. "We've had red tape getting his body, and financial problems, too. But the government and the Olympic Committee have done nothing to help us out."

"Rick represented them all these years, but he's a body to them now. When something happens to someone and they're no good to anyone anymore, I guess it's easy to write them off."

In New York, Henry Wittenberg, the 1948 wrestling gold medalist, commented angrily, "Where's all the talk of Olympic spirit?" "What's going on with Rick is pure callousness."

After a long delay, Rick's body was flown back to Portland Saturday on a commercial flight, with no special honors. To pay the costs, Sanders' half-brother and half-sister had to obtain a bank loan.

Portland State has started a memorial fund to pay for the funeral. It honored Sanders in half-time ceremonies Saturday night at a home football game with Puget Sound.

"Letters have been coming in from everywhere and kids have been writing how Rick was their hero." Said Westcott. "No letter from the International Olympic Committee, though."

The 27-year-old Sanders whose 5 feet, 4 inches and full beard had given him the appearance of a Leprechaun, was a favorite of young wrestling fans.

Sanders: In the Moment

"Rick belonged to this age," said Westcott. "He represented the millions of youngsters today who rebel against the status quo. To call him a hippie would be a cliché. What he believed in was total personal freedom."

Sanders never hid his liking for beer and marijuana, even during Olympic training. And he brazenly wore his smoking pipe, strung with beads, around his neck.

According to Cy Mitchell, a member of the United States Olympic Committee, the committee will honor Sanders by sending an Olympic flag to his funeral.

"Oh, they could do more," he said. "And if his name was Mark Spitz something would have been done. But he was just a wrestler, so I guess they don't care."[41]

Wayne Wells teamed with Sanders for two Olympic Games. In Wayne's recollection, Rick toted a large duffle bag with him wherever he went. "There wasn't anything that he couldn't dig out of that damned bag: sugarless ketchup, wrestling gear, whiskey bottles, marijuana joints." But rarely any money. The total value of assets released by the U.S. State Department in Yugoslavia to David Stockner, executor of Rick's estate, was $26.50. Of that amount, Rick's silver medal was recovered and valued at $19.00. Items such as a miniature chess board, paperback books, jock strap, "Tiger" wrestling shoes, and a flashlight were assessed no value. The balance of the $26.50 was seven dollars and fifty cents—all the money Rick had available to get to Greece.[42] It's likely only Ricky Sanders could appreciate the possibilities in such a tight spot.

Mike Gerald, long-time columnist for Amateur Wrestling News, nominated Sanders to the National Wrestling Hall of Fame in 1986. Gerald's first attempt promoting Rick's induction failed by two votes. Gerald was told previously when approaching Myron Roderick that, "If he had anything to do with it, Sanders would never be inducted int othe hall. Undeterred, Gerald nominated Rick again the following year.

Sanders: In the Moment

Sanders was selected for the National Wrestling Hall of Fame in 1987, his second time nominated for consideration. He was inducted posthumously and entered along with Bill Farrell and Bobby Douglas. Sanders' Hall of Fame Plaque describes his career metaphorically—"like a meteor... a streak of brilliance then, tragically, he was gone."

Sanders' wrestling style was absolutely marked by his unwavering commitment to the exercise of personal freedom. Freedom provides the light for champions to make their way, but it requires accountability. Sanders was willing to be the catalyst to allow some of the esoteric personalities in the sport today to add character, fun, and acceptance to the culture.

Ultimately, eleven members of the 1972 Olympic freestyle team entered the Hall of Fame. Others so honored are Dan Gable, Wayne Wells, Gene Davis, Ben and John Peterson, Chris Taylor, Don Behm, Jim Peckham, and Bill Weick. *Amateur Wrestling News*, commenting on the 1972 Munich Olympics, wrote: "United States freestyle wrestlers won three gold, two silver and one bronze medal in the 20th Olympiad, and the U.S. team finished second in unofficial scoring. This harvest of medals exactly equals the total of those garnered in the last three Olympic Games and is the best showing by a U.S. Olympic wrestling team since 1928." Clearly, U.S. wrestlers were advancing the style of international freestyle wrestling from the familiar folkstyle commonly used in American high schools and colleges.[43]

Mike McKeel, a college teammate of Sanders, recalls chaperoning his junior high daughter's field trip some years after his competition days were over. He had not remained close to Sanders. The Gresham, Oregon class was studying the history of the Oregon Trail. Browsing through a remote roadside cemetery interred with nineteenth-century pioneers, McKeel observed a headstone with five rings. Mike was surprised to find the final resting place of his teammate and two-time Olympian Richard Joseph Sanders.[44] Perhaps it was fitting to be buried among pioneers of the Oregon Trail, those heroes Rick enjoyed reading about in his youth, and, too, for his pioneering of Oregon wrestling across the nation and internationally in the albeit brief period of 1959-1972, beginning as a high school freshman and culminating in his final Olympic performance at Munich, Germany.

Rick was buried at Forrester Cemetery near Eagle Creek, Clackamas County, Oregon—a spare roadside country plot near Estacada, Oregon. The chapel was full with over 150 people paying their respects. Pallbearers included Freeman Garrison, Masaru Yatabe, and Bob Bergen—PSU teammates—and Bobby Douglas and Jim Burke—international teammates. Rick's closed coffin was so light, Bobby Douglas needed assurances that a body was inside. Rick's brother, David Stockner, calmed a distraught Douglas.[45]

The eulogies were prolific. Don Conway, PSU's new wrestling coach who knew Sanders for several years, called him "one of the greatest competitors I've ever been associated with and probably the best wrestler in Oregon…but I don't feel Rick ever really reached his potential, He was capable of being a two-time Olympic champion and a four-time world champion."[46]

Marion Pericin, PSU's basketball coach, commented, "I was close to the young man because he followed basketball and all sports. It's tragic, because he gave so much to the school and the state of Oregon. He was such a loveable little guy."[47]

Sanders' esteemed PSU wrestling coach Howard Westcott said of Rick, "He was one of the sport's great innovators. He developed moves never tried before. Today, everyone uses them. His loss will be felt by everyone associated with the sports world in Oregon and around the nation."[48]

Olympic freestyle coach Bill Farrell remembered, "Rick was the best wrestler in the world at 125… it won't be easy to forget him and his unusual ways. Certainly, all younger wrestlers in this country looked up to him because of his abilities."[49]

PSU advisor, Dr. Earle MacCannell, in his formal chapel eulogy, spoke tearfully of "Rick living 24 hours a day, seven days a week, all year,"—"Rick lived all the time. He thought it was an atrocity to separate yourself. He lived his wrestling and wrestled his living. Many of us knew Rick in parts. He didn't want that. He wanted to be known as one man."[50]

"Rick was a naturalist," claimed Sergio Gonzalez. "He loved the outdoors." They returned west one year from a tournament in Oklahoma camping at the Grand Canyon. Waking at 5:00 a.m., "Rick was awed by the beauty of the landscape," said Gonzalez. They traveled on to play in the snow fields of the Rockies. Gonzalez was amused when Rick posed on top of a sign marking the elevation at the top of the Continental Divide. Later, Rick walked on his hands at the famous Four Corners landmark, touching the states of Colorado, New Mexico, Utah, and Arizona in one acrobatic sweep. Sanders even scrambled two hundred yards down a mountainside to retrieve a souvenir log from a beaver dam. Gonzalez made room in the Volkswagen bug for the trophy, hauling it the rest of the way back to Portland.[51]

Bobby Douglas described one of many fishing trips he and Rick enjoyed. "One time we were out in a boat and we saw an eagle swoop down and pick a fish out of the water," Douglas said. "It was amazing to see that. Rick loved the outdoors."[52] He loved what came naturally, like an eagle capturing a fish out of the great Columbia River within view of Mount Hood, standing snow capped at 11,250 feet before Portland. It is a scene primordial and unchanged. Rick loved it. He was earthy and passionate. His first passion was wrestling—an ancient and revered sport. Yet when the '60s counterculture suggested change, Sanders indulged. He transformed wrestling because he chose to be himself no matter the cost; he changed wrestling because he refused to let it change him.

In the music of the era, John Prine's lyric from *Angel From Montgomery* resonated with Sanders—"Just give me one thing that I can hold on to. / To believe in this living is just a hard way to go."[53] Rick was transformed, and fifty years later, wrestlers and fans are beginning to understand the quizzical Sanders and how his unique approach to wrestling influenced the sport.

"He played with wrestling," said Sergio Gonzalez. "It was never work."[54] Rick's world view was simple, yet its message, especially in the context of his tragic death, is profound.

"Enjoy being in the moment."

Sanders: In the Moment

Endnotes and citations

Introduction
1. Wayne Wells, interview by author, Edmond, Oklahoma, 22 February 2021.

Chapter One
1. David Stockner, interview by author, Estacada, Oregon, 3 March 2021.
2. Stockner, 3 March 2021.
3. Kay Hirons, interview by author, San Luis Obispo, California, 12 July 2021.
4. Patricia Rogers, interview by author, Portland, Oregon, 3 March 2021.
5. Hirons, 12 July 2021..
6. Stockner, 3 March 2021.
7. Stockner, 3 March 2021.
8. http://traveloregon.com (accessed March 5, 2021).
9. Rogers, 3 March 2021.
10. Christopher B. Strain, The Long Sixties America, 1955-1973 (Chichester, West Sussex, UK, 2017), 1.
11. American Psychiatric Association, Desk Reference to the Diagnostic Criteria from DSM-5 (Washington, DC, 2013).
12. Rogers, 3 March 2021.
13. Rogers, 3 March 2021.
14. Rogers, 3 March 2021.
15. Portland State Viking 1968 (Yearbook), 63.
16. Stockner, 3 March 2021.
17. Stockner, 3 March 2021.
18. Rogers, 3 March 2021.
19. Strain, 4.
20. Rogers, 3 March 2021.
21. Oregonian Staff, The Oregon Story: 1850-2000 (Portland, Oregon).
22. Rogers, 3 March 2021.
23. Rogers, 3 March 2021.
24. Wayne Wells, interview by author, Edmond, Oaklahoma, 22 February 2021.
25. American Psychiatric Association.
26. Rogers, 3 March 2021.
27. Rogers, 3 March 2021.
28. David Farber, The Age of Great Dreams: America in the 1960s (New York, New York, 1994), 54.
29. Bob Bergen, interview with author, Ashland, Oregon, 8 April, 2021.

Chapter Two
1. Don Behm, interview by author, East Lansing, Michigan, 26 March 2021.
2. Dale Anderson, A Spartan Journey: Michigan State's 1967 Miracle on the Mat (Chrystal Lake, Illinois, 2016), 159.
3. David Stockner, interview by author, Estacada, Oregon, 3 March 2021.
4. Ron Calhoun, interview by author, Sandy, Oregon, 27 April 2021.
5. John Irving, The Imaginary Girlfriend (New York, New York, 1996), 40.
6. Wayne Baughman, interview by author, Colorado, Springs, 2 February 2021.
7. Jerry Groover, interview by author, Portland, Oregon, 16 March 2021.

8. The 1963 Cardinal Lincoln High School Portland, Oregon (Yearbook), 132.
9. Delance Duncan, interview by author, Portland, Oregon, 15 March 2021.
10. Michael R. Ives, The Oregon High School Wrestling Championships (Portland, Oregon, 1985), 51.
11. David Farber, The Age of Great Dreams: America in the 1960s (New York, New York, 1994), 184.
12. The 1962 Cardinal Lincoln High School Portland, Oregon (Yearbook), 99.
13. The Portland Oregonian, March 1962.
14. The 1962 Cardinal Lincoln High School Portland, Oregon (Yearbook), 99.
15. Ron Iwasaki, interview by author, Portland, Oregon, 12 March 2021.
16. Bob Allen, 55 Years of Excellence: Oregon High School Wrestling (Hillsboro, Oregon), 193.
17. Michael R. Ives, The Oregon High School Wrestling Championships (Portland, Oregon, 1985), 55.
18. Iwasaki, 12 March 2021.
19. Allen, 175.
20. J.R.L. Anderson, The Ulysses Factor: The exploring instinct in man (New York, New York, 1970), 22.
21. Werner Holzer, History of the United States Wrestling Federation/USA Wrestling (2013), 1.
22. Don Schollander and Duke Savage, Deep Water (New York, New York, 1972), 145.
23. Mike Chapman, Encyclopedia of American Wrestling (Champaign, Illinois, 1990), 41.
24. Dale Anderson, A Spartan Journey: Michigan State's 1967 Miracle on the Mat (Chrystal Lake, Illinois, 2016), 159.
25. Kristyn McIvor, Joel Freeman, Luana Hellman Hill, Legacy of the Twenty-Six: A Celebration of the First 100 Years of the Multnomah Athletic Club (Portland, Oregon, 1991), 134.
26. McIvor, et.al., 1991.
27. Timothy Leary, Turn On Tune In Drop Out (Oakland, California, 1966), 2.
28. Farber, 90.

Chapter Three
1. Roy Tomizawa, 1964 The Greatest Year in the History of Japan (2019),19.
2. Delance Duncan, interview by author, Portland, Oregon, 15 March 2021.
3. Arno Niemand, The Dream Team of 1947 (Boulder, Colorado, 2012), 126.
4. Steve Woods, Sorta Tough (Bend, Oregon 2017), 2.
5. Woods, 25.
6. Joe Much, "Respect to Oregon," Salem Capitol-Journal, August, 1963.
7. Mark Hatfield, Governor, letter to Sanders, June 25, 1963.
8. Allen, 192.
9. Oregonian Staff, The Oregon Story: 1850-2000 (Portland, Oregon).
10. Christopher B. Strain, The Long Sixties America, 1955-1973 (Chichester, West Sussex, UK, 2017), 75.
11. Bruce Glenn, interview by author, Tangent, Oregon, 22 March 2022.
12. Glenn, 22 March 2022.
13. Mike Chapman, Legends of the Mat: Stories of 34 of America's Greatest Wrestlers of All Time (Newton, Iowa, 2006), 70.
14. New Training by Olympic Coaches-Russ Houk's International Rules and Holds Clinic, Amateur Wrestling News, (May 13, 1964), 1.
15. Wayne Baughman, interview by author, Colorado, Springs, 2 February 2021.
16. Mike Chapman, Encyclopedia of American Wrestling (Champaign, Illinois, 1990), 28.

17. https://wwwteamusa.org. (accessed April 17, 2021).
18. Bob Welch with Dick Fosbury, The Wizard of Foz: Dick Fosbury's One-Man High-Jump Revolution (New York, New York 2018),34.
19. Ron Calhoun, interview with author, Sandy, Oregon, 27 April 2021.
20. Mihaly Csikszentmihalyi, The Psychology of Optimal Experience (New York, New York, 1990), 10.
21. Chapman, 498.
22. David Farber, The Age of Great Dreams: America in the 1960s (New York, New York, 1994), 191.

Chapter Four
1. Mark Westcott, interview by author, Portland, Oregon, 5 May 2021.
2. Westcott, 5 May 2021.
3. Neil Andersen, "Wrestling's Big-Time Success For Vikings," Oregonian, 1967.
4. Ron Calhoun, interview by author, Sandy, Oregon, 27 April 2021.
5. Masaru Yatabe, interview by author, Portland, Oregon, 26 April 2021.
6. Calhoun, 27 April 2021.
7. Mike McKeel, interview by author, Gresham, Oregon, 25 April 2021.
8. Westcott, 5 May 2021.
9. Bob Bergen, interview by author, Ashland, Oregon, 8 April 2021.
10. Don Behm, interview by author, East Lansing, Michigan, 26 March 2021.
11. Marlin Grahn, interview by author, Portland, Oregon, 5 March 2021.
12. Yatabe, 26 April 2021.
13. Craig Sesker, Bobby Douglas: Life and Legacy of an American Wrestling Legend (Exit Zero Publishing, 2011), 46.
14. https://goviks.com , (accessed May 16, 2021).
15. Yatabe, 26 April 2021.
16. Calhoun, 27 April 2021.
17. Delance Duncan, interview by author, Portland, Oregon, 15 March 2021.
18. nwcaonline.com/naia/naia-wrestling-archive/naia-men-championsip-brackets/ (accessed April 17, 2021).
19. https://wwwnwhof.org , (accessed March 11, 2021).
20. Len Kauffman, interview by author, Portland, Oregon, 6 June 2021.
21. https://wwwnwhof.org , (accessed March 11, 2021).
22. McKeel, 25 April 2021.
23. Bob Allen, 55 Years of Excellence: Oregon High School Wrestling (Hillsboro, Oregon), 192.
24. Kay Hirons, interview by author, San Luis Obispo, California, 12 July 2021.
25. Mike Chapman, Encyclopedia of American Wrestling (Champaign, Illinois, 1990), 41.
26. The Winged M, MAC Wrestlers Win National AAU Freestyle Title, June 1965.
27. Craig Sesker, 76.
28. Wayne Baughman, interview by author, Colorado, Springs, 2 February 2021.
29. Baughman, 2 February 2021.
30. Bill Smith, letter to Sanders, January, 1966.
31. Dean Rockwell, letter to Sanders, 19 July 1965.
32. Christopher B. Strain, The Long Sixties America, 1955-1973 (Chichester, West Sussex, UK, 2017), 67.
33. Freeman Garrison, interview by author, Portland, Oregon, 15 May 2021.

34. Gene Davis, interview by author, Colorado Springs, Colorado, 29 March 2021.
35. Wayne Wells, interview by author, Edmond, Oklahoma, 22 February 2021.
36. John Prine, Beyond Words (Nashville, Tennessee, 2016), 12.
37. Strain, 109.
38. Behm, 26 March 2021.
39. Behm, 26 March 2021.

Chapter Five
1. Amateur Wrestling News- "1966 Mid-Season All-American Teams," (February 23, 1966), 3.
2. cnywrestling.com/ii/hof/halloffamer.php?id=127 (accessed July 11,2021)
3. Amateur Wrestling News-1964 All-American: First Team," (February 19, 1964), 1.
4. https://wwwnwhof.org, (accessed March 11, 2021).
5. Mike Chapman, Encyclopedia of American Wrestling (Champaign, Illinois, 1990), 241.
6. https://wwwnwhof.org , (accessed March 11, 2021).
7. Mike McKeel, interview by author, Gresham, Oregon, 25 April 2021.
8. https://wwwnwhof.org, (accessed March 11, 2021).
9. Amateur Wrestling News- "Oklahoma State Comes From Behind To Win 25 th Title," (April 6, 1966), 3.
10. https://www.teamusa.org/USA-Wrestling/Features/2012/April/30/Remembrance-for-wrestler-and-c-25041 (accessed July 11, 2021).
11. Christopher B. Strain, The Long Sixties America, 1955-1973 (Chichester, West Sussex, UK, 2017), 173.
12. Chapman, 41
13. Dave Buell, "Sanders Earns U.S. Berth", The Oregonian Journal, April 23, 1966.
14. David Maraniss, Rome 1960: The Olympics that Changed the World (New York, New York), 63.
15. George Pasero, "Pasero Says:" The Oregonian Journal (June 22, 1966).
16. Bill Smith, letter to Sanders, January, 1966.
17. Strain, 76.
18. Bob Allen, 55 Years of Excellence: Oregon High School Wrestling (Hillsboro, Oregon), 27.
19. Jess Lewis, interview by author, Corvallis, Oregon, 10 June 2021.
20. Wayne Baughman, interview by author, Colorado, Springs, 2 February 2021.
21. Masaru Yatabe, interview by author, Portland, Oregon, 26 April 2021.
22. Jerry Groover, interview by author, Portland, Oregon, 16 March 2021.
23. Ron Iwasaki, interview by author, Portland, Oregon, 12 March 2021.
24. Marlin Grahn, interview by author, Portland, Oregon, 5 March 2021.
25. Len Kauffman, interview by author, Portland, Oregon, 6 June 2021.
26. Don Behm, interview by author, East Lansing, Michigan, 26 March 2021.
27. McKeel, 25 April 2021.
28. AP, "Variety win potential mark U.S. wrestlers," The Oregonian Journal, August 27, 1972.
29. Sergio Gonzalez, interview by author, Ashland, Oregon, 26 February 2021.

Chapter Six
1. https://wwwnwhof.org , (accessed March 11, 2021).
2. Mike McKeel, interview by author, Gresham, Oregon, 25 April 2021.
3. Mike Chapman, Encyclopedia of American Wrestling (Champaign, Illinois, 1990), 206, 242.
4. Amateur Wrestling News- "Michigan State Wins First NCAA," (April 5, 1967), 4.

Sanders: In the Moment

5. https://wwwnwhof.org , (accessed March 11, 2021).
6. Anderson, A Spartan Journey: Michigan State's 1967 Miracle on the Mat (Chrystal Lake, Illinois, 2016), 233.
7. Bob Burnett, "Sanders: Outside the Ring," The Vanguard, April 29,1967.
8. Burnett, 1967.
9. Mike Chapman, Encyclopedia of American Wrestling (Champaign, Illinois, 1990), 96.
10. Dan Gable with Scott Schulte, A Wrestling Life: The Inspiring Stories of Dan Gable (Iowa City, Iowa, 2015), 62.
11. David Zang, "Inestimable," Amateur Wrestling News, 1997?
12. Burnett, 1967.
13. Bruce Glenn, interview by author, Tangent, Oregon, 22 March 2022.
14. Mike Chapman, Encyclopedia of American Wrestling (Champaign, Illinois, 1990), 56.
15. Chapman, 42.
16. https://www.wikiwand.com/en/1967_World_Wrestling_Championships#/google_vignette, (accessed July 11, 2021).

Chapter Seven
1. David Farber, The Age of Great Dreams: America in the 1960s (New York, New York, 1994), 212.
2. Farber, 210.
3. Sergio Gonzalez, interview by author, Ashland, Oregon, 26 February 2021.
4. Don Behm, interview by author, East Lansing, Michigan, 26 March 2021.
5. Christopher B. Strain, The Long Sixties America, 1955-1973 (Chichester, West Sussex, UK, 2017), 121.
6. Ron Calhoun, interview by author, Sandy, Oregon, 27 April 2021.
7. Wayne Wells, interview by author, Edmond, Oklahoma, 22 February 2021.
8. Mike McKeel, interview by author, Gresham, Oregon, 25 April 2021.
9. Amateur Wrestling News- "1968 Mid-Season All-American Teams," (February 28, 1968), 3.
10. Amateur Wrestling News- "Peninger Named Man of the Year," (March 20, 1968), 1.
11. Portland State Viking 1968 (Yearbook), 63.
12. Mike Chapman, Encyclopedia of American Wrestling (Champaign, Illinois, 1990), 244.
13. Don Bartling, interview by author, Brookings, South Dakoata, 10 September 2021.
14. https://wwwnwhof.org , (accessed March 11, 2021).
15. https://wwwnwhof.org , (accessed March 11, 2021).
16. John Nolen, "Instinct Almost Gave Sanders Win," The Oregonian Journal, March 27, 1968.
17. Gonzalez, 26 February 2021.
18. Dale Anderson, interview by author, via email, 29 June 2021.
19. https://www.nwcaonline.com/d2/d2-wrestling-archive/d2-hall-fame/ , (accessed July 11, 2021).
20. Amateur Wrestling News- 3 Champs Lose As West Wins 21-8," (April 17, 1968),1.
21. Amateur Wrestling News, April 17,1968.
22. Amateur Wrestling News, April 17, 1968.
23. Masaru Yatabe, interview by author, Portland, Oregon, 26 April 2021.
24. Don Fair, "Sanders, Andros, Keck Claim Hayward Awards: Vik Matman Top Athlete in Oregon,
The Oregonian Journal, February 7, 1968.
25. David Zang, "Inestimable," Amateur Wrestling News, 1997?
26. Behm, 26 March 2021.

27. Craig Sesker, Bobby Douglas: Life and Legacy of an American Wrestling Legend (Exit Zero Publishing, 2011), 76.
28. Mezirow, Jack, Transformative Learning: Theory into Practice (1997).
29. Ben Peterson, interview with author, 15 February 2021.

Chapter Eight
1. Amateur Wrestling News-"38 Go To Olympic Training Camp," (May 22, 1968), 1.
2. Amateur Wrestling News, May 22, 1968.
3. Amateur Wrestling News, May 22 1968.
4. Kevin B. Witherspoon, Before the Eyes of the World, Mexico and the 1968 Olympic Games (DeKalb, Illinois: Northern Illinois University Press, 2008), 52.
5. Mike Chapman, Legends of the Mat: Stories of 34 of America's Greatest Wrestlers of All Time (Newton, Iowa, 2006), 83.
6. J.R.R. Tolkien, The Lord of the Rings: The Fellowship of the Ring (New York, New York, 1954),84.
7. Sergio Gonzalez, interview by author, Ashland, Oregon, 26 February 2021.
8. Wayne Wells, interview by author, Edmond, Oklahoma, 22 February 2021.
9. Richard Hoffer, Something In The Air: American Passion and Defiance In The 1968 Mexico City Olympics (New York, New York, 2009), 81.
10. Bob Welch with Dick Fosbury, The Wizard of Foz: Dick Fosbury's One-Man High-Jump Revolution (New York, New York 2018),132.
11. Hoffer, 199.
12. Jairus K. Hammond, The History of Collegiate Wrestling (Stillwater, Oklahoma: National Wrestling Hall of Fame and Museum, 2006), 100.
13. Wayne Baughman, interview by author, Colorado, Springs, 2 February 2021.
14. Dean Rockwell, letter to Sanders, 19 July 1965.
15. Wayne Wells, 22 February 2021.
16. Wayne Wells, 22 February 2021.
17. Don Behm, interview by author, East Lansing, Michigan, 26 March 2021.
18. Amateur Wrestling News, "Oklahoma Wins the Hard Way," (April 22, 1964). 8.
19. Witherspoon, 35.
20. Witherspoon, 22.

21. https://www.sportingnews.com/ca/olympics/news/olympic-athletes-paid-explained/ejr1uhiu1gxkkjujcqwah1qp#:~:text=Olympic%20athletes%20do%20not%20get,bronze%20medal%20is%, (accessed July 17, 2021).
22. Witherspoon, 27.
23. David Farber, The Age of Great Dreams: America in the 1960s (New York, New York, 1994), 221
24. Witherspoon, 104.
25. Hoffer, 25.
26. Hoffer, 30.
27. Hoffer, 48.
28. Witherspoon, 125.
29. Witherspoon, 124.
30. Hoffer, 237.
31. Witherspoon, 138.
32. Witherspoon, 138.

33. Witherspoon, 138.
34. Witherspoon, 126.
35. Hoffer, 173.
36. Hoffer, 99.
37. Wayne Wells, 22 February 2021.
38. https://en.wikipedia.org/wiki/Wrestling_at_the_1968_Summer_Olympics_%E2%80%93_Men%27s_Greco-Roman_52_kg (Accessed July 17, 2021).
39. Amateur Wrestling News- "U.S. Olympic Team 4 th In Freestyle," (November 13, 1968), 1.
40. Craig Sesker, Bobby Douglas: Life and Legacy of an American Wrestling Legend (Exit Zero Publishing, 2011), 67.
41. Amateur Wrestling News, November 13, 1968.
42. Mike Chapman, Encyclopedia of American Wrestling (Champaign, Illinois, 1990), 28.
43. Governor Tom McCall, letter to Sanders, November 26, 1968.
44. Chapman, 42.
45. Amateur Wrestling News, "Tom Evans Chosen 1968 Man of the Year," (March 26, 1969), 1.

Chapter Nine

1. Shelby Steele, Shame: How America's Past Sins Have Polarized Our Country (Basic Books, 2015), 78.
2. Christopher B. Strain, The Long Sixties America, 1955-1973 (Chichester, West Sussex, UK, 2017), 122.
3. David Stockner, interview by author, Estacada, Oregon, 3 March 2021.
4. Mike Chapman, Encyclopedia of American Wrestling (Champaign, Illinois, 1990), 41.
5. Amateur Wrestling News, "36 Wrestlers To FS Training Camp," (February 12, 1969), 4.
6. Amateur Wrestling News, "Freestyle Team For World Games," (March 5, 1969), 1.
7. Chapman, 41.
8. Phil Knight, Shoe Dog: A Memoir by the Creator of Nike (New York, New York, 2016), 96.
9. Craig Sesker, Bobby Douglas: Life and Legacy of an American Wrestling Legend (Exit Zero Publishing, 2011), 67.
10. Wayne Wells, interview by author, Edmond, Oklahoma, 22 February 2021.
11. Amateur Wrestling News-"The Average Wrestling Season" (January 28, 1970), 6.
12. Stockner, 3 March 2021.
13. https://pipiwiki.com/wiki/1969_World_Wrestling_Championships , (accessed August 11,2021).
14. Amateur Wrestling News-"The Average Wrestling Season" (January 28, 1970), 6.
15. Mike Gallego, interview by author, Grass Valley, California, 23 April 2021.
16. Chapman, 41.
17. William J. Baker, Jesse Owens: An American Life (University of Illinois Press, 2006), 59.
18. Don Schollander and Duke Savage, Deep Water (New York, New York, 1972), 148.
19. Werner Holzer, History of the United States Wrestling Federation/USA Wrestling (2013),26.
20. Amateur Wrestling News, "Roderick Takes Federation Post," (September 24, 1969), 1.
21. Amateur Wrestling News, "Dan Gable Chosen 1969 Man of the Year," (March 25, 1970), 1.
22. Abraham H. Maslow, A Theory of Human Motivation (Mansfield Centre, Connecticut, 2013),1.
23. Kay Hirons, interview by author, San Luis Obispo, California, 12 July 2021.
24. Stockner, 3 March 2021.
25. David Zang, "Inestimable," Amateur Wrestling News, 1997?

Chapter Ten

Sanders: In the Moment

1. https://en.wikipedia.org/wiki/Angela_Davis (Accessed 15 August 2021).
2. Ellis Amburn, Pearl: The Obsessions and Passions of Janis Joplin (Central Grand Publishing, 1993), 203.
3. Kareem Abdul-Jabbar and Peter Knobler, Giant Steps: The Autobiography of Kareem Abdual-Jabbar (New York, New York, 1983), 112.
4. Mike Chapman, Encyclopedia of American Wrestling (Champaign, Illinois, 1990), 95.
5. Chapman, 98.
6. Amateur Wrestling News, "Bill Farrell Briefs Potential FS Squad," (March 4, 1970),6.
7. Chapman, 98.
8. Amateur Wrestling News, "NYAC Dominates USWA Freestyle," (May 13, 1970), 1.
9. Amateur Wrestling News, "Training Camps Planned for U.S. Team Selection," (May 13, 1970), 12.
10. Bill Farrell, letter to Amateur Wrestling News, 18 November, 1997.
11. Mike Chapman, Encyclopedia of American Wrestling (Champaign, Illinois, 1990), 35.
12. Chapman, 43.
13. Martin A. Lee, Smoke Signals: A Social History of Marijuana- Medical, Recreational, and Scientific
(New York, New York, 2012), 41.
14. Kevin P. Hill, M.D., Marijuana: The Unbiased Truth About The World's Most Popular Weed (Center City, Minnesota, 2015), 24.
15. Lee, 52.
16. Lee, 6.
17. Hill, M.D., 36.
18. John Prine, Beyond Words (Nashville, Tennessee, 2016), 12.
19. Sergio Gonzalez, interview by author, Ashland, Oregon, 26 February 2021.
20. Mike McKeel, interview by author, Gresham, Oregon, 25 April 2021.

21. Hill, M.D., 22.
22. Lee, 6.
23. Lee, 13.
24. Amateur Wrestling News, Hair rule- Camaione,1969
25. Werner Holzer, History of the United States Wrestling Federation/USA Wrestling (2013),26.
26. https://henryehooper.blog/witness-post-rick-sanders/ (accessed July 11, 2021).
27. Gene Davis, interview by author, Colorado Springs, Colorado, 29 March 2021.
28. Amateur Wrestling News, "Wayne Wells Named 1970 Man of the Year," (March 17, 1971), 6.
29. Amateur Wrestling News, "Myron Roderick Named 1971 Man of the Year," (March 11, 1972),1.
30. Mike Chapman, Encyclopedia of American Wrestling (Champaign, Illinois, 1990), 113.
31. Bob Hurt, "Sanders Really Flies When He Jogs," The Oregonian Journal (July, 1970).
32. Wayne Baughman, interview by author, Colorado Springs, Colorado, (2 February 2021).
33. Amateur Wrestling News, "Visiting Russian Team Wins First Three Duals," (March 24, 1971), 21.

Chapter Eleven
1. Oregonian Staff, The Oregon Story: 1850-2000 (Portland, Oregon), 107.
2. David Farber, The Age of Great Dreams: America in the 1960s (New York, New York, 1994), 188.
3. Mike Chapman, Encyclopedia of American Wrestling (Champaign, Illinois, 1990), 69.

4. Chapman, 99.
5. Amateur Wrestling News, "Sanders and Wells Head Pan-Am Team," (May 19, 1971),1.
6. Chapman, 54.
7. Sergio Gonzalez, interview by author, Ashland, Oregon, 26 February 2021.
8. Don Behm, interview by author, East Lansing, Michigan, 26 March 2021.
9. Gonzalez, 26 February 2021.
10. Behm, 26 March 2021.
11. Chapman, 44.
12. Chapman, 489.
13. https://en.wikipedia.org/wiki/1971_World_Wrestling_Championships (accessed July 11, 2021).
14. Werner Holzer, History of the United States Wrestling Federation/USA Wrestling (2013),41.

Chapter Twelve
1. Patricia Rogers, interview by author, Portland, Oregon, 3 March 2021.
2. Christopher B. Strain, The Long Sixties America, 1955-1973 (Chichester, West Sussex, UK, 2017), 94.
3. https://www.nytimes.com/2003/01/28/opinion/wrestling-with-title-ix.html (accessed August 23, 2021).
4. https://wwwnwhof.org, (accessed March 11, 2021).
5. "Express Your Appreciation," Amateur Wrestling News, (September 30, 1972), 2.
6. Amateur Wrestling News, "USSR Wins All Four Duals With U.S. Teams, (April 8, 1972), 1.
7. John Musemeche, "Japanese Defeat U.S.A. In Wrestling," Advocate, (September, 1971).
8. Journal Staff, "Sanders Has A Roadblock To Olympics," The Oregonian Journal (September, 1971).
9. Masaru Yatabe, interview by author, Portland, Oregon, 26 April 2021.
10. Mike Chapman, Encyclopedia of American Wrestling (Champaign, Illinois, 1990), 100.
11. Werner Holzer, History of the United States Wrestling Federation/USA Wrestling (2013),77.
12. https://www.olyclub.com/, (accessed September 11, 2021).
13. https://www.olympedia.org/affiliations/5850, (accessed September 11, 2021).
14. https://www.nyac.org/, (accessed September 11, 2021).
15. Bill Farrell, "The Inside Story- Our Olympic Team," Amateur Wrestling News, (November 11, 1972), 14.
16. "The Road To Munich- 433 Entries In Final Olympic Team Trials," Amateur Wrestling News, (September 30, 1972), 22.
17. Chapman, 31.
18. https://en.wikipedia.org/wiki/Wrestling_at_the_1972_Summer_Olympics, (accessed September 11, 2021).
19. "The Road To Munich", 38.
20. James V. Moffatt, Wrestlers at the Trials-Their stories of trying to make the U.S. Wrestling Team 1960-1988 (Zero Publishing, Inc. 2007),86.
21. https://intermatwrestle.com/articles/3054, (accessed July 11, 2021).
22. Moffatt, 87.
23. Moffatt,87.
24. Moffatt, 87.
25. Jeff Callard, interview by author, Idaho Falls, Idaho, 31 October 2021.
26. Don Behm, interview by author, East Lansing, Michigan, 26 March 2021.

27. Behm, 26 March 2021.
28. Sergio Gonzalez, interview by author, Ashland, Oregon, 26 February 2021.
29. David Zang, "Inestimable," Amateur Wrestling News, 1997?
30. John Peterson, interview by author, Comstock, Wisconsin, 7 December 2021.
31. Leo Davis, "A remembrance of things past," The Oregonian Journal (November, 1972).
32. Sergio Gonzalez, interview by author, Ashland, Oregon, 26 February 2021.
33. Callard, 31 October 2021.
34. Gonzalez, 26 February 2021.
35. Davis, November 1972.
36. Ben Peterson, interview with author, 15 February 2021.
37. John Peterson, 7 December 2021.
38. Behm, 26 March 2021.
39. Leo Davis, "Sanders: Master craftsman at doing his thing- wrestling," The Oregon Journal (August 29, 1972).
40. Davis, August 1972.

Chapter Thirteen
1. David C. Large, Munich 1972: Tragedy, Terror, and Triumph at the Olympic Games: Munich 1972
(Lanham, Maryland, 2012), 11.
2. Large, 21.
3. Large, 26.
4. Large, 32.
5. Large, 38.
6. Large, 45.
7. Don Behm, interview by author, East Lansing, Michigan, 26 March 2021.
8. https://www.teamusa.org/USA-Wrestling/Features/2017/August/16/Hall-of-Fame-Coach-Bill-Weick-passes-away-at-age-85 (accessed July 11, 2021).
9. https://buhuskies.com/honors/hall-of-fame/russ-houk/127 (accessed July 11, 2021.).
10. David W. Zang, "Inestimable," Amateur Wrestling News, Vol. 47 No. 8 (February 8, 2002), 5.
11. Wayne Wells, interview by author, Edmond, Oklahoma, 22 February 2021.
12. Myron Roderick, "An Open Letter To U.S. Wrestlers, Coaches, and Fans," Amateur Wrestling News, (September 30, 1972), 13.
13. Lynn Marr-Moore, "The Gentle Giant: The Chris Taylor Story (Ames, Iowa, 2001), 56.
14. Bill Farrell, "The Inside Story- Our Olympic Team," Amateur Wrestling News, (November 11, 1972), 14.
15. Leo Davis, "Sanders: Master craftsman at doing his thing- wrestling," The Oregon Journal (August 29, 1972).
16. Davis, August 1972.
17. Marlin Grahn, interview by author, Portland, Oregon, 5 March 2021.
18. Behm, 26 March 2021.
19. David W. Zang, "Inestimable," Amateur Wrestling News, Vol. 47, No. 7 (February 22, 2002), 6.
20. John Peterson, interview by author, Comstock, Wisconsin, 7 December 2021.
21. Munich (AP), "Sanders wins silver medal in wrestling," The Oregonian Journal (September 1, 1972).
22. David C. Large, Munich 1972: Tragedy, Terror, and Triumph at the Olympic Games: Munich 1972

(Lanham, Maryland, 2012), 160.
23. Peterson, 7 December 2021.
24. Ben Peterson, "Road to Gold: The 1972 Olympic Journey of Ben and John Peterson," (Watertown, Wisconsin, 2015), 165.
25. A Bill Farrell, "The Inside Story- Our Olympic Team," Amateur Wrestling News, (November 11, 1972), 14.
26. Dan Gable with Scott Schulte, A Wrestling Life: The Inspiring Stories of Dan Gable (Iowa City, Iowa, 2015), 63.
27. Sergio Gonzalez, interview by author, Ashland, Oregon, 26 February 2021.
28. Jeanmarie Bettencourt, interview by author, Seattle, Washington, 26 April 2021.
29. Gonzalez, 26 February 2021.
30. Christopher B. Strain, The Long Sixties America, 1955-1973 (Chichester, West Sussex, UK, 2017), 99.
31. Wayne Baughman, interview by author, Colorado, Springs, 2 February 2021.
32. Gonzalez, 26 February 2021.
33. Eddie Hart with Dave Newhouse, Disqualified: Eddie Hart, Munich 1972, And The Voices Of the Most Tragic Olympics (Kent, Ohio, 2017), 170.
34. Large, 187.
35. Large, 190.
36. Large, 251.
37. Large, 267.
38. Large, 156.
39. Large,176.
40. Large, 201.
41. Large, 207.
42. Large, 208.
43. David W. Zang, "Inestimable," Amateur Wrestling News, Vol. 47, No. 7 (February 22, 2002), 7.
44. Gonzalez, 26 February 2021.
45. Department of State Foreign Service of the United States of America: Report of Death of an American Citizen, Belgrade, Yugoslavia, (December 19, 1972).
46. Mike Chapman, Encyclopedia of American Wrestling (Champaign, Illinois, 1990), 29.
47. Mike McKeel, interview by author, Gresham, Oregon, 25 April 2021.
48. David Stockner, interview by author, Estacada, Oregon, 3 March 2021.
49. John Nolen, "European Car Crash Kills 'Lovable Little" Sanders," The Oregonian Journal (October 20, 1972).
50. Nolen, October 1972.
51. Nolen, October 1972.
52. Nolen, October 1972.
53. Nolen, October 1972.
54. Gonzalez, 26 February 2021.
55. Craig Sesker, Bobby Douglas: Life and Legacy of an American Wrestling Legend (Exit Zero Publishing, 2011), 77.
56. John Prine, Beyond Words (Nashville, Tennessee, 2016), 22.
57. Gonzalez, 26 February 2021.

Sanders: In the Moment

Sanders: In the Moment

Photographic Credits

Photographs in this work are used by permission and courtesy of the following:

Front book cover: John Hoke Amateur Wrestling News, July 1972.
Back book cover: Amateur Wrestling News, November 1972.

David Stockner, pages 4, 7, 10, 29, 43, and dedication page.

Amateur Wrestling News, pages 50, 72, 83, 86, 92, 105, 107, 115, 131, 143, 167, 186, 216 (both) 240, 247.

Wrestling Hall of Fame and Museum, pages 64, 107, 148, 158, 159, 173, 234, 241.

1962-1963 Cardinal Lincoln High School Portland, Oregon yearbook, pages 21, 22, 27, 101.

Portland State Viking 1968 Yearbook, page 199.

Mike Gallego, page 173.

Mike Ives, page 112.

Masaru Yatabe, page 109.

Jeanmarie Bettencourt, page 251.

Sanders: In the Moment

Acknowledgements:

It was an honor to talk with several of Sanders' family members, teammates, and friends in the eighteen months it took to bring Sanders' biography to fruition.

I began my research by reading Rick's obituary. Sanders' half-brother David Stockner of Estacada, Oregon was named. I found a land line number for Stockner and left a message on his answering machine. Stockner, who was 87 at the time, called me back. I was encouraged, but even better, he invited me out to Portland to review the scrapbook he had on Rick. I spent a week at Dave Stockner's house as his guest. We drove together to Oakridge, Oregon where Sanders lived and went to elementary school. We viewed Rick's grave site at Eagle Grove Cemetery. I visited Lincoln High School where Rick won four city championships and three state titles. The high school was razed in 2022 and rebuilt on the same grounds. I met Patricia Sanders, Rick's full sister, during the Portland visit, and spoke with her several times by phone. Patricia passed away in January 2022. I was also honored to talk with Masaru Yatabe, Rick's PSU teammate on the Portland visit as well as PSU D-II Hall of Fame coach Marlin Grahn, who was a workout partner with Sanders.

Sanders: In the Moment

The Sanders' biography is supported by data from several eminent sources. Amateur Wrestling News captured Sanders' career quite well beginning in 1963 with the Japanese High School exchange tour through the 1972 Olympics. John Hoke at Amateur Wrestling News provided valuable insight. South Dakota State University Briggs Library contains the Jim Koch archived copies of all AWN issues. There are very few copies of AWN beginning in 1965 through 1972 that do not have some mention of Rick Sanders.

Mike Chapman's Encyclopedia of American Wrestling was absolutely golden for the Sanders project. Rick wrestled so many different venues—Collegiately: NAIA, D-II, D-I; AAU, Pan American games, World Championships, and Olympic Games. The results of these tournaments are found in the Chapman treatise. Chapman's Legend's of the Mat was also a wonderful source for background information on contemporaries of Sanders. He also provided excellent proofreading for the book.

The History of Collegiate Wrestling by Jairus K. Hammond was a valuable source as well. U.S amateur wrestling is a microculture, and threads to that culture can be gleaned from Hammond's work. Wrestlers are profiled, but so too are collegiate power programs.

Specific to Oregon is 55 Years of Excellence - Oregon High School Wrestling by Bob Allen. Oregon wrestling has always been dynamic. Collegians in top U.S. programs recruited out of Oregon include—Fred Fozzard, Tony Russo, Larry Owings, Mike Grant, Andy Foster, Mat Gentry, Nick Amuchastequi, and Tyler Berger. The venerable Oregonian grappler Robin Reed may have been America's best during his era of the 1920s, some say the best of any era. Bob Allen makes the case for Sanders' legacy in his fine work.

Sanders: In the Moment

Another Oregon source document on Sanders was produced by Michael Ives entitled The Oregon High School Wrestling Championships. Rick's high school career is chronicled in Ives rather esoteric volume.

Former PSU coach Marlin Grahn donated the copy to me from his impressive backyard museum of wrestling memorabilia.

The National Wrestling Hall of Fame was integral in providing contact information on distinguished members who knew Sanders and were willing to reflect on Rick. Jack Carnefix, Operations Manager at the Hall of Fame, was prompt, professional, and enthusiastic about lending a hand in the research effort.

I conducted over thirty interviews with Sanders' teammates, friends, family, and acquaintances to establish an accurate profile of Sanders. Not all of Sanders intimates were willing or able to respond to my inquiries. Most are in their middle seventies and beyond. Health issues frustrated the ability of a few to answer the call. I found the vast majority enthusiastic about the opportunity to be part of the Sanders project. To these hallowed contemporaries, Sanders was special.

- Ben Peterson—Munich Olympic teammate ("Sanders was a 'wrestling machine,' he played in it.")

- David Stockner—Older half-brother (Rick was late for the plane, so he ran out on the runway and the plane stopped for him to get on.")

- Patricia Rogers-—Rick's full sister ("We lived on 3rd avenue which at the time was skid row in Portland.")

- Marlin Grahn—Work-out partner and future Portland State D-II Hall of fame Coach ("He was one of the greatest friends I ever had.")

- Masaru Yatabe—Portland State University teammate ("Success did not change him.")

Sanders: In the Moment

- Wayne Wells—Mexico City, Munich Olympics and World Championships teammate ("Rick was the most interesting wrestler I ever saw.")

- Wayne Baughman—Mexico City, Munich Olympics, and World Championship teammate ("Wrestling was Rick's total reason for life.")

- Len Kauffman—World Championships teammate ("He was a free spirit without coaches because he learned on his own.")

- Sergio Gonzalez—Munich Olympics teammate (Rick was a chess piece in motion, he didn't overpower with strength, he could innovate in a moment.")

- Delance Duncan—Oregon High School and Japanese Cultural Exchange coach ("Rick was the greatest Oregon wrestler, with the possible exception of Robin Reed.")

- Jerry Groover—Portland Interscholastic League High School competitor ("I saw Rick 15 miles outside of Portland running.")

- Ron Iwasaki—Oregon State All American ("He got tougher…sometimes while on top he'd 'relax' to see what you might try to do…but if he was on a mission…it seemed unrelenting.")

- Mike Lund—Portland State Athletic Information Administrator.

- Jack Elder—Oregon State Sports Hall of Fame Director.

- Jack Maugan—NDSU Senior Associate Athletic Director.

- Bobby Douglas—Olympic and World Championships teammate ("Rick had terrible technique, but he was a scrapper and a fighter. He would find a way to beat you. He was one tough son of a bitch.")

Sanders: In the Moment

- Dana Barton Cress—Lincoln High School Alumni Association Archivalist.

- John Hoke—Editor, Amateur Wrestling News ("Sanders was doing things at the trials that he probably shouldn't have been doing.")

- Don Behm—Mexico City, Munich Olympics and World Championships teammate ("It was the crowning moment in my career. Even though I lost, I was, and forever will be, part of one of the best wrestling matches ever!")

- Gene Davis—Munich Olympics teammate ("Rick genuinely did not care how he was perceived by others.")

- Ron Calhoun—Portland State University teammate ("Rick was tactile with friends-touchy, feely. He was just a sleek, loving, little guy.")

- Bob Bergen—MAC and PSU workout partner ("I helped him put up some plywood in an attic in downtown Portland. All his medals were in a box. Rick said, 'take them—they don't mean anything.' They included his 1968 Olympic Silver medal.")

- Freeman Garrison—Portland State University teammate ("We went swimming in the summertime—jumping off a waterfall into a pool.")

- Henk Schenk—Mexico City, Munich and World Championships teammate ("Rick was not wrestling near what his capability or style was like against Yanagida.")

- Mike Gallego—Fresno State All American (Rick was a free spirit; ornery.")

- Jeanmarrie Bettencourt—sister to Hellene Antoinetta "Toni" Torres ("Toni was a flower child, earthy, wasn't a big pot smoker, was a good student, didn't do drugs.")

Sanders: In the Moment

- Mike McKeel—Portland State University teammate ("Sanders, at the 1967 national tournament at Kent State, worked out all night at the YMCA to lose seven pounds. He won the tournament and OW award.")

- Jess Lewis—Mexico City Olympics and World Championships teammate ("I want to tell you at the get go, Sanders was the toughest guy I've ever met.")

- Kay Hirons—Rick's older half-sister ("Rick got into trouble until he found wrestling.")

- John Peterson—Munich Olympics teammate ("Rick wrestled similar to Dave Schultz-very relaxed on the mat and seeming to enjoy the experience, where many wrestlers do not.")

- Mark Westcott—PSU coach Howard Westcott's son ("He was homely, ears stuck out, not at all a physical presence, but when he got in a crouch- he became a ballet dancer who could go beyond thrilling.")

- Bruce Glenn—AAU teammate ("Rick loved an entrance.")

- Jeff Callard—All American ("Rick showed me how to whittle sumac beads.")

- Dale Anderson—All American ("He had so much talent. So even though he was doing immature stuff, he still beat everyone.")

-

The initial drafts of the manuscript were edited by developmental editors Emily Jones and Michael Larson, and proofreader Lindsay Peterson.

Sanders: In the Moment

I am grateful to Sergio Gonzalez, Don Behm, Masaru Yatabe, Marlin Grahn, Wayne Wells and John Peterson for reviewing and offering comment on the manuscript rough draft. Josephine Funk edited successive drafts, completed the copy editing, assisted with the final book layout and facilitated the publication process. Ms. Funk's assistance was extraordinary.

About the Author

Bahne Bahnson, Ed.D., J.D.

Bahnson wrestled for the Northern State College Wolves during the middle 1970s. He is a long-distance hiker and bicycler, thru-hiking the AT in 2014 and completing the GDMBR in 2017. Bahnson also enjoys poetry, fishing, and motorcycles. He is retired and lives with his wife Kay in rural South Dakota.

Sanders: In the Moment